Mediterranean
Summer

~ ~ ~ ~

Mediterranean Summer

~~~~~

A Season on France's Côte d'Azur and Italy's Costa Bella

David Shalleck
with Erol Munuz

Foreword by Mario Batali

Broadway Books/New York

PUBLISHED BY BROADWAY BOOKS

Copyright © 2007 by David Shalleck and Erol Munuz
Foreword copyright © 2007 by Mario Batali

A hardcover edition of this book was originally published in 2007
by Broadway Books.

Published in the United States by Broadway Books, an imprint of
The Doubleday Publishing Group, a division of
Random House, Inc., New York.
www.broadwaybooks.com

BROADWAY BOOKS and its logo, a letter B bisected on the
diagonal, are trademarks of Random House, Inc.

Book design by Donna Sinisgalli

Maps by Ben Pease, Pease Press, www.peasepress.com

Library of Congress Cataloging-in-Publication Data
Shalleck, David.
Mediterranean summer : a season on France's Côte d'Azur and
Italy's Costa Bella / David Shalleck with Erol Munuz.
        p.   cm.
Includes bibliographical references.
1. Shalleck, David. 2. Cookery, Marine. 3. Cooks—Biography.
4. Sailing—Mediterranean Sea. 5. Mediterranean Sea—Description
and travel. I. Munuz, Erol. II. Title.
TX840.M7S53 2007

ISBN 978-0-7679-2049-0

PRINTED IN THE UNITED STATES OF AMERICA

1   3   5   7   9   10   8   6   4   2

First Paperback Edition

To my mother and father
—D.S.

For my family
—E.M.

Although I didn't know it at the time, the story I tell in *Mediterranean Summer* took root the day I decided to leave my steady restaurant job in the States to travel to France and Italy. I had set out to find an answer to what transforms one into a chef and at the same time had only a vague notion of the culinary discoveries I would make. Once abroad, I cooked during a few summers on a gorgeous classic sailing yacht—the main setting in this book—that proved most significant in fulfilling my desire. I remain grateful to the owners for the opportunities they gave me when I was on board. For storytelling purposes, those seasons and actual events that occurred have been consolidated here into one summer at sea. Moreover, out of respect for the privacy of those involved, the names and many physical characteristics of the owners, my fellow crew members, the yacht, and other yachts in the story have been changed. I'm grateful to all of those I encountered during my tenure abroad, many of whom appear in this narrative. I shall forever carry the wonderful experiences and lessons learned from what turned out to be a life-changing culinary journey on the Mediterranean.

David Shalleck
San Francisco
November 2006

Contents

When my old friend, chef cohort, and comrade David Shalleck, whom I've known for twenty years, asked me if I'd write the foreword to his first book, I immediately responded positively. I expected a solid and interesting collection of recipes gathered and developed along his amazing journey throughout Europe from an American cook's point of view—spritzed with interesting anecdotes, spicy and zippy headnotes filled with tidbits of lore, and stories of the fun and hazards of cooking around the Mediterranean on a yacht. When he finished the manuscript several months ago he popped it in the mail, and I let it sit on my desk, confident I would whiz through it in a few minutes to get the feel of it and knock out a perfunctory testimonial to good cooking and experience in the real world.

Instead, I read the entire tale on a flight from New York to Paris on my way to Alba for a weekend of truffles and reacquaintance with Italy, as I do several times a year, and was struck by the many ways this timeless story echoes my own experiences. How delightful to find David had written real literature, with clear language, strong sentiment, his stories varied and fun—a book filled with sage cooking advice, travel anecdotes, and, most important, a young and vibrant voice chronicling the world from a delicious new perspective.

Like *Heat, Down and Out in Paris and London,* and *Kitchen Confidential,* David's prose in this picaresque tale provides an intimate back-of-the-house look at the constant ride between the catastrophic and the successes of what is true life in a modern kitchen.

I first met David in San Francisco when he started at Campton

Place under Bradley Ogden in the very middle of the California cooking revolution of the eighties. He had a New Yawk accent and a very
East Coast sentiment about him but was all about the food and the
style of the times. I was working at the Four Seasons Clift Hotel as a
sous-chef, and most of my real pals at that time were sous-chefs or
line cooks to the greats of the era such as my heroes Jeremiah Tower
at Stars, Mark Miller at Fourth Street Grill, Judy Rodgers at Zuni, and
Bradley at Campton Place. We had an informal kind of club and
would meet at each other's restaurants to try our cooking, snack together on days off, and stay up late after service talking incessantly
about food, waiters, bartenders, farmers' markets, wine, foie gras, and
tacos. It was a time when we all learned to eat, to share, and to support each other. And this mutual admiration club continues even now.
Looking around San Francisco, and the country for that matter, it is
quite enjoyable to see how many of our peers have gone on to their
own incredible and well-deserved successes: Mark Franz at Farallon,
Loretta Keller at Coco500, Traci Des Jardins at Jardinière, Bruce Hill
at Pico and Bix, Dave Robins at Chinois and Spago in Las Vegas.

From San Francisco, I moved first to Santa Barbara, and then on
to my own grand tour in Italy, landing outside Bologna, infused with
enthusiasm by Faith Heller Willinger's writing and consulting her
book *Eating in Italy* in every town of my journey. During this time, I
lost direct contact with David. I traveled east to Turkey in search of
Byzantine mosaics, then discovered a bit of the world of yacht crew-
ing in Bodrum, and actually considered trying to find a job by visiting
a crew agency in Antibes, France. With no luck in the offices, I hit the
docks looking for the biggest and most beautiful boats in search of em-
ployment in a new environ. Knocking on the door of one of the most
magnificent yachts in the whole port, I met an Australian deckhand
who told me to wait a minute while he went to get the chef. Lo and
behold, up from the galley emerged my old pal David. He was busy
making a base for bouillabaisse, so we agreed to meet for a drink later

that day. Many details of what eventually became this very book became clear in the midst of great celebration and much festivity over
the next couple of evenings in Antibes.

So our entangled journey continued in Europe, both of us on our
grand tour of Italy, kitchens, culture, and self. Several years later we
met again in New York, when David was touring as a culinary television producer and chef, working the margins in his constant research
of food, cooking, and the intellectual pursuit of the delicious.

This book is many things to me—primarily it is David's excellent
adventure and a joy to read for both style and content. But mostly I
find it a wonderful barometer of what makes my generation of cooks
and chefs so special: the thought processes, the constant improve-
ment, and the delight of introspection in the face of remarkable and
unique personal experience, a luxury to read about, but most important, to live.

Mario Batali

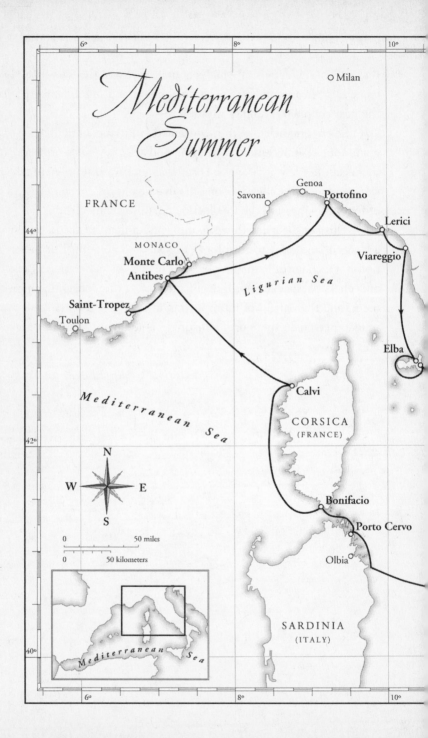

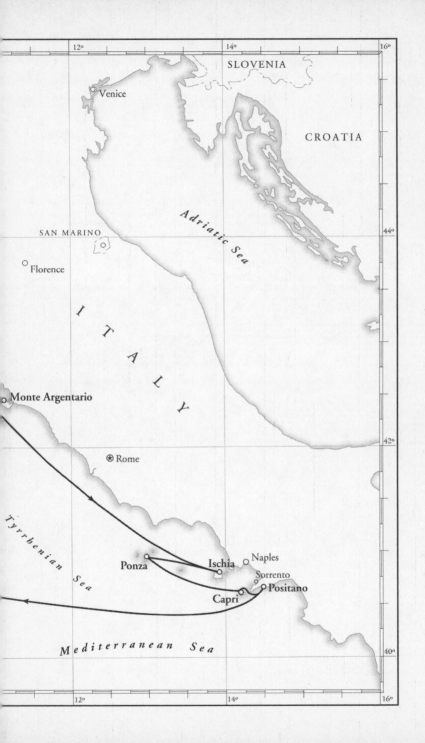

Serenity

~ ~ ~ ~

The dawn's stillness is all around me as I start my exercises on the foredeck of *Serenity*. Barely half an hour after first light, the anchorage remains quiet. It's still too early to see those famous crystalline blues of the Mediterranean Sea, but here and there small rings of concentric circles interrupt the glass-like surface of the water. Probably fish snatching for food.

I glance up and see the faint stencil of last night's quarter moon stubbornly resist being washed away by a brightening sky. Across the cove, another boat arrived sometime in the middle of the night, its white anchor light still illuminated at the top of its mast. About a hundred yards to shore lies the town.

The view of Positano from the sea has to be one of the world's great vistas. With virtually no harbor, it's a picturesque village sitting in a sleepy alcove on the Amalfi coast. Just offshore, several small, brightly colored fishing boats are tied to moorings and rest in the same direction. Others are lined up to one side of the pebble beach that fronts the town, sharing it with rows of beach chairs. At the far side, a string of restaurants, all with alfresco dining areas, together seem like a retaining wall, preventing the arched terraces of the colorful villas that are built into the cascading hillsides behind from sliding into the sea. High up in the distance, near the top of the town and too far from the anchorage to be heard, a small orange bus makes its way along a road of sharp turns cut out of the steep terrain.

The sun hasn't yet crossed over the landmass of the peninsula. The decorated majolica dome of the church next to the beach is cast in a dark mauve shadow beneath the ravine. When *Serenity*'s anchor was dropped last night, the amber glow of the setting sun rendered it blue-gray.

The silence is broken by a lone fishing boat that cuts a wake as it moves to the open sea, its small outboard motor humming. A seagull follows it, and then two more appear. Old friends going off to work. I watch as the wake becomes a ripple by the time it reaches *Serenity.*

Precious moments like these, before the owners, guests, and crew come on deck, are mine. They are a necessary break I have arranged for myself to help me get through the pressures of the job.

I finish my exercises, remaining quiet so as not to wake the others below. The thin layer of dew on deck is slowly evaporating as the sun begins to warm the teak planks. I stand up and take one last sweep of the scene in front of me. But it is time to go below to change into my uniform, grab the keys to the launch, and head to shore. On days when there is much provisioning, I bring one of my crew members with me. But today I don't need much, and I want to be alone.

The ride is short, and I have learned how to shut the launch's engine at just the right speed and distance from the dock so that as the boat drifts toward shore, I can grab my things and in one quick move step off with the bowline in hand and quickly tie it to a cleat. I manage it perfectly. Too bad there isn't anyone on the dock to serve as witness.

The *caffè* near the beach hasn't opened yet, so I make my way up the narrow road to the town center. There the streets are being cleaned by workers in blue jumpsuits using long-handled brushes that resemble witches' brooms. A few shopkeepers have already opened their metal gates, and small delivery vehicles are making their stops. It won't be long before Positano's narrow, pedestrian-only streets fill up with townspeople tending to their morning chores. And just a short while later the tourists will be out, checking the shops or making their way down to the beach.

My morning onshore will begin with a cappuccino—strong, hot arabica coffee properly extracted from a commercial machine, covered with a dense, hazelnut-colored layer called *crema,* then blended with a mousse-like infusion of frothy steamed milk. I find a *caffè* busy with locals.

"*Buon giorno,*" I say to the barista in the *caffè.*

"*Buon giorno,*" he answers back with a nod of "what can I get for you?"

"A cappuccino with *poca schiuma*"—not too much foam—"*per favore.*"

A few men look over at me. I can sense they know, by virtue of my uniform, that I have come from the yacht anchored just offshore.

The barista delivers a perfect cappuccino, and we begin to talk. He is pleased to learn that I come from New York and asks if I know so-and-so, who grew up in Positano but left for Brooklyn four or five years ago. I explain that New York is a big place. Another man cuts into the conversation and mentions he has a sister in New Jersey. A third wants to practice his English. "How are you?" he asks me, and then says he remembers when American soldiers landed at Anzio, near Naples, to help push the Nazis out during the Second World War.

Being in such a remote location, one can feel a long way from home. But listening to the men in the *caffè* volley their kind words and ideas about where I am from makes me feel welcome. The Italian way is to try to make you feel *at* home. My extended journey abroad has also helped me understand what it means to *be* home, even when not there.

There is an orange pay phone on the wall, and I suddenly get the urge to call my family.

"Do you sell phone cards?" I ask the barista.

"How many would you like?" he asks.

"Enough to call New York for ten minutes or so," I say.

"It's two o'clock in the morning there! Who are you going to call now?"

Lost in my reveries, I have completely forgotten about the difference in time zones. I am relieved the barista has stopped me. I'll call when it's better for them. Instead, I finish my cappuccino, put a few thousand lire under the saucer, wish everyone good day, and go on my way.

I had better concentrate on provisioning what I need for today's meals: the day's bread, a couple kilos of tomatoes, zucchini, some bell peppers, melon, and I noticed a flat of beautiful figs when I passed the *frutta e verdura*—fruit and vegetable—stand before. I also need to stop at the fish market to see what I will be able to get over the next few days while we're here.

Walking toward the dock, I stop outside the church of Santa Maria Assunta to get a closer look at the tiles covering its dome. Bright spots in yellow and green. How different it looks from the sea, when all the tiles blend into one monochromatic image. Not so different from my journey, a summer where countless small experiences make up a picture I can't see while still so close.

It's time to get back to the boat. In an hour, the anchor will come up, and *Serenity* will be on her way to a secluded spot along the coast.

I drive a little slower on the ride back and admire the beauty of *Serenity* with her smooth white hull, shimmering with reflections from the water at her side. Her masts, booms, and rigging lines silhouetted against the bright morning sky while she sits at anchor still impress me. I feel a certain pride in having this boat as my home as well as my workstation. It has given me a summer I could never have imagined.

I cut the engine, glide toward the galley porthole, and then maneuver the launch against *Serenity*. As I stand on one of the inflated sides of the launch, I put the bowline through an opening in the top of the yacht's hull, reach over the mahogany rail, and tie it to a cleat near the edge of the deck. I pass my market bag on the boat, and then lift myself on board. I hear awakening movement and voices from down below.

It's now time to retreat to the galley and prepare another set of meals, different from those I prepared the day before and those that will follow. But I am not thinking about yesterday's meals or tomorrow's shopping. I take a last few seconds for the here and now: one last look at the glorious panorama of Positano.

Then I go below to start my day.

One

~

Five-Year Summer

~ ~ ~ ~

The restaurant was in downtown London, a couple of blocks from the Savoy hotel. Although it was close to a landmark, its side street address gave it the sense of being a hideaway spot off the main road. The interior decor was simple and clean, adorned with colorful paintings by California artists that accented contemporary furnishings. In the back of the dining room, a semi-open kitchen featured a mesquite grill—a new trend in restaurant design in the States and a fresh addition to the London restaurant scene.

From the beginning, I felt apprehensive. It was the first time I would be responsible for all the back-of-the-house operations—from scheduling, ordering, equipment maintenance, and service—as well as the most important, the quality of the food. The departing sous-chef hinted that things might be a little "sensitive" in the kitchen.

After a couple of days on the job, I got the picture all too clearly. From my training in other restaurants, I learned that great kitchens are silent kitchens, the air thick with concentration. The only competition for your own thoughts are the sounds of knives chopping, whisks whisking in stainless steel bowls, and food sizzling in hot pans—all under the hum of the exhaust hoods and refrigerator compressors. I also believed it was the best way to get the most productive work out of a staff.

But each afternoon long before service began, this kitchen was abuzz with a cacophony of endless, needless, and distracting chatter. It was clear the staff enjoyed each other's company far more than the work. Something else was clear. No one was looking to impress the new guy in charge.

Then again, why should they? They knew I was there for only a couple of months. And I wasn't confident enough of the support I'd get from the owners if I told everybody to just chill out, that until they heard otherwise I was the boss and quiet was the way I liked it. Or maybe it wasn't confidence I lacked, but a natural assertiveness.

One afternoon about a month into the job, on what was supposed to be my first day off since starting, I stopped at the restaurant to reassure myself that I could go and enjoy the rest of the day in peace. I was in the chef's office, looking over the week's food invoices, when one of the line cooks dropped on me that he had heard Alice Waters had reserved a table for dinner that night. Yes, the same Alice Waters who by any measure was one of the most respected figures in American cooking. I went to the hostess stand and checked the reservation book. It was true. Next to her name, in letters the hostess could not miss, the day manager had written "PPX"—*personne particulièrement extraordinaire*—the restaurant's version of VIP. My evening's plans would have to wait.

I had met Waters several years before, first at a charity event in New York, and then again after I moved to San Francisco. One day, while flipping through a popular food magazine, I noticed an article describing a small, intimate cooking school in the south of France run by a self-taught authority of the cuisine, Nathalie Waag. What particularly caught my attention was the article's description of how Nathalie took small groups of students to open-air markets in Provence to shop for the ingredients that they would use to prepare dishes that evening in her *mas,* a Provençal farmhouse. It was mornings in the markets, a leisurely lunch at a nearby café or an impromptu picnic made up from market finds, afternoon drives in the countryside, informal classes in the kitchen with aperitifs, and long evenings at the farmhouse table in the dining room. It sounded pretty good to me.

I was working as a sauté cook in one of the celebrated hotel restaurants in San Francisco, Campton Place. By all outward appearances, my life was good and my career was progressing nicely. In fact, a couple of weeks earlier, I had been offered a promotion to sous-chef. I hadn't yet accepted the offer, but I hadn't turned it down, either. Among their many responsibilities, sous-chefs are the ones who do the daily food ordering, which requires that they know and manage the kitchen's inventory of ingredients. I had visions of spending more time with clipboard in hand counting the portions of meats, poultry, fish, produce, and dairy in the walk-in refrigerator, then moving on to counting the groceries in the storeroom, than actually cooking the food.

By comparison, the image of life described in the magazine article was far more enticing, and I wondered if there was some way I might get to speak with Nathalie. The article mentioned that she was a good friend of Waters's, and that she spent her winters across the bay in Berkeley hanging out at Alice's respected restaurant, Chez Panisse. I thought Alice would remember me and take my call. She did, and when I asked if she knew how I could get in touch with Nathalie, she said, "Sure," and passed the phone to her. By an amazing coincidence, Nathalie happened to be sitting next to Alice at that moment. I introduced myself, and we agreed to meet over coffee a few days later at Fanny, Alice's small café also in Berkeley.

When I arrived for the meeting, Nathalie was already seated. Once the pleasantries had been exchanged, she went about describing the simple ways of Provence. We spoke about cooking, markets, and ingredients. It didn't take long to realize this was a lifestyle that had to be seen firsthand. Without ever having planned to do so, I offered to be her assistant if she ever needed one.

A couple of months later, it came—an invitation from Nathalie. She suggested I spend a "spring-summer school term" with her. I would be getting room and board—no salary or stipend, but that didn't matter. Her reputation as a devout practitioner of Provençal cooking was unquestioned, and I knew that working side by side with her would broaden my cooking palette. I accepted immediately, figuring I would work with her for a few months and then see if I could find another opportunity in France, extending my European stay to six months, nine at the most.

A number of my fellow cooks scoffed at the idea of leaving an established position to take an unpaid internship. However, Mark Franz, a friend and well-known chef who ran the popular and busy kitchen at Stars in San Francisco, had a different take.

"It won't be a waste," he told me. "Short detours can be good for a career. Even if she has you in the back of the kitchen doing nothing but dicing tomatoes. Forget your ego; forget what the others are saying; just concentrate on cutting those tomatoes and watch. This could turn out to be the most important trip you'll ever take."

My excursion from San Francisco to the south of France included a weeklong stopover in New York. It was early spring, a nice time of year to visit and see my parents, friends, and some of my cooking buddies. The trees were starting to bloom, and those pesky dandelions were all over my parents' yard. Coming from the temperate climate of the San Francisco Bay Area, I realized how much I missed the change of seasons.

During my week in New York I received a message from Nathalie telling me that I would have to delay my arrival at the school for a couple of months. Something about her classes starting late that year. Sitting around and waiting has never been my best game, so I called around looking for something to fill the gap. Within a day Larry Forgione, my former boss at An American Place in Manhattan and one of the true pioneers of the American food revolution, came through for me. He knew of the perfect situation.

A friend of his had just sold the London edition of his restaurant, and the new owners needed an interim *chef de cuisine* to run the kitchen for a couple of months until their own chef could start. The irony that this job would entail much of the clipboard work I was running from didn't elude me. But what the heck. It was a short-term job that filled the empty slot in my calendar, and then I'd be off to the south of France. I called Larry's friend, who in turn put me in touch with one of the new owners, and we agreed to a two-month arrangement.

With Alice Waters in the reservation book, I quickly changed into my kitchen whites, and when I entered the kitchen, I was glad I had. Everywhere I looked things that should have been taken care of had been let go. The walk-in was a mess, dirty pots had built up into a huge pile at the dishwasher station, and the garbage bins were overflowing. Damn it, I thought. I had left the place in good shape only the night before. How fast things can go south in an unsupervised kitchen. Even more troubling was that after I informed the staff that we had one of the world's preeminent chefs coming to dine that night, everybody from the dining room manager to the pastry chef went on with a "What, me worry?" routine, breezily going about business as usual.

At five-thirty that evening, the hostess poked her head into the kitchen to say that the Waters party had just been seated, half an hour before their reservation time. Their early arrival caught me in a pre-service scramble, not really ready for them. I looked at my line cooks, who held my fate in their hands but had so far evinced no interest in pleasing or protecting me. But hope springs eternal, and I thought maybe, if for no other reason than to impress a world-renowned culinary figure, they might somehow find it in themselves to put out a special effort to match the occasion.

I decided to send a plate of hors d'oeuvres to Alice's table. I was late getting them out, but at least this gesture would let her know that I wasn't oblivious to her visit. Just as the hors d'oeuvres left the kitchen, the computerized dupe machine began spitting out the kitchen copy of the Waters order. It showed that one of the dishes was the same as what I had just sent out.

As I look back on that night, and I have done so many times, I wonder if I should have sent the manager to their table to ask if they wanted to change their order. But that night, under pressure, unsure of myself, I thought I had no choice but to go forward. I called out the entire order, first to the salad and appetizer station and then to the line cooks. "Ordering: red pepper crab cakes, a bacon and Stilton salad, and a pasta followed by a salmon, a lamb medium-rare, and a chicken. Ordering a cheese plate after the entrées." The order was in.

My first indication that the night would be a long one came early. The server, a hip East End fellow with a punk hairstyle, placed the scallops with angel-hair pasta on the counter next to the salad and the signature crab cakes. The pasta, I could see, looked limp and lifeless, a dead giveaway to anyone in the business that it was over-cooked. The scallops around the pasta revealed another problem— they appeared milky, not caramelized, telling me they had not been placed on the grill's hot spot. Too late now.

The salad had its own troubles, being overdressed. The surplus vinaigrette had smeared all over the rim of the plate.

"I need another salad right away," I said.

The salad maker replied that he needed to leave his station and go to the walk-in refrigerator to get it.

"Why aren't you ready for service?" I asked him. "It's past six. Didn't you think anyone would be having a salad tonight?"

He didn't even bother to answer me. I had to settle for transfer-ring the salad to another plate. Fortunately, the crab cakes were fine. I wiped the rims of the plates clean and sent the waiter out with them. After about ten minutes, I fired the entrées, hoping to dovetail the second course on the back of the first, all the while wondering if I could be lucky enough to have Alice miss the pasta and salad defects.

I didn't have long to wait for the next piece of bad news. The salmon was put up on the shelf way before the lamb. As should have been anticipated, the plate was too hot, which made the citrus butter sauce—a delicate liaison of reduced orange and lemon juice with carefully melted butter—boil, creating a mesa of light and dark yellow around the fish. I transferred the salmon and garnishes to a warm plate and added some new sauce, a quick solution to the problem, even though there were remnants of the broken sauce near the edges of the sauce pools. When the lamb was finally out of the oven, I squeezed the rack from the sides between my thumb and my forefinger. My panic ratcheted up yet another notch. It was slightly firm, almost resisting the pressure from my fingers and bouncing right back from the indentation instead of being a little softer. It had been cooked to medium, not medium-rare as ordered. By the time we carved it, the lamb would be medium-well.

Through clenched teeth, I asked how a dupe with the word "medium-rare" on it could have produced an item that was not and could not ever again be medium-rare. No one answered. Of course no one answered. I was talking to myself.

The chicken was a needed bright moment. Except for some slight charring on the end of its wing bone, it looked fine nestled next to a cluster of watercress. But when I looked at the standard vegetable garnish on the plate, I failed to ask myself why I was serving winter vegetables in spring to the woman whose creed was that all good cookery should be in harmony with the land and its season.

I knew I should have refired the course, but by this point I was in a tailspin. When the entrées for the Waters table were out, the kitchen staff seemed to exhale as one, not because they particularly cared how well their work would be received, but because my tension level was off the chart and they hoped I would now ease up on them.

When the manager reported no complaints from our distinguished guest, I indulged myself in a prayer that I had dodged a bullet with my name on it. When it came time for the post-entrée cheese course, I thought, *At least we can't blow this*. The pantry cook handed the cheese selection to me. I was wrong. We didn't even get that right.

The first rule of serving cheese is to have it at room temperature. The assortment of California cheeses specially brought in included a couple made by Alice's friend Laura Chenel. They had all been left in the walk-in refrigerator. I had no choice but to transfer the cheese from the chilled plate they were on to one that was room temperature. I said to the hipster waiter, "Take it."

Because I could not see Alice's table from the line, the hostess signaled when she and her family had finished dessert and were sitting with their espresso. I walked out into the dining room, past the waiters' marking station—the place where flatware, glasses, and table linens are stored—and saw Alice's sweet but formidable face at a corner banquette. I walked over to greet her.

"Thanks for coming in, chef," I said, happy to see her. Alice politely introduced me to her husband and daughter, mentioning they were on their way to France and Italy, but wasted no time.

"This was not very good tonight, David," she said. She gave me the name of the hotel where she was staying and said, "Call me tomorrow."

Her tone was not as unpleasant as her authoritative message, and I sensed that she understood and had taken into account all I had to deal with—temporarily running a kitchen past its heyday with an insubordinate staff over which I had little influence and no power.

The next morning I called her, thinking we would share a laugh over how impossible our profession can be at times. I went in that direction, trying to set a confident, relaxed tone. "Hi, Alice, it's David. What a night!"

Alice's voice held none of the pleasant friendliness of the previous evening; in fact, it was outright cold. "Don't you ever let that happen when you are chef of a kitchen," she admonished me. "The owner is a friend of mine. I was embarrassed for him, but mainly I was embarrassed for you."

She didn't leave it at that, going on to a meticulous critique of each part of the meal, missing nothing—not even the parts I had tried to fudge. She was indignant about the out-of-season vegetables, finishing on the cheese and the dessert.

"And the cheese was cold, David, COLD! That's inexcusable. And I could taste food odors in the cake!"

Yes, I knew that keeping cake in the walk-in with the rest of the food was bad practice. It's something any good kitchen knows not to do, but with a staff that needed watching at every step, I had let it go.

"You are responsible for everything that comes out of that kitchen," she chided me, "and that has to be your first priority."

She was right and I knew it. I had known it that night as I sent out dish after dish of substandard quality. She must have heard how totally deflated I was, all my cockiness knocked out of me. But she wasn't finished. "Before you call yourself a chef," she went on, "remember what the word means." It means "chief," and in the restaurant business it's where the buck stops. My heart was pounding so hard that after a while I could no longer process her words. But no matter. Her tone of voice carried her message loud and clear. I had blown a huge opportunity, humiliating myself in front of a woman every cook in America studies and idolizes. And worst of all, I had stupidly tried to charm my way out of a dismal failure.

Of course she was right, about the bad meal and the cold cheese and the poorly stored cake and about the fact that I—not the line cooks, not the pastry chef, not the server—was responsible for everything that came out of the kitchen. From the moment the call was over, I tried to salvage something from the debacle, allowing my mind to take me back to an old expression: "A whipped dog is a wiser dog." I vowed I'd never again come to the game unprepared. But I couldn't help wondering about another possible fallout. Alice would no doubt be visiting Provence and might share with Nathalie her disenchantment with me. I had invested so much in the hope that in Nathalie's school I would become more than a good cook. I wondered if I had blown my chance for success before even getting there. The thought of failure on my journey had never entered my mind until that Saturday night. And Alice's implicit judgment was clear: I had a long way to go before I could call myself a chef.

Reflecting on what brought me into this demanding profession of cooking for the pleasure of others, I realize that it was not just my love of food. The restaurant business, at least back when I entered it by way of a first summer job as a dishwasher, abounds with opportunity for those hungry to get ahead. But the work also provides a hefty dose of pressure for those trying to get by. As with early television shows that aired live, what you serve your guests has to come off right the first time, and that requires top performances from all of the support staff.

Over a succession of summer jobs and part-time during school, I moved from dishwashing to plating the salads, but the night I remember most clearly was when I was assigned to my first post "on the line," kitchen talk for stations under the exhaust hood, working on the hot appetizers. From "hot apps" to fish then meats, from sautéing and roasting to grilling, I still have fond memories of being exposed to some of the very best mentors in the business, a brigade of dedicated cooks at a beautiful restaurant at the foot of the Brooklyn Bridge named the River Café.

It was there that I was also exposed to just how much time the chef, Larry Forgione, put into finding unique, fresh ingredients that were grown or raised in the States. I was endlessly intrigued, but at the end of each summer I went back to college. Later I learned that Forgione left to open An American Place in Manhattan, named by James Beard, the chef's mentor and one of the foremost cookbook authors in America. College graduation brought me a job at a lighting and set design firm and I thought my kitchen days were over as I looked for a break into show business. But a few months later, Larry called and offered me a full-time position on the line at his new place. Unhappy with my job as a draftsman—where it seemed as if I would have to pay my dues in an office job for an eternity—I decided to cook and maybe one day become a chef.

For the menu at An American Place, Forgione was creating dishes with ingredients I had never heard of, things like nasturtium leaves, fiddlehead ferns, and morel mushrooms. "Where did you find them?" I asked him. They came from California and northern Michigan, he told me, and added that in Europe all chefs learn to be foragers. Most of them, he said, regularly wander through markets and out-of-the-way places to find something interesting or unique, and then create a dish around it. As the cottage food business grew and foragers throughout the nation contacted Forgione, his repertoire continued to expand.

At the same time, the California cuisine trend hit Manhattan. Simple, robust food came out of open kitchens with mesquite grills and wood-burning ovens. Reduction sauces gave way to flavored mayonnaise, and sprigs of fresh herbs were the garnishes instead of fluted mushroom caps. The entertainment of watching cooks prepare food while wearing black baseball caps in lieu of a toque—the classic French chef's hat—added to the signature of this new wave of cooking that brought the high-quality dining experience many steps closer to being casual. Larry would say that what I was witnessing in New York was only a part of the California food world.

The idea of heading west to check out firsthand the restaurant scene in San Francisco began to form in my head. When I told Larry, he urged me on.

Once in California, I quickly found work at the Campton Place hotel under Chef Bradley Ogden, a friend of Larry's. But any conversation about California cuisine's beginnings invariably came around to the schoolteacher-turned-chef Alice Waters and Chez Panisse, her influential restaurant across the bay in Berkeley, where she successfully compressed the time it took to get food from the ranch or farm to the tables in her dining room.

In the introduction to her first cookbook, *Chez Panisse Menu Cookbook,* I read that her food was inspired by travels in France and by the cookbooks of Richard Olney and Elizabeth David. To that end, Chez Panisse was originally a French restaurant, modeled after the rustic dishes of the south of France, in particular the cooking of Provence. The influence showed in the dining room as well, where the walls were adorned with posters for films by Marcel Pagnol, the French filmmaker who had written stories based in Provence. I later learned that Waters was so inspired by these films and the lives of the characters that she named the restaurant after one of them, Panisse.

France and food were bound up together for me as well, though in my case the link involved only vicarious travel to France during my childhood. In our home, as in most American homes, Sunday night television with Disney was a ritual. But as a child of two off-camera television professionals, I also watched some shows that were not what you would expect a kid to be watching. One, aimed at an adult audience, mesmerized me. It was called *The Galloping Gourmet* and was hosted by the happy, funny, and well-dressed gourmand Graham Kerr. It ran in our area just about the time I usually came home for lunch.

The Galloping Gourmet was a show about a flamboyant but skilled chef going through a hectic routine each episode as he deftly prepared a grand gourmet meal inspired by some exotic locale or classic technique. His hammed-up facial expressions and zany ways, along with his interactions with the live audience, made for an amusing show. I was captivated by the way he transformed raw ingredients into finished dishes—peeling, chopping, slicing, then pots and pans jangling on the stove, working two ovens as he made a meal around the main event, like roast duck with a sauce of pinot noir or shallow-fried turbot with lemon and parsley butter sauce. But what I remember most vividly were the short segments devoted to his sojourns overseas, mostly in France and Italy—the famous harbor of Marseille, where he bought the fish for bouillabaisse, the Burgundian countryside as he spoke about dishes *à la dijonnaise,* and the open-air markets where he shopped for fresh ingredients. Even if I had no idea what he was talking about when he referred to what went into dishes like *escargot truffière,* it did not matter. What did matter was that he always made cookery fun.

On the train from Paris to Provence, I obsessed about the possibility that Alice had told Nathalie about my fiasco in London, going over all my failures of service that night, one by one, as she had with me. And so I was relieved when Nathalie met me at the Avignon train station with her son Jerome, greeting me with a hearty, "Welcome to Provence!"

She looked different from how I remembered her—she stood a little taller than she appeared at our first meeting, but was thinner and balanced her weight on a cane. She pointed to the cane as the reason for the two-month delay—knee surgery. Swiss by heritage, Nathalie had discovered Provence in her twenties and adopted the region's sun-drenched lifestyle with the same dedication as a native. Her long, free-flowing auburn hair, angular features, wise brown eyes, and wide smile may have been a nod to the gypsies of the Vaucluse valley. She had even named her home after one of their patron saints, but since we met in Berkeley, she had moved into an apartment in town.

As we set out in Jerome's little Peugeot station wagon, she told me that we had to make a few stops on the way home. "We must pick up some wine," she announced, "then visit a *huilerie* for some olive oil and a nursery to get starter plants of basil and parsley. It's unfortunate when all I need is a sprig or a few leaves that I have to buy a whole bunch. Unless I am making *pistou*"—pesto—"and I need a lot, it's wasteful. Plus, the flavor is best when you can go to the source."

Jerome drove swiftly through the valley as we passed meadows of bright red poppies, asparagus fields, vineyards, and cherry orchards. It was too early in the season to see the famous purple rows of lavender that Provence is known for. But its nascent fields were everywhere. I could just make out the medieval hilltop villages—Lagnes, Gordes, Ménerbes—far off in the distance. They all shared a similar architectural style of stone and terra-cotta except for Roussillon, which rose from the red rock of nearby cliffs. "You'll get a chance to visit them during your stay," Nathalie said as she watched me gaze in awe through the open car windows. "We have to move fast because the vendors all close at noon for their midday break."

"Where is everything else going to come from?" I asked.

"There are excellent shops in some of the towns, and just down the street from the apartment is a great *boulangerie*," Jerome was quick to reply over his shoulder.

"Unless of course when we go to the markets we get everything there," Nathalie said from the passenger seat. She directed Jerome in French to turn left at the next intersection. She preferred to travel in the valley on the "D" routes as opposed to the "N" routes of the national system. "It might take a little longer, but there is much more to see on the *département* roads."

A short while later, Nathalie pointed to Bonnieux, a town that capped a lone hill ahead, our final destination. The winding two-lane road to town took us past fruit and nut orchards, grass fields, restored farmhouses, and old stone barns. The car's diesel engine labored to make the final steep grade. Near the summit a clear vista of the valley of the Vaucluse opened up. I looked across to Lacoste, another hilltop town close by, and saw the jagged ruins of the Marquis de Sade's castle, which dominated the vista from high above the village. Recalling the twisted madness chronicled in Peter Weiss's modern play *Marat/Sade* that I read in college, I wondered how this exquisite environment could have produced such a tortured soul.

It didn't take long to adjust to the daily rhythm of living in Provence. Early each morning I'd walk down the street to the patisserie to get warm breakfast pastries or brioche to have with café au lait, which we drank out of bowls, a local custom. We would leave by eight o'clock to go to the markets, buy what we needed for lunch and dinner, and then return to the apartment with an occasional detour through one of the villages that dotted the hilltops of the valley.

At the end of my first month, all seemed on track until one day Nathalie asked me, "Is there anything you want to make while here?"

I replied, "No, I like your choices. I like what you're doing."

"But didn't you come here to learn the food of Provence?"

"Of course," I answered. "That's why I try to follow your lead in the kitchen."

Nathalie dismissed my response with a somewhat chilly "okay" and went back to her work. That seemed to resolve the issue, but just what might have motivated her question continued to nag at me.

I didn't understand what her problem was. I was eager to go to the market each morning, help with the prep, even help with the clean-up, all the while trying to adhere to my mother's warning not to be a pushy American.

"Remember," my mother had advised me, "you will be living in this woman's home, working in her kitchen. Don't come on like a know-it-all, telling her that this isn't how they do it in San Francisco or New York. You are there to learn."

"What are you thinking about?" Nathalie asked me the next day as I chopped some mirepoix vegetables and tried my hand at making the "house" salad dressing.

Maybe because her question took me by surprise, or because I didn't know what answer she was looking for, I replied, "Nothing. I was just thinking about how different eating at home is."

"David, I didn't invite you here to chop vegetables and season lamb. Cooking, you know, is not about recipes. It comes from my heart. You have never asked me why—why I do things, why I want it done this way and not that way. What's in your heart, David? Did you leave it at home?"

I didn't know quite what to say. I must have searched too long for an answer, for Nathalie went on.

"Maybe you might want to think about other things to do in Provence. But that is for you to decide."

With that, she left the kitchen.

I quickly finished up the vegetables, wiped my hands, left the apartment, and briskly walked up the narrow cobblestoned road to the village peak. I perched myself on the top of a wall overlooking the entire valley and began to assess what just happened. I had been invited to find something else, my services no longer required. Yes, despite the polite words she had used, I had been fired, and not from a glitzy restaurant with a demanding clientele, but from a job without pay. I had no idea why, other than that in some way I failed to measure up. I didn't know what to do. I thought for a minute about trying to repair the situation with Nathalie, but she had left me no such opening, her demeanor communicating that she had made her decision and it was final. I had been let go, told to find some other place, not just to work but to sleep as well.

I had to make a decision. Going home after having been stamped a total loser by a world-recognized food authority likely meant leaving cooking forever. And I wasn't able to explain Nathalie's judgment of me, even to myself. The problem was I still didn't quite know what I had done wrong.

As much out of embarrassment as courage, I wanted another chance in Europe. But in order to stay, I needed a connection—someone who could open a door for me to another position. As if guided by a kindly saint who had taken pity on me, I remembered that my mother had mentioned during a call home that one of her colleagues had a sister, Faith Heller Willinger, who was a food writer living in Tuscany. Just in case I considered going to Italy, my mother had passed on her address. The next day I sent off a letter.

Faith was close to the Italian restaurant business and had become a respected expert in food and wine. Although I didn't know it at the time, my letter arrived while she was busy reading galleys of her soon-to-be-published guide to Italian regional cuisine, *Eating in Italy*. Yet she took the time to speak to me by phone. I told her about my embarrassing experiences with Alice and Nathalie. She took the time to buck me up, to restore a little of my lost confidence. But the help she offered me was not limited to confidence building.

She suggested that I meet her in Florence and maybe she could help arrange an itinerary of internships in some of the best Italian restaurants, providing that my priority was to learn, not to make money. I assured her this was so, that I had come to Europe to broaden my skills and see Mediterranean cooking at the source.

During our first meeting in Florence, she began to educate me. "You must realize when we talk about *la cucina italiana*"—Italian cuisine—"it's about cookery from twenty different regions rather than a single, national cuisine."

She went on to explain that Italy has been united as a republic only since the mid-nineteenth century, almost a century after the United States became a nation, and every region still held on to its own specialties and traditions.

"During the twentieth century," she added, "in the largest cities, this interesting palette of distinct regions has been a little blurred by modern transportation and a new generation of young chefs who strive for innovation."

I had originally left the states to experience Provence and the south of France. Being in Italy was completely unexpected. I was excited by the prospect of a new challenge, but at the same time my failure to meet the last challenge had left me vulnerable. Faith must have read this on my face.

"Okay," she said, shifting gears. "Have you ever cooked with white truffles? Know how traditional balsamic vinegar is truly made? Made pesto in a mortar and pestle? Have you ever heard of the regions of Friuli or Liguria, the dairy belt of the Po valley, or know that Chianti is a place and not just a wine?"

While she spoke, I realized how little I knew about Italian cuisine and that I had accepted as fact many of the worst clichés about the Italian menu.

"Tomatoes came from the New World, not Naples. *Peperoni* are bell peppers, not the sliced salami disks on a pizza. Bologna is a city, and the deli meat you know is really a derivative of mortadella," she continued. "And a true Florentine steak is a very thick porterhouse that doesn't need to be served with spinach."

When she realized just how little I knew, she figured out how to help me.

"I believe it would suit you best," she said, "to move around for a while, in rural parts, and experience the variety this country offers from its core." Over the next few days, she tirelessly worked the phone, creating an itinerary of internships that would expose me to what she considered the heart and soul of true Italian food. This would take me to areas of the country where the best examples of regional cooking could be found, and where restaurant owners and chefs were dedicated to preserving the cookery of their respective localities.

Only room and board was offered, except in the rare case where a generous owner might provide a small stipend for pocket money. I would start in Piedmont, and then move on to Friuli, Tuscany, Lombardy, Campania, and Lazio, not in big-city restaurants but in restaurants and wineries in small towns and back-road rural areas where the menus featured time-honored local fare.

The first stop would be in Piedmont. It was truffle season. I was going to a restaurant among the vineyards of Barbaresco, in the valley of the Langhe—fertile soil for the pricey *Tuber magnatum,* the white truffle of Alba. I had no idea what to expect, what working in a foreign kitchen with strangers beside me was going to be like. Especially since I didn't speak a word of Italian.

Once off the train I showed the address to the uniformed stationmaster. He led me outside to get a clear view and pointed to a winding road that seemed to end at an old town on top of a nearby hill. As I gathered my bags, trying to distribute the weight evenly shoulder to shoulder, he raised his eyebrows, and then shrugged a smile at me. I thanked him and set out.

I finally dragged my three bags up the last incline to the small piazza where the restaurant was located. I found the back door and went into the kitchen, soaked in sweat even on that cold and foggy November day. The staff was in the final hectic stages of getting ready for a lunch banquet, and the chef had no interest in my heroic feat of getting me and my luggage up that road. The first words belted out of her mouth in French were *"Bienvenue, es-tu ici pour regarder ou pour travailler?"*—Welcome! Are you here to watch or work? She handed me an apron. Like most folks so close to the border, she was bilingual. We could communicate, at least enough to be understood in French.

She wasted no time. "Go help in the pasta station!"

Virtually no one spoke English. Italians speak Italian, and among themselves they communicate in their own rapid-fire local dialects. I heard a language full of emotion, but my lack of vocabulary deprived me of the nuance each emotion was driving home. I heard the stream of words as little more than white noise. It was easy to tune out what I was having so much trouble understanding.

During the internship, I sensed snide comments were being made behind my back, and sometimes to my face. I kept hearing *"il Americano,"* and since I was the only American on the staff, it didn't take long to connect the dots. I stayed silent, trying to be polite by responding with what I thought were appropriately timed *sì*'s. I probably said yes to being an arrogant, selfish, rich, greedy, spoiled American cowboy more times than I would ever care to know about. "Cowboy" seemed to be a favorite label for Americans, curious because the Italians had a love-hate relationship with America's legendary wide-open West, knocking the brawny cowboy mind-set but making their own Westerns, called spaghetti Westerns, based on the creations of Hollywood.

I watched the other cooks and tried to rely on common sense to get through the day. Although one time when a chef asked for eggs, I came back with grapes, wondering why he needed them for a dish that didn't seem to call for fruit. He, along with everyone else in the kitchen, doubled over in sidesplitting laughter. To my untrained ear, *uove*—eggs—and *uve*—grapes—sounded similar, especially when spoken quickly with an unfamiliar accent. I went along with it good-naturedly, concealing my embarrassment.

I got through that first internship with a better familiarity with the Italian words for eggs and grapes, certain cheeses, sage, and keeping things clean. But each new internship exposed me to yet another variation of regional Italian food. And the very different personalities of Italian kitchens. Some kitchens were accustomed to *stagiaires*—the French word that Italians used for "interns." Others were not. In some kitchens I felt the chef had some minimal interest in me, while in others I was just ignored. But in each kitchen you also had the line cooks to win over. Some welcomed me. Others simply did not want to be working alongside a *straniero*—foreigner. My first week at each new place reminded me of a first-day-of-school shakedown—sorting out the show-offs from the helpful, the wise guys from potential friends. The former talked *at* me, whereas the latter spoke *with* me.

Some kitchens thrived on chaos, others were organized and efficient. At one place the chef ordered a code of silence. Arguments that turned physical were infrequent, but could happen at any time, the explosive outbursts sometimes startling me. I once saw a chef throw ladles of boiling pasta water at her tuxedo-clad maître d' husband. At another, the owner broke a toe kicking a pot, then broke his hand punching a wall—in the middle of service! In Friuli, there was a sous-chef who cried miserably all the time. No one could figure out why. One night an owner in a drunken passion actually put a loaded pistol to the center of my forehead to make sure I fully appreciated the brilliance of his wife's cooking.

Living conditions, something I didn't consider when I began, were another matter. There were rooms with minimal heat, poor mattresses, or "hot" showers that at best achieved a temperature you could call no more than tepid. At one place, the water from the bathroom sink smelled as if it had been pumped up from a swamp, while at another the staff cottage flooded when it rained. There were no televisions, music systems, telephones, or newspapers in English. But there were snoring roommates and cooks' quarters that reeked of cigarette smoke. At one hotel restaurant I regularly had to sleep in the linen closet down the hall from the cooks' quarters.

But I was learning.

I did a short stint in Florence at a hidden gem of a restaurant called Da Noi—meaning "from us"—that had thirty seats and one star from Michelin. The owners kept their kitchen lean, employing only one other person to help cook. They used no fancy equipment and cooked with normal household cookware, including a pressure cooker for one of the entrées. It wasn't about the gear in that kitchen. It was about the food and a deft hand at the stove.

"*Un piatto, un gusto*"—one dish, one flavor—is what Franco Colombani used to say to me as we had dinner together in one of the family rooms at the highly regarded Albergo del Sole in Lombardy. The hotel and restaurant had been in continuous service since 1464. It was the blending of only a limited number of ingredients, chosen carefully to blend harmoniously, that preserved the dishes' distinctive taste. One example was an antipasto on the menu, *insalata di cappone*. Poached, then sliced, white meat from a capon is gently tossed with softened golden raisins, thinly sliced candied lemon or orange peel, some Tuscan extra virgin olive oil, a splash of high-quality balsamic vinegar, sea salt, and a few turns of freshly cracked black pepper. After resting for an hour, it was finished with a splash of red wine vinegar and, when plated, an extra drizzle of olive oil. All of the components balance into a very satisfying one-flavor result. Franco was one of very few outside of Modena authorized to make traditional balsamic vinegar. His coveted barrel room was above a barn on the premises.

In the hills outside of Lucca, at Il Vipore, I listened to the story behind Etruscan meat curing from the chef, Cesare Casella. While he explained the time-honored practice, he said that many of the recipes he used were hundreds of years old. "*Semplice ma buono*"—simple but good—was his cooking mantra.

One day I asked a line cook at the restaurant in Friuli how long he had worked there. I would watch him, focused on every dish he made, tasting as he cooked. He didn't talk much, and it was clear that he was very proud of his work. "Nineteen years," he told me. Then I asked how often the menu changed. "My station, never," he said.

Many places used ingredients I never knew existed as foodstuffs. Duck eggs for pasta. *Cee*—tiny, just-hatched freshwater eels netted from a tributary. *Gamberetti*—small shrimp, no larger than my pinkie, deep-fried with the head on and in their crispy shells. Little game birds called *tordi* consumed whole, bones and all. *Filoni*—veal spinal cord. *Brovada*—fermented turnips. A rare and very expensive mushroom called *ovolo*, whose colors and form resemble a poached egg. A marjoram-like herb found in the woods called *nepitella*. One kitchen used black truffles with onions and celery in a base trio of aromatics for stews and soups. I worked with ingredients still used from lean times—wild greens, plant sprouts, flowers, nuts, seeds, roots, grape must, and even kernels from the pits of stone fruits. Understanding the constant recycling and reusing of natural resources brought home the idea of a nation at one with its ecosystem.

I kept in touch with Faith all through my *stages,* letting her know not only how grateful I was but how much I had learned. One day she announced that I was ready for a particularly important *stage.* She was prepared to arrange a stay for me at the Michelin three-star Dal Pescatore in Lombardy.

"This one is truly special. Pay attention," she told me. I was excited to see what it takes to receive the highest restaurant rating from the world's most influential dining guide.

Antonio and Nadia Santini, the owners and operators of Dal Pescatore, had both left graduate studies in economics to run the family restaurant. Antonio's mother and father, Bruna and Giovanni, had opened the original restaurant as a gathering place in the dairy-farming community of Canneto sull'Oglio, halfway down the train line from Brescia to Parma. With Antonio up front and Nadia in the kitchen, the restaurant built its reputation until it became one of Italy's most important.

The cooking was firmly based in the classic menu of the Po valley repertoire, with a respect for tradition evident everywhere. The ivy-covered stone building housing the restaurant abutted the road, with only a brass plaque by its arched wooden door attesting to the continuity of cooking methods going back decades. The kitchen was warm, not only from the heat of the grill, but also because it served as the family hub. Nadia and her mother-in-law's strong yet nurturing personalities were the soul of the restaurant, while Antonio administered and attentively watched over the sumptuous dining room.

During a slow weekday lunch service about two weeks into my *stage,* Nadia watched me take some quick notes between plate-ups. At night after service, I would elaborate on these notes in my journals.

But that day she interrupted me, not upset that I was taking a break from work, but with a peculiar observation.

"David, I don't understand why you write so much down. How can you make words for what I do?" she asked while basting a duck breast in a small sauté pan with a sweet-and-sour sauce known as *agrodolce*. She had a very pure and clean look to her, or what the Italians describe as *acqua sapone*—a nice compliment translated as "water and soap."

"I am cooking from my soul, so there is no recipe for what I make. Tomorrow night be a little different because I don't know how I am going to feel."

I wondered if there would ever come a time when I would feel sure enough about my cooking that I, too, could cook from my soul. If there were ever a place to learn that skill, this certainly seemed to be it, for the owners made me feel more like extended family than an unpaid employee. One morning, however, toward the end of my two-month stay, I was offered the choice of two tasks: breaking down a large freshwater pike (time-consuming and I didn't know how) or preparing a signature cake, *pipasener* (easier and part of my station). I chose the latter.

Something about that day's service in the kitchen was different. It was quieter than normal, and Nadia and Bruna kept to themselves, saying very little to me. I could feel some tension. As I began cleaning my station after lunch, Nadia signaled me. "Come outside with me, David. I want to talk to you."

I followed her outside, drying my hands on a precious kitchen towel, precious because Bruna was the caretaker of the restaurant's linen supply. "Why did you choose the easy task?" she asked. I instantly knew what she was talking about. That morning my instinct told me to tackle the fish.

"I thought it was one or the other. What did I do wrong?"

Nadia blew right by me. "It's not about the task," she said. "It's you—your strength and how you feel about being a bigger person than the job."

Could there have been an adequate response to what she had just said? If so, I couldn't come up with it. I looked at her for a moment, processing what should have been clear. I thought of her and her husband as friends as well as mentors. Now I had to face that I was their employee. If they thought me unproductive, they had a right to send me packing. I was prepared to do just that, hit the road. I needed no explanation that would give me more pain than information.

But she did want to give me an explanation, and she continued one notch higher in intensity.

"I want someone with strength in my kitchen! Where's the chef in you? A chef is strong!" she said, clenching her fist and gritting her teeth. "Look at what I do. I have three jobs. I am the chef of the restaurant, but I am also a wife and a mother. I want to feel that I work for you when I come into the kitchen."

Nadia went on. "Faith told us there would be a *bravo ragazzo*"— a great guy—"coming to the restaurant. Where? I don't feel someone is here who wants to run it all."

Once again I had been found wanting in some set of skills I just didn't seem to have. And exposed to attitudes I had never known existed. Larry Forgione had never asked, "Aren't you eager to fill my shoes?"

Nadia's voice, with a new quality that pulled me up short, interrupted my thoughts, almost as if it were coming from deeper inside her.

"A chef has control over the whole thing. Everyone needs to feel there is a person that's guiding every day of the business. Even if you feel like you don't know what you are doing, make everyone feel like you do. Don't be a follower. Be a leader. I want a leader in my house!"

We were in front of the restaurant next to the side of the road.

Occasionally a car or truck would whiz by. At one point, Antonio poked his head through the restaurant door and said, "Nadia, stop already."

"No," she responded, starting in English and switching to Italian. "I have more to say."

Antonio quickly retreated. I wondered if he had witnessed this scene before. I became tight, motionless, and just listened. And then finally all I could think to say was, "Sorry, I thought I was taking care of my station."

"That's not a chef's answer!" she came back at me. "That doesn't make me feel there is a chef in my kitchen."

Nadia's face softened while she fixed her apron. "David, you have it in you. Faith told me you took a risk and left a fancy job in San Francisco because you want to be a real chef, someone whose cooking is a vision into his soul. What happened to the person with courage who walked away from a good situation at home? Where did this *bravissimo* young man lose his *figura?*"

Figura is one of those Italian words that doesn't translate well. It can mean the impression you make on others, your personage. The way she used it, the best translation might be "unshakable belief in oneself."

Maybe I didn't have it was all I could think.

"Don't be so solemn," Nadia went on, her tone now motherly, smiling, almost teasing. "You are leaving us soon." She took me inside and pulled an Italian cookbook from a shelf in the library. Before handing it to me, she said, "Just know I say what I say to help you, not hurt you. We will always be friends." And then she reached for a pen and began to inscribe the title page. In Italian, she wrote: "*Per Davide. Buona fortuna. Ti auguro di diventare un grande chef*"—For David. Good Luck. I hope you become a great chef.

I went up to my room to think about what had just happened. Nadia's eyes and words cracked the shell. It was three in the after-

noon, and the bells in the local clock tower down the road started to
ring. I recalled having seen the words in large letters painted under the
clock: È L'ORA DI FAR BENE—It is the hour to do well.

Seasons changed one into the next. My language skills increased, although to some Italians I had a Spanish accent. My clothes
all bore the "Made in Italy" label, although I could never quite figure
out how to wear them as well as the locals. I eventually became a le-
gal resident with a work permit and an identity card. I began dream-
ing in Italian.

Italians feel an immense pride that tends toward the regional
rather than the national and reveals itself in more than just the cooking. From cosmopolitan Milan in the north to history-laden Rome,
each region has its distinct identity, style, and attitude.

My trip introduced me to many of these differences, and I knew
I would be coming home a vastly better cook. Given the right ingredients, I could prepare numerous regional recipes. However, even
though I had learned a great deal about Italian food, I wanted the opportunity to choose ingredients and write menus, if for no other reason than to reassure myself that my culinary grand tour had been
worth one of the longest sabbaticals ever taken by a cook.

I thought about contacting some of my bosses in Italy to see if
they had any real jobs for me, not another internship. But I didn't love
the idea of starting at the bottom. And once in, I wasn't sure how long
I could get away with the white lie a friend of mine recommended I
tell people for acceptance in a class-conscious society: "Tell them
you're the chef, not a cook." In a small town, I was bound to get
caught.

While working in Milan, I contacted a yacht charter agent
whose name I had been given by a friend in San Francisco. There
were large yachts that plied the Mediterranean, he told me, and many
of them had private chefs on board. The idea was intriguing.

The agent, Annie, was based in Antibes on the Côte d'Azur. I told her what I had been doing and that I was interested in possibly cooking at sea. She invited me to her office for an interview. She said my timing was good because the yachts were starting to return from the winter in the Caribbean. I made an appointment and went to Antibes during my next days off from work.

As the train made its way from Genoa west along the coast, I had a nonstop view of the Mediterranean. The most romantic body of water on the planet was right in front of me. Two vivid tones of blue—water and sky—filled the train windows. By the time I got to my destination, I would have said anything to get work on or near the sea.

At her office, Annie immediately asked me two questions: "Have you ever worked on a yacht before?" and "Do you get seasick?"

The truth came out like a reflex. "No, I haven't. But I believe seasickness is a state of mind."

She cracked a smile and probably sensed I was eager to get a job. We talked a long while, and then she said she would try to find something for me.

I went back to Milan seduced by what I had seen. The famous Côte d'Azur. Huge yachts. A thriving international community. The idea of an offshore adventure was alluring. Several days later, Annie called. "I found something."

When she told me that the new owners of a sailing yacht called *Serenity* were looking for a chef that summer, I asked to hear more. The money was good, Annie assured me, but the owners would make demanding bosses. With scant tolerance for anything except the very best, they were the types of people who didn't suffer fools gladly.

"*Serenity* was purchased by a very wealthy and socially prominent Italian couple," Annie explained. "The boat will now be based on the Côte d'Azur."

She instructed me to refer to them always as *il Dottore* and *la Signora*. She also told me that *la Signora* was, in her own right, one of

Europe's most successful and admired businesswomen. Annie cautioned that she had heard *la Signora* could be quite blunt in voicing her dissatisfaction when something wasn't done the way she wanted it.

"Think carefully, David," Annie said. "I know you've spent four years in Italy learning the cuisine, but these people will know in an instant if you can't meet their standards."

All I could think about was the opportunity this offered for me to finally have my own kitchen and run my own show. I would be fully responsible for everything that went out of the galley. Another dozen *stages* could not make me any more qualified than I believed I was at that moment.

I asked Annie to set up the interview.

"Ciao!" *the elegant, tanned* woman greeted me as I stepped from the dock to the boat.

"*Ciao!*" I responded and wondered if Annie had stressed that I was fluent in Italian.

It was warm even for late March, with an occasional strong gust whipping across the boat. Unruffled by the wind, *la Signora* indicated that I should follow her to the cockpit.

I was surprised by her appearance. Her high cheekbones and forehead, which in class-conscious Europe were said to confirm both breeding and intelligence, were accentuated by dark brown, almost black hair tied back in a long ponytail. Her untucked bright blue blouse was striking over beige slacks and white moccasin-type shoes. Born of a people who created it, style draped across her effortlessly.

At the cockpit, with an extended hand, palm up, she directed me to a cushioned seat. I stepped down into the sun-filled area that wrapped around the binnacle—the polished brass housing for the compass and steering wheel. *Il Dottore* was seated, and she introduced him to me.

Il Dottore appeared to have a medium build, a skin tone that looked like a perennial tan, wavy gray hair that covered his ears, a nice smile, and an easy way about him—the casual demeanor of success and confidence. Dressed in a short-sleeve, button-down shirt and slacks, he augmented the very put-together presence of *la Signora*.

I positioned myself on the seat across from both of them. The folding cockpit table was fully opened between us, with what appeared to be *Serenity*'s blueprints and the sail plan. *Il Dottore* was reading them before I sat down.

I affected an attitude that I hoped would convey total ease. But perhaps they sensed a little nervous tension in the fact that I kept looking from one to the other, trying to determine which of the two would be making the hiring decision. I also didn't understand why they would even consider a young American cook and not an Italian chef.

This would be their first season as owners of *Serenity*, which they were apparently rushing to make ready for the May opening of the Riviera yachting season, less than two months off. Angry cries of the French, Italian, and British day workers on board, arguing about whose way was the right way to rewire the running lights from the navigation station, flew across the boat. But *la Signora* just tuned them out and began the interview in flawless Italian. I knew enough Italian to understand most Italians, but understanding a foreign language is always easier when the person speaking is highly articulate. This is especially so with Italian, some of whose regional accents only vaguely resemble Tuscan Italian, considered the most proper.

"So, Davide, what kinds of things do you like to cook?" She pronounced my name "DAH-vee-day."

"Well, I am inspired by many things," I answered. "I love to cook—am fascinated by—first courses and pastas. My whole perception of what pasta is—as a course, as a flavor, integral to a meal—has been rediscovered since I've been living in Italy. But what I like cooking most are game birds."

"What kind?" she asked.

"Quail, pigeon, duck, and guinea fowl. They're a great challenge to master," I went on. "I've been exposed to a wide range of ways to prepare them." Now, really wound up, I rambled on about how preparing special regional dishes allowed me to take the academic knowledge I had picked up during the various *stages* of my training and apply it to my own creations.

But mostly I spoke of ideas and a refined palate, confident this would distinguish me from a dockside adventurer looking to sling galley grub for tax-free cash. I paused, ready for *la Signora* to compliment me on my broad knowledge and interesting cooking ideas. No such compliment came. Instead, she sat quietly, patiently waiting for me to finish saying all I wanted to say.

When she was sure I was done, she said, "*Allora*," pushing up to the edge of the cockpit bench, posture erect. I also edged closer to the lip of my seat both to signal attentiveness and to hear her above the workmen's din. *Il Dottore* had long ago turned his attention back to the plans he was studying.

There was no question about who would be making the hire.

La Signora cleared her throat and held forth:

"This is what we like to do in the summer. We like our food to be very light, very clean. We like it to be well prepared. We want it to be fresh, to be Italian. We don't eat a lot of meats or heavy things in the summer.

"We want lots of fish—there is no reason why we shouldn't have fish—we'll be at sea!" she said, smiling and gesturing to the Mediterranean on three sides of us. Now I wished I hadn't run on about game birds.

"Lots of fish and seafood, plenty of vegetables—we love tomatoes—and fruits. Simple things done beautifully.

"We'll let you know when we want to have a pasta, so don't think that we'll have pasta or risotto at every meal, as you may have done at some of the restaurants where you worked.

"No onions are to show in dishes and no snails, red beets, or mussels.

"No meat sauces.

"No cold plates for dinner entrées. Occasionally you may serve a dish *tiepido*"—tepid—"if it makes sense for the menu."

Il Dottore mentioned something to her as she was talking. "Oh yes," she added, "don't be shy with *peperoncini*"—chile peppers.

"Have different snacks available and an assortment of canapés to be served every day with cocktails before dinner service. Make many and rotate the offerings so that repeats are spaced no closer than once per month.

"We'd like to have three or four courses for both lunch and dinner. Everything will be presented on platters and served Russian style." Russian style, I knew, is where a server offers and then serves each person from the platter. That didn't surprise me. No family style on this boat.

La Signora leaned forward to emphasize her most important dictate. I found myself completely taken with her. She became very focused, her brown eyes locked onto mine, her perfect Italian coming off her tongue like the snap of crisp biscotti.

"There is no reason to ever, *ever* repeat a dish throughout the summer." She explained that the season would officially begin in late May at Monte Carlo, during the weekend of the Grand Prix auto race, and end in October, during the Voiles de Saint-Tropez classic yacht regatta. From May through July, she and *il Dottore* would be flying from whichever of their residences they happened to be at the end of the workweek to meet the boat for weekends at predetermined places along the French and Italian coast, but come August, they would be on board for the entire month. The itinerary would take *Serenity* around the Côte d'Azur, then down the west coast of the Italian boot to Portofino, the Cinque Terre, along Tuscany from Viareggio to the Argentario via Elba, the islands of Ischia, Ponza, and Capri, the Amalfi coast, then after, the longest water leg, across the Tyrrhenian Sea to Sardinia along the Emerald Coast, to Corsica, and finally back to Antibes.

"As the cuisine changes in each port of call," she told me, "you should be able to alter your menu to take account of the indigenous offerings of each place we visit. *Hai capito?*"—do you understand?

Clearly they wanted to enjoy the seasonal, regional, and local attributes of *la cucina italiana*. This created one of the most exacting criteria for cooking I had ever been given, requiring me to know what to look for in the markets at every port of call, then figuring out what local preparation to make out of what I'd be able to find.

I had learned that Italian cooking is all about place. Each region has its own flavors and even its own style of cooking, and she was now asking me if I thought I could vary my own cooking to accommodate this very Italian way of preparing food. I thought I could. After all, I had been preparing meals for Italians in my years in Europe. But then again, I never had sole responsibility for the menu. Nor had I ever cooked day after day for people who knew precisely what regional Italian cooking should taste like.

The extent of detail she had gone into, along with her flat-out directness, encouraged me to believe I had at least made the short list. I was happy with that. I wanted the job, but I didn't know whether to tell her that I thought I could meet her requirements or wait for her to say something further. I decided to say nothing.

Finally, shifting from her *padrona* tone in Italian to the first English phrase she used during the interview, she added: "Make sure you have *an emergency menu*. If six guests turn to ten or fifteen, you must be prepared. Keep some cheeses, fruits, bread sticks, and crackers on board. Some canned tuna, canned tomatoes, *salumi,* and maybe a kilo of frozen shrimp. Enough to enable you to prepare a beautiful and simple meal on short notice." I made a mental note to record this list in my journal to cover myself in case I got the job.

"Also, always have pâté on board." The word "pâté" exploded from her mouth—more an order than a suggestion. "I like to have it on board at all times."

She turned and asked *il Dottore* if he had anything to add. Solely by his facial expression, without a spoken word, he indicated she had covered everything.

She turned back to me and extended her hand. *"Grazie, Davide,"* she said warmly. Then, with the first smile she had shown me, she added, "See you in two months, okay?" I nodded my agreement. "The yacht manager will contact you about details."

I wasn't surprised when not a word about my pay was uttered. I had learned that the Italian way is that if you don't trust your employer to do right by you, why even waste time on an interview? As I left the cockpit and walked down the *passerelle,* I took a last look back. *La Signora* had rejoined *il Dottore* in reviewing the blueprints and sailing plans.

With that, I had the job.

Two

~

A Season to Taste

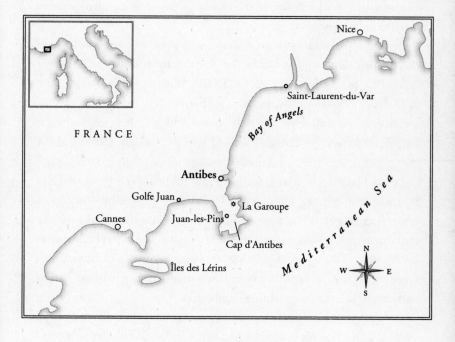

Antibes and the Bay of Angels

As the coastal train rolled into Antibes, I caught sight of the tall, cascading masts of *Serenity* berthed at the Yacht Club d'Antibes, on the far side of Port Vauban. The boat had been moved since I was on board for my interview and was now in a new extension of the harbor built to accommodate mega-yachts, some among the largest in the world. A few of the motor yachts berthed near *Serenity* were many times her size.

The walk from the train station was a long one, but I welcomed the opportunity to get a better feel for the town that would be my home port for the summer. As I made my way toward *Serenity*, I took in the activity of the busy harbor. The hundreds of motor yachts, motor sailers, and sailing yachts, tied up one after the next, gradually got larger and longer the farther I walked into the marina. On just about every one it seemed maintenance was going on. Sun-bleached teak decks and bright white hulls were being scrubbed clean by tanned and fit crew members in uniforms; a few riggers worked at the top of masts; cranes lifted and lowered smaller craft into the water near the harbormaster's building; little Renault marine service vehicles were everywhere. The noise of sanding, spraying, fairing, and honing was constant. It was just another busy late-spring day in a working harbor catering to the serious yachting community.

Serenity was parked stern-to in her slip almost at the end of the quay. When I was on board the first time, she was undergoing a complete makeover—restoration work on the rig, deck, interior, and mechanical systems—or what's called in the yacht business a refit. When the owners said that she would be ready for the opening of the summer season, my reaction, which I kept to myself, was disbelief. To my eye, too much remained to be done to meet that target date. Now I had to concede that I had been wrong. Although a lot of finishing work was still going on, I no longer doubted she'd be ready. This confirmed the reputation and my original impression of the owners: that these were people who knew how to get things done.

Sitting high and proud, *Serenity* was a magnificent yacht, seemingly ready to handle whatever the sea threw at her. Having sailed the Mediterranean and Caribbean for decades, this 124-foot, gaff-rigged schooner had been commissioned and built in the United States during the early 1930s, the worst years of the Great Depression. A model of classic design, she enjoyed a reputation in the yachting world as having "great lines." Now, as the refit neared completion, the sanded teak deck, varnished woodwork, replicated solid brass hardware, polished fixtures, new masts, booms, ropes, blocks, and virgin white sails made her shine.

I was looking forward to spending time in this major hub of the sailor's world. Situated between tony Cannes and bustling Nice, Antibes was founded by Greek colonists as Antipolis—the city across—possibly because it lay across the Bay of Angels from the earlier-settled Nice. Control of the city later fell to the Romans, who ruled it for many centuries, then in turn to nearby Italians, the Ligurians, and the house of Savoy. Not until the mid-nineteenth century did the region officially become a part of France, which accounts for the city's culture being so strongly Italian.

Beyond *Serenity*'s bow, I could see Fort Carré, a sixteenth-century stone fort across the harbor. When I first came to Antibes, Annie had given me a tour of the area and noted a few landmarks, the fort being the most prominent. Napoleon spent some time there, both in front of and behind bars. I looked to the other side of town and saw Phare de la Garoupe—the famous lighthouse on top of Cap d'Antibes. This aid to navigation has kept seafaring vessels from having their hulls ripped on the beak-sharp peninsula rocks that lurk in the shallow waters along the coastline. I soon learned it had a land-based navigational role as well, guiding drunken crewmen back to their boats from Juan-les-Pins, the wild nightlife town on the other side of Cap d'Antibes. Down along the seafront side of the old town is one of the most distinctive landmarks, the ramparts, the shoreline fortification that protected the town against invaders and against the high sea swells driven by the legendary mistral winds.

Whether experienced on land or sea, the force of a mistral can be nasty. The mighty gales come roaring down the Rhône valley, then split offshore in the Golfe du Lion, with one half fanning easterly while the other blows to the west. But Annie calmed any concerns I had about being caught in the tempest by promising that an advanced mistral is rare in the summer.

This beautiful and brackish port city overlooking the Mediterranean Sea has been attracting creative people for more than a century. Jules Verne wrote *20,000 Leagues Under the Sea* in Antibes, and from the 1920s on it was a playground for movie stars, artists, and writers. Ernest Hemingway, F. Scott Fitzgerald, and Gerald and Sara Murphy dug their toes in the sand while sipping pastis, and Picasso, like Monet before him, found his time in Antibes inspiring and restorative. He generously left behind his collection of work done at Antibes, the city turning his prominent old-town residence, Château Grimaldi, into Musée Picasso, a museum dedicated to these objets d'art. Jacques Cousteau used Antibes as home port for his research vessel, the *Calypso,* when he was working in the Mediterranean.

Behind the facade of glamour lent it by artists and writers, Antibes stayed true to its heritage: first and foremost it has always been a sailor's town. As the harbor grew into one of the most important in the world for yacht sales, berthing, chartering, and maintenance, a labor force to fulfill these services made the area home. This citizens-of-the-world confluence of captains, sailors, specialists, and day workers, all drawing handsome paychecks from their wealthy employers, kept perpetual smiles on the faces of the local shopkeepers, landlords, crew agencies, restaurateurs, and bar owners. I looked forward to becoming part of this community.

I don't recall how long I had been standing there on the quay admiring *Serenity* before a broad-shouldered man with a military bearing and a serious look called out to me from the deck. "Can I help you?" he asked in very British Queen's English.

"I'm David," I answered. "The owners hired me a couple of months ago."

"The cook, right? I heard you might be joining today."

Following yachting protocol, I asked permission to board. When it was granted, I took off my shoes before ambling up the *passerelle*— the gangway. This is not a universal maritime practice, but dark-soled street shoes can mar and scuff a yacht's soft and stain-prone teak deck, so removing them before being asked to do so, I hoped, would be taken as a sign of my respect for the stately *Serenity*.

"Kevin, the mate," he said, offering a firm handshake. As the mate, he was second in command. "Welcome aboard."

"Pleased to be here," I responded. He said nothing further. I stood awkwardly, making sure I at least made a good impression. He caught the eye of someone on deck farther forward and waved him over to us.

"Scott, the engineer," he told me. To Scott, he said just as simply, "David, our cook." So much for small talk.

Direct from the Isle of Wight, Scott was more cordial than Kevin, even cheery, with the weathered and chiseled looks you find in many men who live on the sea. He was tall and thin, had a receding hairline, and a neatly groomed beard. He volunteered to show me around, inviting me, with a sly smile, to go with him for the "cook's tour."

I followed him almost the length of the boat, carefully plotting my way past the day workers on deck, trying not to interrupt their work. At the bow, we climbed down the crew ladder into the fo'c'sle, short for forecastle (pronounced "FOLKS-ul"), the small crew quarters in the bow. I noticed that Scott was as sure-footed as a mountain goat, leaving me feeling like a landlubber. It would take a few days for me to get my sea legs.

The slightly raked floor and support structure for the deck above made ceiling height below just under six feet. The camber of the space created a feeling of being inside an elongated pyramid on its side. We moved aft through a bulkhead, and I put my bags on the mess table. One step farther aft Scott opened the thick metal door to the engine room to let me have a look at *Serenity*'s new artificial heart—a loud, vibrating diesel generator that provided electricity and charged the boat's batteries while under way or at anchor. Then he showed me other newly installed equipment: a drive axle, water desalinator, electric panels, alarm systems, and a wall of meters, digital gauges, and switches. For a long moment he stood before all this new equipment with a look of pure love in his eyes.

I would guess he saw no such look in my eyes, because he quickly moved on, to the galley, my new office. It was an L-shaped space on the port side just across from the mess area that led into the pantry. All around us, the floorboards had been removed to give workers access to the utility lines under the flooring. We had to move around by balancing ourselves on the support structure. He showed me the refrigerators, known as "reefers"—one a hull-mounted reach-in, the other top-loading, built like a deep chest, not my favorite design in fridges, since whatever you need in a hurry will invariably be found crushed at the very bottom.

I was introduced to an appliance I was surprised to find in a yacht's galley—a shiny new commercial-grade dishwasher. Whoever was in charge of the refit must have figured an onboard dishwasher would add a nice touch of modernity. But every new convenience comes with a price. Part of the challenge of cooking at sea is resource management. Dockside, a dishwasher can draw electricity from shore service, but once under way it's a discipline of power trade-offs, and in this game it was a fair guess that the captain would choose his radar over my rinse cycle. Plus, the owners wouldn't want to be worrying about whether there was enough available power for them to watch a video or play music. I suspected this dishwasher was going to enjoy a nice, easy life as a large bread box.

Standing in the galley, I had a different take on the progress of the work being done. As magnificent as *Serenity* looked from the quay, here below she reeked of a foul combination of varnish, brass polish, and diesel fuel. The small portholes on either side of the galley were open, but clearly not up to the job of ventilating the area. One of the first chefs I ever worked for used to say that taste is also appearance and aroma, or as he also liked to say, "Smell the flavors!" Would every dish I prepared taste like the odors now permeating the galley?

Scott interrupted my thoughts, giving me what he thought was good news. "We just installed a new marine stove for you," he said, beaming.

Yep, it looked new, and expensive, too—mostly made of stainless steel—but damn it, once again there was bad news mixed in with the good. The stove wasn't on gimbals, gyroscope-like devices to keep an onboard stove horizontal in heaving seas. "No gimbals?" I asked.

"No, we can't do that," he answered nonchalantly. The stove had been installed parallel with the beam (width) of the boat, rendering gimbals useless. Great! I had visions of sauce sloshing over a pot's rim with every sea swell. Scott mentioned that a custom-designed system of bars and adjustable guards was to be installed within days to keep the pots over the burners. I would quickly find out that the system was only good for pots, since fry pans were shallow enough to slip under the guardrails. This system would prove useless unless I gave some forethought to menu needs, the sailing schedule, prep time, and the size of the cookware. And the ventilator hood above sounded at best like a decent desk fan.

Scott would have made a good poker player. Ignoring the serious concern that must have been written all over my face, he went on with the tour, noting one by one each of the galley's features. He proudly pointed to where my oven hooked into the gas line and to the butane tanks housed in a locker on deck. He emphasized a sequence of manual valves that were automatically monitored. Escaping gas that went down into the bilge could be very dangerous, so an alarm system, a high-pitched screech audibly very different from the other bell alarms, had been installed. Scott pointed out a space under the floor just above the bilge that had new shelves installed: my nonperishable food and beverage storage area. Getting to it meant pulling up the heavy floor plank then climbing down with only enough space to spin in a squatted position.

We headed aft to take a look at the areas I would not be entering as part of my work. The salon and dining area were given an indulgent amount of space across the entire beam. Farther aft, there were four luxurious cabins, each with its own head, or bathroom. A staircase provided access to deck level. From the glorious woodwork of the rails and posts, it was clear that this was for owners and guests only; the crew would use the forward ladder.

Newly installed carpet was a steely blue that made a nice match with the matte-finished wood paneling of the walls and off-white painting of the boat's metal superstructure that supported the deck. Not masking the rivets, bolts, and beams gave the interior a true nautical feel, and the polished brass hardware of the portholes looked smart. The upholstered furniture and the bedcovers were in sumptuous fabrics of coordinated beiges, golds, and whites to go with the rest of the interior, except for a few pieces like the banquette at the dining table, which was covered in fitted, dark navy blue leather. All the guest heads had marble bathtubs and sinks with newly cast brass fixtures based on the original style. It was very elegant, a completely different ambience from the crew quarters in the fo'c'sle.

Once the tour was complete, and Scott was off somewhere else,

I sat at the mess table, trying to think through all that had to be done. This was going to be tough. When I was here for the interview, I didn't even think to come down to have a look at where I'd be working, what equipment I'd have available as I set about putting together the series of culinary miracles *la Signora* had made part of the job description. And I had to pull this off in a galley that served as home for seven crew members trying to coexist for the summer in tight quarters. Small bunks with a minimum of storage space. One head for all of us. A mess table that could not seat everyone at once. And most important in terms of my job, a galley that was far from the ultimate in convenience.

I wasn't yet sure about the maximum number of guests the owners might be entertaining at any given time. In this problematic work space I could cook for up to eight guests staying on board and the crew. More than eight guests and I'd be in trouble. At my interview, *la Signora* had made a reference to my being prepared for any emergency. What if she decided to have an afternoon party of fifteen or even twenty? Somehow I would have to manage.

Serenity's galley may have been small, poorly equipped, and ready to confound me in the first rough seas we hit, but it was the first chance I had to run my own kitchen and do it right, gimbals or no gimbals. I had learned from more than one hard experience how important it is to get on top of everything right off, how quickly high hopes can go sour when a chef doesn't control his kitchen. I wasn't going to make that mistake again.

La Signora had made it clear during my interview that she wanted an all-Italian menu, a challenge I embraced. I'd have to create one great meal after another, all from scratch, which meant planning every menu around the fresh ingredients I could find at each port of call. I'd also need all the right seasonings, aromatics, and condiments. So a well-organized list of staples was crucial. Once under way, there would be less opportunity to run out and pick up a needed item to finish a dish I was preparing.

Many ingredients and styles of cooking along the Côte d'Azur, especially *cuisine niçoise,* go back to when the area was Italian, not French, so I expected I'd be able to get most of the basics I needed close by. The flavors of this region are so close to those of Liguria just over the border that except for certain dishes like the ubiquitous *salade niçoise,* the pizzalike flat bread called *pissaladière,* and the chickpea-based crêpe-like snack called *socca,* the Italians left a grand impression when the border was created. So it is no wonder culinary heritage shows in what's available in the markets and shops. And if I couldn't find something in Antibes, I could sign out one of the leased crew cars and drive across the Italian border to Ventimiglia or San Remo.

I carefully went through my notes and the few cookbooks I brought on board to help me find all the pantry ingredients I would need for the season. At the top of the list were a variety of olive oils, a few vinegars, and the essential seasonings of the Italian repertoire: anchovies, capers, hot red pepper flakes, and dried porcini mushrooms to use for a delicious porcini mayonnaise on baked or poached fish. The spice rack consisted of a selection totaling no more than ten, and a visit to the international grocery store in town gave me access to the condiments I needed, including Worcestershire and, for one recipe in particular, soy sauce. Then there were the shelf-stable items like canned tuna, rice, dried pasta and beans, olives, and the ingredients needed for simple baking. Dairy was kept to the basics, including a short list of cheeses, and I could pick up the *aromi*—the fresh aromatics—in ports along the way, confident they would not be hard to find. Once procured, these items would give me the base I needed to prepare *la cucina italiana* and, more specifically, the summer repertoire along the coast. I taped a copy of the list in my journal to commence the recording of the season's menus.

Serenity Pantry List

Base Ingredients, Seasonings, and Condiments

Pure olive oil	Cornichons
Extra virgin olive oil	Pitted Niçoise olives
Sunflower seed oil	Picholine olives
Red wine vinegar	Concentrated tomato paste
Balsamic vinegar	Whole peeled tomatoes (canned)
Champagne vinegar	Spanish piquillo peppers (canned)
Anchovies in salt	Chickpeas (canned)
Capers in salt	Tuna in oil (canned)
Hot red pepper flakes or peperoncini	Arborio rice
Dried porcini	Dried pastas
Dried oregano	Cannellini beans
Bay leaves	Borlotti beans
Herbes de Provence	Dried bread crumbs
Saffron	Pine nuts
Fennel seeds	Almonds
Whole nutmeg	Golden raisins
Vanilla	Unsweetened chocolate
Fine sea salt	Flour, semolina
Coarse sea salt	Sugar
Black peppercorns	Powdered sugar
Dry mustard	Honey
Dijon mustard	Dry yeast
Worcestershire sauce	Savoyard cookies
Ketchup	Amaretti cookies
Soy sauce	Dry white wine
Harissa	

Dairy and Cheese

Milk

Heavy cream

Unsalted butter

Eggs

Parmigiano-Reggiano

Aged pecorino

Mascarpone

Ricotta

Ricotta salata

Fresh Aromatics

Pancetta

Yellow onions

Red onions

Garlic

Shallots

Celery

Carrots

Italian parsley

Lemons

Oranges

Potatoes (always on board)

Of course, I couldn't forget the crew. Food is the great comforter under way, so I'd have to do my part to hold up morale. The food would be Italian in style but adjusted to the hearty, carb-needy appetites of my co-workers. I planned on creating crew menus from what I was preparing for the owners by extending things like sauces and side dishes and replacing the obscure ingredients like rare and expensive seafood with more substantial fare, like meats and pasta dishes. They'd also want different cereals, cookies and biscuits, jams, chocolate, snacks, soft drinks, spring water, and, of course, plenty of beer.

Getting the base ingredients on board was only the half of it. Michele, *Serenity's* land-based money manager, gave me an open ticket to go into town and buy whatever kitchen supplies the galley required: pots, saucepans, casseroles, and sauté pans (the high sides are great when cooking while under way). I measured my new "marine oven" to make sure the roasting pans, sheet trays with grills, and ceramic baking dishes that I bought would fit inside. Molds for tarts, canapés, and *panna cotta;* a rolling pin, pastry brushes, mixing bowls, and a two-kilo scale (the easiest thing to use when cooking in metric); knives, ladles, kitchen spoons, whisks, and strainers. I wished for spring-loaded tongs that all cooks swear by in American kitchens, but I had never seen them in any of the Italian restaurants where I worked. If I couldn't find them, so be it. Out of necessity I had developed the dexterity to use a large fork and spoon like tongs, and discovered how versatile the technique can be. Then I went through my journals again, marking the pages where I thought certain dishes or recipes would work for the season's repertoire and making a mental note of what kinds of kitchenwares they would require. I didn't rush completing my lists. *La Signora,* who had come off in my interview as a woman with scant tolerance for incompetence, had made it clear that she expected me to be ready for any eventuality within reason. I had little doubt that if something I prepared failed to meet her standards, she would not be interested in why.

Kevin came down to take a break and reintroduce himself while getting a drink from the reefer. He took a place at the mess table, looked around the galley, inquired about my lists, and made some comments about the challenges I faced. He agreed that the dishwasher would be better used as a storage space. Then he asked if I would be cooking Italian food this season.

"Not only do I want to, but according to *la Signora* I have to," I said, and then added, "I'd like to pull this into crew menu, too."

"Great. I like pasta. Especially a nice carbonara," he responded, and then left.

His preference was noted, but a little tweak in seasonal eating would be in order, something I preferred to furnish in practice rather than by explanation. A rich carbonara sauce based on pork fat and egg yolks was perfect in winter but would give way to a lighter summer alternative based on olive oil and tomatoes and no less shy in flavor.

With all of the activity of the refit going on, mechanics, electricians, and other installers passed continually through the galley. Eventually, I met our two deckhands, who were both in their twenties. Nigel was a burly New Zealander who stopped in Antibes for the season while on a world tour, and Ian was a happy-go-lucky Australian day worker turned crew member. Ian came off like a seasoned pro who had worked on boats his entire life. A few days later, I was surprised to learn that this would be his first job at sea.

I spent most of my first two days in the galley writing equipment lists and preparing menus, taking an occasional break from what had come to feel like school homework to go up on deck, get some sun and fresh air, check out what was going on, and get to know the crewmates with whom I'd be spending the season. I picked up that among the crew, *everyone pours the coffee,* so I made sure to help out wherever I could. Also, from my past experiences in restaurant kitchens, I knew that everyone's eye was always on the new kid, to see if he thought too much of himself. A good way to show that I didn't see myself as better than the rest was to pitch in with the grunt work where needed.

Patrick, the captain, ducked into the galley to welcome me on board. An American, he called the Côte d'Azur home and made his living as a full-time sailor. His clean-cut features and stocky military build gave him an aura of authority, like someone who was thorough and did things by the book. Having skippered some beautifully maintained classic yachts in both the Mediterranean and the Caribbean, he had originally signed on to manage the refit. That day, he brought my work attire, which would constitute my daily wardrobe for the rest of the summer: shorts, pants, polo shirts and T-shirts, a couple of sweaters, a high-tech Italian Windbreaker, two pairs of boat shoes, and foul-weather gear. Everything had the *Serenity* name and logo printed or embroidered on it and was navy blue, gray, or white. He mentioned that before the first weekend with the owners, we would also have our formal uniforms that would be worn when they were on board.

"They'll be cotton, right?" was my immediate question to Patrick.

I couldn't imagine wearing polyester in what I sensed was going to be a hot summer in the galley.

"No, poly," he said.

"The heat down here is going to be rough," I emphasized.

He tried to allay my concern by saying, "Let me see what I can do."

At the end of the second day, even after everyone else had packed it in and headed to the bars, pubs, or their apartments in town, I stayed on board. It took a while to plan where to put things. There wasn't a lot of storage space, and I wanted to be familiar with the space I had before the provisioning began. Satisfied that I had done my best with this stage of my prep, I decided to get some sleep so I'd be able to get an early jump on my pantry shopping in the morning.

Six bunks lined both sides of the crew quarters. When Patrick suggested I pick a bunk in the small but separate captain's quarters, my first thought was that the owners had told him that I should be treated as someone of rank. Such hopes were quickly deflated when a more likely explanation occurred to me: that maybe he knew something about the owners I didn't and might be showing compassion for a condemned man.

I climbed up into my top bunk, turned on my side, and looked out of the cabin at the dimly lit crew quarters. Over a hundred yards of heavy anchor chains would run through steel tubes in the middle of the fo'c'sle and into lockers under the floor. I imagined how much space would be left after everyone brought their gear on board. The open hatch on deck let in the evening chill and the briny smell of seawater. It reminded me that one thing high and low alike would be forced to share on our voyage was the pervasive dampness that goes with living at sea.

As I lay there waiting for sleep, I focused on keeping my elbow clear of a thick iron deck beam that ran two feet above my chest. With the boat all to myself, I hoped I would get the uninterrupted night of rest I desperately needed. I knew this luxury wasn't going to last.

Three

The One Without the Tan

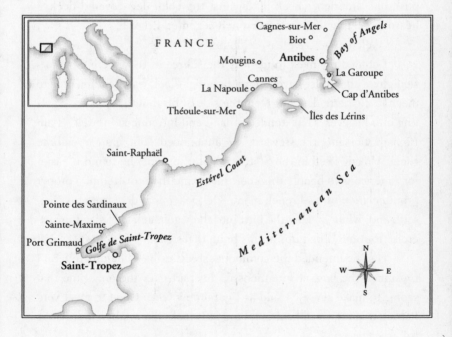

Cap d'Antibes and the Estérel Coast

*I*t was six-thirty in the morning, and I was on the foredeck trying to get through my daily routine of stretches and exercises. The night spent in the damp fo'c'sle had left my joints more than a little stiff, and my elbow ached from being banged against the overhead beam every time I rolled over in my bunk. Resting between sets of push-ups, my right cheek flat against the cold, dew-covered deck, I heard a greeting delivered in French-accented English.

"Welcome to *zee* pleasure dome!"

I craned my neck to identify the source of the greeting. A frazzled guy with a must-have-been-a-late-night look was standing next to me, a lit cigarette dangling from the side of his mouth, the smoke getting into his eyes. He extended a hand and introduced himself. "I am Richard Corsaire, the steward," he announced, "but you can call me Rick." Having lived in the States, he later told me, he found it easier for Americans to handle this short nickname than to attempt a proper pronunciation of his French name. He took a final drag from his cigarette and, while flicking the butt into the water, acknowledged my exercise routine: "Push-ups at this hour, that's good."

Had he intended the comment sarcastically? I couldn't tell. So I presumed the best of intentions on his part. "It's the only time that seems to make sense," I said as I got on my feet. "Good to meet you. Patrick told me you'd be around today. It looks like we have our hands full to get set up."

"I will help you, but don't worry," he assured me. "It won't be all work." He had obviously misread my concern. "I can show you the Côte d'Azur you've never seen!"

The idea was intriguing. It would be a few weeks before the real cruising began that would take us out of France for the rest of the summer. I had heard a great deal about the sheer opulence of this coast and its famous cities—Nice, Cannes, Monte Carlo, Saint-Tropez. I had been to parts of the Riviera over the course of my years in Europe, and the glint in Rick's eye suggested he knew of special sensory delights lurking off the beaten path. But I had a galley to equip, I told him, and that would have to come first.

"As you wish," he said and went below.

A couple of hours later he invited himself to go to town with me to get my kitchenwares and check out the open-air market. As we walked toward the old town along the wide quay of the yacht club, Rick could take only so much work talk before changing the topic. "Listen, let's get this done so we can go to the beach clubs on the Cap d'Antibes." The exclusive beach areas on the coast are like the VIP rooms at trendy nightclubs, and Rick was eager to demonstrate his easy intimacy with such places. I'm usually not one to turn down an opportunity to go to the beach, but I held my focus on why I was there. "Maybe we can go after I'm set up," I said.

Rick wasn't buying. "David, look where we are!" His arm swept in a wide arc. "On the French Riviera, Europe's summer playground! The eggs can wait."

"Don't you have stuff to do below to get ready?" I asked him. As steward, he had the owner and guest cabins to set up and common areas to help organize and maintain. When the owners were on board, he would be server, butler, valet, and house cleaner. Beverages, floral arrangements, and laundry were also in his domain.

"Why so fast? You are too nervous," he said as he cleaned the lenses of his sunglasses with his shirt. "The owners are not fools. They wouldn't have hired you if you couldn't handle the job."

"Maybe, but I'm not taking any chances."

Finally convinced that I intended to work at outfitting the galley *today,* with or without his help, he shrugged and said, "Okay, I will not desert you. The French shopkeepers will see the American coming and pick clean his pockets." He wanted it understood that it was only for me that he was giving up on the idea of spending the day at Plage Keller, his favorite beach club. His body language suggested that as a Frenchman he had made a generous sacrifice for his new friend.

As we walked, Rick started to sing a jingle celebrating life in the south of France: "The women are so hot, hot, hot 'cause they make you feel good, good, good!" And he lived what he sang. Each woman we passed got a sultry *"Bonjour, madame"* or *"Bonjour, mademoiselle"* from him. I was surprised at how often he got a smile and a pleasant *"Bonjour"* in return. Or at least a saucy flip of their hair.

Even though I was tense and eager to get to work, this guy was hard to dislike. Rick was an authentic French bon vivant. A passion for la dolce vita was clearly his motivation. Curious to know what went into making him the man he was, I encouraged him to tell me about his background. He didn't need any arm-twisting.

"I am a sailor by blood," he explained. Born into a shipping family, he had grown up in Bordeaux and on the Atlantic coast. His father had skippered ferries from Calais across the English Channel to Dover. As soon as Rick was old enough, he went to sea, he said, to follow in his father's footsteps as a sailor.

"I worked on one of the French America's Cup challengers," he added with unmistakable pride, "and had a great time in Newport, Rhode Island, then in the maxi circuit." If there is a hierarchy among sailors who serve on yachts, those who have raced competitively on large maxis—sixty-foot, high-performance, and technologically advanced racing boats—make up the top tier. Then, as if to concede that his life had not been all highs, he told me in a confidential tone, "After that I made a big mistake. I got married." His short marriage to an American took him to Washington, D.C., where his new in-laws owned an upscale restaurant. He promptly went to work running the dining room and learning the finer points of elegant service. "The marriage was *très mal,* but I picked up good skills. And," he continued,

"the marriage has given me a son, so it was worth it." No false sentiment here—the mere mention of his son seemed to cause Rick to
stand a little prouder. He volunteered that his ex-wife and son still
lived in America.

"How did you get to *Serenity*?" I asked.

"I know Patrick for long time. We ran into each other a few
months ago, and he told me he was looking for a steward. I was working on one of the boats down the quay from us. Life got a little too wild
in the Caribbean and I had to get off." He broke stride to greet a server
in an open-air café, then caught up to me. "I know these people from
the inside out," he said, referring to the owners of the mega-yachts
lined up alongside *Serenity*. "They work hard, and when they are not
working, they want to be made happy, to be entertained. I can take
care of this for them. *Il Dottore* and *la Signora* are no different from
other people around here."

I pressed him on what he knew of our bosses. He filled me in,
as much as he could, telling me that *il Dottore* had been born into
moderate wealth, which he then multiplied many times over. Under
his guidance, the family's original textile business grew into one of
Europe's largest and most profitable privately held blue-chip compa-
nies. It was through his business dealings that he met *la Signora*. They
had been married for many years.

"I will buy nice wine for the owners," Rick assured me. "That will
make them happy. Don't worry. It will be easy to please them. You'll
see."

I envied Rick's confidence but didn't share it. I had met the owners only once, during the job interview, and had definitely come away
with the sense that they were not going to be easy to please.

Now, walking through the old, narrow cobblestoned streets in
the free commune of Safranier—a town within a town whose seces-
sionist pride was expressed in the abundance of plants and flowers

draping from overflowing window boxes—Rick and I arrived at a small but well-stocked kitchen supply store with the name Fournitures C. Quillier written across its awning. Inside, I carefully examined the copper and *inox* cookware and the large selection of professional kitchen tools they carried. How important was having the best kitchen equipment? There was no consensus among the chefs I had worked with. Bruno at Da Noi in Florence made magic using the humblest wares, while Larry at An American Place in New York never skimped on the quality of his equipment. It was Larry's assertion that consistent results require a reliable *batterie de cuisine*.

The *inox* pans were good because they were stainless steel both inside and out, making them easy to clean and resistant to corrosion from the salty air. I then found what I wanted most: a stainless set with clad layers of copper and aluminum sandwiched inside and stay-cool, ergonomically shaped handles. They would be up to the task of good heat retention and even distribution on my marine stove with low BTU's. Because of the stainless steel interior, they would not cause food with high acidity like tomato sauce to have any off flavors. And their flanged rims around the whole circumference would make pouring sauces while under way in a rolling sea much easier.

Working from my lists, I sized the pots and sauté pans, selecting each with a capacity two sizes larger than needed. Yes, each pot would do less work than it was designed to do, but the over-sizing would help avoid spillovers when my gimbal-less stove pitched in rough seas. Rick helped by pulling from the shelves stainless bowls, strainers, and a selection of ceramic baking dishes. In addition to a food processor, I chose a nice-sized marble mortar and pestle. Given the marble fixtures in the guest heads on the boat, a little extra weight forward in the galley might even add ballast to the waterline of the boat.

Rick, once again being a true charmer, engaged the shopkeepers in a conversation about food and the good life. When they found out I was the cook on board, they gave me a couple of classic coastal

French recipes, insisting that I absolutely had to have them in my repertoire if I would be sailing and cooking along the Riviera—*brandade de morue,* a whipped salt cod and potato preparation, and rouille, the rust-colored mayonnaise-like condiment for Provençal fish soup and poached seafood.

We retraced our steps to *Serenity* to drop off our purchases, a hundred pounds of nesting sauce pots, stacked sauté pans, and bags of kitchen tools. Rick came back to town with me, this time to the *marché Provençal*—Provençal market—that was set up under a long paned-glass roof supported by ornate wrought-iron columns in front of city hall in the old town. Once there I reminded him that we needed to work fast. "But first things first," he corrected me as he filched a handful of strawberries from a stand. "You have to stay healthy," he explained, pulling on his cigarette between bites. "It helps you party longer."

The crowded market teemed with color, and the claylike smell of freshly picked produce was heavy in the air. Vendors greeted prospective buyers and shouted sellers' talk to one another. The items marked *"fermier"* and *"de pays,"* which meant they were from the area, like the strawberries Rick snatched, were available from the local farmers along the center aisle.

All of a sudden I was back in the valley of the Vaucluse. Those initial Technicolor days when life in the south of France made its first impression. I'd shadow my host, Nathalie, on her daily open-air market expeditions, leaving early in the morning to go to a different market each day—Apt, L'Isle sur la Sorgue, Cavaillon, Saint-Rémy, Aix-en-Provence, Arles, and, once on a Sunday, Coustellet, where predominantly peasants and gypsies sold their goods from makeshift tables or from the backs of their little blue Piaggio Ape farm vehicles.

Those markets shared similar characteristics with the endless rows of stalls winding through the streets. Butchers, fishmongers, bakers, produce vendors, cheese sellers, *charcutiers,* and florists sold from tables, crates, baskets, and modified delivery trucks with sides that opened to reveal wonderful displays of food in long glass cases. Selling and buying were both very cordial: greetings were exchanged, choices made, quantities weighed, items wrapped, and cash paid.

Nathalie made a point to walk the market and survey the stalls before making any of her purchases. During this first pass she would start to plan her menus, based on what caught her eye in the various stalls. She also had a short list of vendors to whom she always gave business: the cheese maker who sold chèvre—goat cheese—in various stages of ripeness; the young fellow of Cambodian heritage who introduced himself as Louie and made endless varieties of *saucisson*—salami; the couple who sold perfumed herbs and seasonings, had a company called Provence Vie et Santé, and foraged the local hillsides for the aromatics that would compose their different blends of herbes de Provence.

It was the same time of year as when I arrived in Antibes, and I remembered my first glimpse of local agriculture. Perfectly handled, displayed, ripe, and scented produce—peak-season asparagus, artichokes, leeks, strawberries, cherries, and melons—were piled high in pyramids or prepackaged in small crates and wooden baskets. Shiny Mediterranean fish were lined up next to each other on ice tables under colorful makeshift canopies. Bakeries brought different kinds of breads displayed in large wicker baskets lined with traditional Provençal printed fabric, each crust looking crispier than the last. The *saucisson* vendors with their edifices of cured meats were never shy about offering a sample. And the cheese sellers in their customized trucks had so much variety it was hard to choose.

I'd follow Nathalie through the markets as she looked, sniffed, lightly pressed, and rejected, until she settled on the firmest green vegetables, evenly marbled meats, handcrafted local cheeses, and sun-ripened fruits that had to be consumed within a day or so. She gently handled all of the purchases, paying respect to the hard work of the farmers who nurtured such wonderful foodstuffs and proudly brought them to market for the enjoyment of people looking for quality.

One day, I was immediately drawn to a table covered with piles of white asparagus and purple-tipped artichokes. When I picked up an artichoke, the woman behind the table said, *"Tirez une feuille."* Nathalie explained that I was being invited to pull a leaf off to see how fresh they were. I obliged. It squeaked when it snapped off.

"I have never seen anything so perfect in my life," I said, and bought a dozen for us to eat that evening, so tender we ate them raw with Dijon mustard vinaigrette.

"It starts with choice," Nathalie said as we walked past a table laden with big ceramic crocks full of different varieties and blends of olives. "When the ingredients are optimum, the cooking can be simple."

It struck me that this same food had been feeding Provençal citizens for hundreds of years.

In just two days, Serenity was going on a short trip to nearby Cannes and back before dark. This would be the first sea trial with the owners on board—a finish inspection, test of the systems, and check of the sailing apparatus to make sure the rig was set up properly. As we walked past the local produce vendors, I struggled to come up with a menu for that day's lunch. A slightly heavyset farmer with bold features popping out of a round face topped with a captain's hat was offering high-quality local produce, mostly different blends of mesclun salad greens, bunches of fresh herbs, and piles of red tomatoes.

"Bonjour, chef!" he greeted me. Rick and I wore our gray *Serenity* polo shirts and dark blue cargo shorts, the working uniform when the owners were not on board that clearly identified us as yacht crew. To this day, I don't know what made him think I was a chef, but I found myself inwardly pleased that one look at me and he immediately jumped to that assumption. Even if he was just blowing smoke at me

in promoting me to chef, he at least saw me as a cook and chef wannabe. He owned a small farm in Biot, he told me, just off the coast behind Antibes. These were his homegrown vegetables. No wonder he displayed so much pride in his wares.

"Look at these zucchini blossoms, perfect for delicious beignets!" he assured me. Crispy beignets. Might be a great idea, but I was not about to deep-fry anything on my first day at sea. Then the farmer directed my attention to a small table covered with tomatoes. "Take this one, go ahead, feel it. In one day, they'll be perfect for salad." It was late spring, and his vegetables were bursting in color. "*Viene ici*"—come here—"look at this beautiful early-season green garlic."

I was so locked onto thinking about what I would be preparing for that first lunch at sea that I was barely able to follow his stream of chatter. I reminded myself what a friend of mine, a chef in San Francisco, once said to me: "Whenever you find yourself in a can't-fail situation, do what you know!"

I thought of a *grand aioli,* a Provençal dish made with poached salt cod and periwinkles served with an assortment of cooked, usually boiled, vegetables and aioli—a heady garlic mayonnaise. It's a pretty rustic dish, so I decided to do a slight variation. I'd make the aioli much more subtle by using the young green garlic before the bulb starts to form, thrice blanched, and local extra virgin olive oil. And by making it a day ahead would give the flavors a chance to fully bloom. In lieu of the cod and snails, I could poach some nice fish fillets like *grondin,* a popular rockfish found in the Mediterranean, along with some shrimp. Then I'd arrange small new potatoes, tender leeks, green beans, and a few hard-cooked eggs for tradition around a bowl of the aioli. I'd offer another platter with sliced tomatoes and a cluster of lightly dressed field greens. To finish, tart and juicy strawberries, crunchy deep red cherries, *calisson*—a Provençal confection made with almond paste—and maybe some madeleines, too. This should keep the folks in the cockpit happy on this first day under sail and give me a chance to get used to serving meals on platters.

Not knowing exactly how many guests would be on board worried me, and I found myself thinking back to a small piece of culinary lore that Jacques, the proprietor of the inn in Provence where Nathalie arranged for us to cook, used to recite to me: "However many people you must feed, always add a portion for the *berger"*—the shepherd—"who may pass by." While we weren't going to be running into any shepherds on the Mediterranean Sea, prudence told me that in my first chance to flash my skills to the owners, I couldn't risk not having enough food. With three confirmed guests and a possible fourth, I took Jacques's advice and doubled it, meaning that I would prepare enough for six.

For the crew, meat-filled ravioli tossed with great French butter, Parmesan, and a few turns of black pepper. A small variety of sliced meats from the charcuterie, some cheeses, baguettes for sandwiches, and, for local flavor, a celery root salad made with a creamy dressing using some of the aioli. This would add some heft to the meal and provide the deckhands with needed carbohydrates. Fresh fruits would be an easy finish, and Kevin, Scott, Ian, and Nigel—the commonwealth contingent—had already told me they wanted tea and English Hob Nob biscuits to finish their meals, especially at lunch.

I worked through the crowd, selected the items I wanted, waited to have them weighed, pulled a wad of cash out of my pocket, did the transaction, and moved on. It was going to be a pleasure having this market minutes from my galley. Rick was sitting on a vegetable crate watching the world go by, at least the female half, and for a brief moment I thought about telling him how relieved I was to have gotten so much done. But I held back, knowing that any sign of showing I was ahead of schedule might invite another hard-sell pitch to hit the Cap.

Rick and I turned down a pedestrian-only side street lined with *traiteurs,* prepared-food shops; *boucheries,* butchers; a *fromagerie,* cheese shop; an *épicerie,* spice shop; a rotisserie; and one shop I expected I would need often. Called La Boîte à Pâtes—the Box of Pasta—it was an Italian-inspired food shop run by a young and enterprising French couple. I could get the ravioli here, and this would become my resource for many Italian ingredients when in Antibes.

I had to admit I was off to a good start. Although the overall provisioning would take a couple of weeks, I had enough on hand to make my galley a working kitchen. Once back at the boat, I lounged on the foredeck with Rick for a few minutes before going below to set up the galley. I looked around at the boxes and bags of pots, pans, small wares, and food spread out around the crew way and began to figure out where to put everything. I wanted to get started with my prep work before sea trial day. Rick joked at my meticulousness but knew he would soon have to be working just as diligently. Well, *almost* as diligently. He took one look at the rest of the crew working on the rigging and decided he didn't want to be spotted and pressed into service. Making himself as small and inconspicuous as possible, he sneaked aft along the scuppers, down the *passerelle,* and onto the quay, no doubt off to the beach.

Saturday morning came, and Michele arrived early. He called a quick meeting with the crew at the mess table. His tone was all business.

"Good morning, gentlemen," he said. "The boat looks beautiful, and everyone has done a great job. The owners are very proud and are looking forward to a grand inaugural season. As you know, we have a strong presence in Europe. It is very important that you understand how to act since you are their representatives onshore. There is a code of ethics that you must follow so that we can enjoy what working on *Serenity* is all about." He proceeded to list his rules and made clear there was no room for discussion or debate:

Always remember as crew, we represent the owners.

When onshore, do not mention the owners' names publicly.

Any display of the boat's name in public is to be respected as an extension of the boat.

Be aware of how to act onshore whether on boat time or personal time.

Be aware of personal hygiene; that is, stay clean and shaved.

Respect your fellow crew members and those on other boats.

Anyone that is discovered to have taken any kind of payment for information about the owners or the boat will be fired immediately.

"Does everyone understand?" he asked rhetorically. Everyone nodded. "Thank you and have a great season."

At precisely nine o'clock, as scheduled, the owners' helicopter arrived, circling a couple of times at low altitude before landing on the roof of the yacht club, not far from our berth. The entrance was exhilarating, and they made the door-to-*passerelle* transit look easy. Even though this was an "informal" visit, everyone seemed a little stressed and guarded. Patrick received the owners when they came up the *passerelle* as if he were the captain of the *Queen Mary*. It felt like we had dignitaries on board. Only Rick seemed perfectly calm.

La Signora and *il Dottore* were very much at ease when they stepped on board. Judging by their casual dress—she in a just-above-the-knee skirt and a colorful printed silk blouse, he in pleated slacks and an open-collar button-down shirt—they looked as if they had casually boarded the helicopter in their backyard. Later in the day, Patrick told me that was indeed how they traveled. Michele greeted them on the aft deck as they removed their shoes. They were all smiles as they looked up the masts and around the deck, gazing at the restored brilliance of their new acquisition.

Il Dottore came up to every crew member to shake his hand, but *la Signora* didn't stray too far from the cockpit at the outset, saying, "*Ciao!*" to everyone from the distance while getting herself settled in. I hadn't seen them since the interview, and I was hoping that she would approach me and ask how it was going, find out if the galley was going to be sufficient, and ask if I had everything I needed. But there was none of that. This sea trial was not only a test for the boat and crew; it was also the first time my new employers would taste my food. And I needed her confidence since I felt I had to prove she made a good hire. More so, I had put it upon myself to show there *are* good cooks from America, something many Italians I had met over the years found hard to believe. This second-guessing and insecurity kept me from approaching her, and as a result I found myself walking on eggshells.

The day became an education for everybody. From what Patrick, Kevin, and Scott said, everything seemed to be functioning properly as we sailed gently in a light wind. They tried to have all the work finished before the owners arrived, but there was still some tweaking to be done in the rig. My job description might have been cook, but it was quickly made clear that everyone's first obligation was to help keep the boat afloat and operating, especially during docking procedures, sailing maneuvers, and if we, or the boat, faced any possible trouble. I realized quickly that working on a sailing yacht with a small crew meant double duty for the cook.

Up on deck, Kevin had his own ideas about assigning tasks while we were under way in the marina, including inflating huge fenders with an air compressor that protected the hull if we bumped into neighboring yachts when leaving and returning to our slip. Once beyond the breakwater, I was introduced to *Serenity*'s new Dacron sail wardrobe—the huge mainsail aft, the foresail that filled the space between the masts, then the headsails, including the staysail just forward and the upper and lower jibs that were rigged at the very front of the boat, creating a sail area that covered about five thousand square feet—and learned the systems for untying, changing, and handling most of the sails while under way, then flaking and storing them. Patrick, the ultimate authority, indicated how lines were to be coiled and stowed—down to which knots were to be used where. A few of them were easy to remember since they were exactly the same as ones I used for tying meats and fowl before roasting.

It was important that the rest of us knew exactly what the captain and mate wanted. Most tasks were not assigned to one crew member in particular; having everyone trained to perform all the sailing tasks made for good seamanship on board. Having worked in many kitchens with a similar etiquette, I found this easy to grasp.

Kevin coached us on raising and lowering the sails in succession from aft to forward—almost in a marching drill cadence. *Serenity* was gaff-rigged, meaning she needed two halyards (lines) on both the main- and the foresail to raise their heavy timber gaffs with the sails. There was a lot of weight to pull—three of us on each line, two guys to haul and one to tail the thick nylon-coated rope. Everyone had to pull in tandem. We got into position. Kevin tailed a line and would watch the sails go up to make sure we were raising them evenly. He started to call the hauling order: "Let's go, guys! Two-six, PULL! Two-six, PULL! Two-six, PULL THE BASTARD! Come on! Two-six . . ."

I later found out the main- and the foresails with their respective gaffs, ropes, and blocks weighed somewhere in the neighborhood of three tons each. The higher and lighter side was the peak. But close to the mast, the throat was heavier since it took most of the weight of the gaff. Rick and I were given this assignment and decided between ourselves that the deck crew were hazing the "hospitality" staff by giving us the heavier side to haul. Rick mumbled and grumbled a steady stream of wiseass comments while we worked—work that turned into a vigorous physical workout. With the owners on board, this would become a twice-daily task. But I didn't want the rest of the crew to see me as cracking on the first assignment I had been given, so Rick's tirades and expletives made me pull all the harder.

After the lower sails were up, Ian and Nigel climbed the ratlines at each mast to the spreaders seventy feet above deck and proceeded to open the topsails, which then had to be tied off and trimmed at the pin rails located near the base of the masts. These added more sail area in which to catch precious wind. In heavy air, their lines could be tough to trim and make fast given the extreme forces on them. Raising the full suit of sails took us about forty-five minutes. Then we practiced using the large brass winches, the only electric equipment on deck, which were used for trimming the headsails. Throughout the day, we reviewed our repertoire of knots—bowlines, half hitches, clove hitches, locking hitches, slip hitches, square knots—and where to use them.

For anchor and chain procedures one of us had to go below and open the chain lockers in the fo'c'sle to pack the chain, while another had to rinse it off with a seawater hose while it was brought in with the windlass on the foredeck. Getting the huge anchor on board took three of us to haul it up with a block and tackle then put it in its crutch. There were steps for hooking to moorings, managing the bow while the anchor was being let out when we backed into a slip, knowing the hand signals from the cockpit, fender placement, stern lines, spring lines, *passerelle* raising, lowering, and stowage, then deck washing and specific ways to dry the varnished wood with chamois. The docking procedures were our version of coming home, opening the electric garage door, and setting the parking brake.

Throughout the whole process of getting the boat out of the harbor and under sail, piles of line were everywhere on deck. *Il Dottore* and *la Signora* remained in the cockpit with Michele in an effort to stay out of the way until the lines were coiled and stowed. During these procedures, I quickly came to understand what was expected of me as a crew member, which meant that I had to stay ahead in my work down below. Once the cruising began, I needed to be available for deck duties whenever Patrick or Kevin wanted me up top. At the same time, I didn't want the owners to think I was straying too far from the main reason I was on board.

Just after midday we anchored between the Îles de Lérins in front of Cannes. *Il Dottore* came forward for a little while to chat with his crew. He explained that on one of the islands, the landmark Fort Royal had held the Man in the Iron Mask, the prisoner made famous by Alexandre Dumas in the novel of the same name. There is still debate, he said, over his actual identity, and the mask was apparently not made of iron. It was a nice gesture on the part of *il Dottore,* a little bonding with his crew, sharing a bit of lore about the area we were calling.

Rick served lunch to the owners and Michele in the cockpit while the crew ate family style around the crowded mess table. Rick and I had to stay in service, so it appeared our eating times were going to be before or after the others and most likely always on our feet. With the crew in the galley area and all the juggling of food, kitchenwares, and platters, my work space shrank by half. But the owners' lunch looked fine. Fresh and simple, more knife work than cookery as I only needed one pot with one change of water—the first time for cooking the vegetables and eggs, the other for poaching the fish. When Rick brought the platters back to the galley, a decent amount of food remained, probably because I sent more than I needed to. I had prepared enough for six, but held back and sent out enough for four. But no word came back regarding the meal. Maybe because so much was happening on board that day, this was a working lunch.

We took a break for an hour, then pulled up the hook and once again raised the sails to take long, leisurely downwind reaches back to Antibes. By early evening *Serenity* was tied up in her home slip. The skipper came below and told Rick and me to be on deck when the owners and Michele departed. Like clockwork, the owners' jet-powered helicopter landed on the roof of the nearby yacht club to bring them back to Italy. It made a different noise, more like a soft, rhythmic *whoosh,* and I mused that for incredibly wealthy people even helicopter noise can be engineered for maximum comfort. *Il Dottore* and *la Signora* waved as they circled over the boat before heading east. Then we cleaned the deck and Michele arranged for us to have dinner in town with lots of rosé to celebrate a job well done.

Day one with the owners, and I survived, though I hoped that my daily tasks would become more habitual. I needed to master all the lines, knots, coils, hand signals, and procedures so I could maintain the demanding balance between cooking and sailing.

That night, back at the boat, I had a sinking feeling when Rick told me that from scraps of conversation he had overheard from the cockpit, he guessed that the owners would be entertaining a lot this summer. Running out of food was something I simply could not let happen. But I pushed these concerns out of my head as I ended the day sitting on the bowsprit all the way forward and enjoying a nightcap. I felt a certain degree of elation while looking aft along the convex lines of the deck, like barrel staves, on this restored beauty—like the high you experience after a vigorous workout.

A few days later Rick showed me the veritable bank vault of service ware that *la Signora* had been sending from Paris and Milan: Baccarat glasses, hotel-weight Ginori china, and Sambonet silver cutlery, serving pieces, and platters. There were table decorations and a beautiful caviar bowl made of heavy glass crystal from Lalique. Two handblown Murano glass vases were anchored in the corners behind the banquette. Patrick later told me they were extremely costly. To think this was all for everyday use. The Bernardaud porcelain for formal dining was kept in a separate cabinet in the salon. It was also hotel weight, which was better suited for use at sea since it was a little heavier than standard home china. The complete set was personalized with detailing that replicated the decorative blue line pattern that was painted along the hull of the boat.

While we were sorting through the platters, Rick finally convinced me that I would deeply regret not experiencing all the Côte d'Azur had to offer. He reminded me that now was the time because once we began cruising, the opportunity would be lost.

"Lighten up," he had said to me on more than one occasion. "You need to check it out. It's good, good, good!" By then, I was in decent shape in the galley and even starting to feel a little cabin fever. So we jumped in the old hatchback Peugeot crew car and headed to the Cap. We drove on some of the exclusive residential streets, and Rick pointed out the perfectly manicured villas whose owners he knew of, all flanked by beautiful French landscaping. "Here is the famous Hotel du Cap Eden-Roc—rooms are eight hundred bucks a night and they only take cash." He said the word "cash" with deep inflection, almost with reverence. We weren't in the car five more minutes when Rick returned to his familiar refrain, "How about we stop by Plage Keller for a couple of hours?"

We came around a bend on a coastal road, and in front of us was a long, secluded inlet. "This is la Garoupe," Rick proudly declared. There were five or six beach clubs next to each other at the end of the cove. Along both sides were a couple of villas back from the water's edge. Small boats were anchored and moored just outside the swimming area, bobbing like fishermen's floats. The water was turquoise blue with a white sandy bottom. It was quiet, clean, and very civilized. No radios, screams, Frisbees, or plastic coolers of beer.

Rick marched onto the beach like a determined general and rented two *matelas*—comfortable beach chairs lined up in the sand— at the half-day price, about twenty bucks each. I followed in tow, curious to see if the experience would match the level of expectation Rick had set.

"This is the same beach where Hemingway, F. Scott Fitzgerald, and Picasso used to hang out," Rick said as we got settled. "Lots of good history." I envisioned writers and painters coming to unwind here after a long day in their studios and dens.

It was the perfect recipe for everything I thought the Riviera would be: the secluded spot, the azure blue of the water, and warm sand giving way underfoot. Then there were the women. Topless in small bikini bottoms and a few in scanty one-piece bathing suits. Their tanning bodies silhouetted against the glistening calm of the Mediterranean Sea.

"Hot, hot, hot," Rick said as if summarizing what this place was all about. Then he confided, "I like older women. Much more mature."

I must admit, I had to agree with him. This scene *was* hot. Why did I put off coming here?

My eyes continued to sweep across the tapestry of sun worshippers while I absorbed the seascape in front of me. Everyone seemed to mind their own business. Mostly adults—singles, not too many groups, and a few young families. It was very calm with the occasional sound of small waves splashing against a floating platform in the swimming area. There were tanned men in great shape, all suave with their black thick-rimmed sunglasses. The women were napping, reading French magazines, or chatting with friends. They were clearly comfortable in the surroundings. Rick, as if giving big brother advice, quietly said, "Nothing tacky, okay?" having caught me eyeing a few *dames* that had just come out of the water from a swim.

I watched as the stylish women enjoyed their place in the sun. When it was time to go for a dip, they put their bikini tops on, then after, took a freshwater shower to rinse off the salt water. They walked in the sand back to their *matelas* in what looked like slow motion. They put their hair in a ponytail, took their tops off, and put their sun-

glasses back on. A waiter from the beachside café would show up minutes later with a bottle of spring water. The very picture of repose. The
only thing missing was "The Girl from Ipanema" playing in the background.

"When are we going back to la Garoupe?" I asked Rick the next
morning.

"See, you believe me," Rick said good-naturedly. "Now maybe
you trust me when I tell you about something good." Having a partner
to share in his fun elevated Rick's mood. He seemed to polish the silver that morning with extra vigor and less complaint.

It is said one can always tell who the cook is on a boat—the one
without the tan. From that day on, Rick and I got in the habit of dis-
appearing for a few hours in the afternoon, telling our crewmates we
were going shopping. It never occurred to me that after each "shopping" trip I came back increasingly darker. My crew members probably noticed this before I did. And just for cover, I always made sure I
came back to the boat with something in my market bags. My ratio-
nale was that we were taking a deserved siesta since I'd have to return
to make dinner for the crew. Plus, Rick reminded me that when the
owners were on board, we would have long workdays both serving and
sailing. It didn't take long to discover that our shared attitudes toward
some of the finer things in life were in fact bonding the battery of
Serenity's service team. If Rick's motive was to get on my good side, his
methods were solid. Those were some of the best days I have ever
spent on a beach.

Michele dropped down the crew ladder early one morning
while most of us were at the mess table. He poured himself a coffee
and after a brief greeting declared that we needed to get to the uniform shop *soon* for sizing. "The owners expect everyone to be in formal attire when they are on board from here on." His tone was

expressly boat-manager-like—this was not a suggestion but an order. I decided to go get it over with that morning on my way back from the market.

The shop was in a mini arcade of yacht businesses: a marine hardware store known as a chandler, charter brokers, designers, crew agents, and the international grocery store. When I entered Dolphin Uniformes, no one was inside except for a tall, slender, short-haired brunette who was arranging polo shirts on a display.

"*Bonjour,* may I help you?" she asked with a heavy French accent.

"Yes. I am here to try on the uniforms for the *Serenity* account."

"You need them soon I've been told." She was very attractive and had a model's posture when she stood straight up.

I quickly became less interested in the uniforms and more interested in talking with her.

"Nice earrings," I said. "I like black pearls. They remind me of the South Pacific."

"Have you ever been there?"

"No, not yet. One of these days." There was a slight pause, and I needed to say something fast because all of a sudden I had her undivided attention. "What's your name?"

"Véronique," she replied with a nice smile.

"My name is David. It's a pleasure to meet you," I said and extended a hand.

"And you," she said with a firm handshake, then excused herself to get the uniforms from the back.

I checked the labels when she returned. Patrick did me a solid— all cotton. I started with the shirts and took mine off in the middle of the shop, thinking nothing of it. I heard a soft "huh" from her now that she was behind the register counter.

"Is everything all right?" I asked.

"We have changing rooms over there," she said with a grin, pointing to a small curtained area next to the jackets at the back of the store.

"Oh, pardon me," I said, "but given how the dressing is at the beaches here, I didn't think this would be an issue."

She asked what beach I was going to and said that she liked to go for an hour or so every day to a little beach in Antibes near the ramparts. It was her lunch break ritual.

"Are you from here?" I asked.

"No, but I have lived here for a while. I grew up near Paris."

"What brought you here?"

"I like the sun and the sea. After college I was a stewardess on a yacht for a couple of years owned by a French family." She paused for a moment with a look of reflection, and then continued, "I didn't want to go home after, so I stayed. Working here is a nice way to be in the business without moving around so much. Where are you from?"

"I grew up in New York, and then lived in San Francisco for a couple of years."

"I like California," she cut in, then added, "Did you know Newport Beach is the sister city to Antibes?"

"No, but only because I haven't spent a lot of time in Southern California."

"And now you are in the south of France!" she said. "What do you do on the boat?"

"I'm the chef."

"An American cooking for Italians. That's interesting. Your owners must like your food."

"I don't know yet. I've only prepared one meal for them so far."

"Then you have a challenge."

"I do?" I asked with a little bit of dry wit but was curious as to what she had to say.

"Well, you know, part of your job is to make them look good."

"I haven't even thought about that."

"*C'est normal.* You never know who they will have on board. But your boss was very pleasant when she came to the shop to choose your uniforms. And she knew exactly what she wanted."

It was a brisk walk back to the boat. At least for a short while, any concern about *la Signora,* the season ahead, and my galley disappeared from my thoughts.

As I approached *Serenity,* a unique sound from an incoming jet caught my ear and pulled me out of my waking dream. The noise gave off a generated pitch higher than a standard commercial jet. I looked up and saw why. The beak-nosed Concorde was on its approach, flying across the bay to Nice. Then I noticed Rick on the foredeck locked into watching it pass over us. All of a sudden, Rick stood at attention and saluted, loudly saying, "*Vive la France! Vive la France!*"

"What are you doing?" I asked.

"I love this!" he proudly replied. "This is French progress!"

I found Rick's heartfelt pride in a French-built mechanical object admirable. As much as the French focus on their historical legacies of culture and food, often looking backward to celebrate the present, the sight of a homegrown modern spectacle could really turn people out. I realized Americans were so used to innovation that we often took it for granted. Rick smiled as the plane dipped over the Bay of Angels toward the airport in Nice, making a rare landing on the Côte d'Azur.

After a day off, I woke up with a throbbing headache from a potent combination of sun, alcohol, and a fitful night of sleep. Rick's influence had once again overpowered me, and we ended the evening on unsteady legs. I had joined Rick, Patrick, and Ian on a late-night binge in Juan-les-Pins. Patrick walked into the crew quarters with an aura of seriousness but looked a little pale when he told us the owners would be flying down to the boat the upcoming Friday evening.

This was a different Patrick from the party-boy American we drank with the night before. His tone could only be described as curt, especially to Rick, and he left no question in anyone's mind that we were his subordinates.

On Saturday, he said, we would take *Serenity* out on her first overnight run with the owners for a trip past the Estérel coast to the region of the Var and Saint-Tropez. I'd be preparing a full rotation of dinner, breakfast, and lunch for two days. This gave me a couple of days to plan the menus and do the major provisioning. By Thursday, everything seemed to be in order. I went over my notes about what *la Signora* had told me the day of my interview, and the word "pâté," underlined, jumped out at me. I felt a rush of panic. I didn't have any on board yet.

I grabbed some cash and went to town. Rick came along since he needed teas and confiture from another shop that sold products from Fauchon in Paris. There was a shop near the market called La Ferme de Foie Gras—The Foie Gras Farm—that sold high-end charcuterie from Gascony: duck and goose liver in all forms of terrines, mousses, and pâtés. They had a wonderful selection of *saucisson*, game pâté, and all of the accoutrements for the Gascony table: mustards, cornichons, and pickled onions, along with a nice selection of wines and liquors from the southwest of France. Rick mentioned that a piece of confit or a pâté sandwich was right up his alley and asked if I could keep some on board for him. I said no problem and grabbed a bottle of Armagnac for me.

The stylish saleswoman matched the put-together decor and furnishings of the shop. She spoke very formally as she presented the line of food items that were house specialties. Then she gave us samples to taste—*goûtez*—of the selections of pâté from the glass and polished brass case: a smooth duck terrine, pheasant with pistachios, venison with black truffles, and a country pâté of pork *au cognac*. She pointed at the rabbit pâté with green peppercorns, but Rick immediately waved her off. There is a superstition about never having rabbit on board a sailing vessel. Even the mention of it could spell doom.

Like many superstitions, this one began rationally. In early sailing days, rabbits were kept on board as food. Once in a while, they would escape their cages and chew on the hemp lines below deck and in the bilge. This weakened lines, which in time caused them to break, collapsing the rigging and suddenly throwing the boat out of control. In rough seas it could even cause a vessel to sink. Over time rabbits came to symbolize bad luck and were banned from boats. Rick told me I was not even supposed to think about the subject while at sea.

I made a nice selection, five different kinds, about half a kilo of each. I added a few jars of condiments to complete the presentation I envisioned—just like the photos of food on silver platters in the seminal encyclopedia of cookery, the *Larousse Gastronomique*. I looked at Rick for his reaction. After all, pâté was French.

"I think maybe you are killing them with kindness," he said with a smile.

"How so?"

"This is a very nice selection," he said.

"*La Signora* was very specific about having pâté on board," I said, then turned to the *madame*. "*C'est tout, merci*"—That is all, thank you.

The owners arrived late Friday, so I abandoned the full dinner menu and prepared a light supper for them: baked rockfish with Madame Quillier's rouille on the side and some roasted new potatoes dressed with a little oil from Vence and coarse sea salt—everything really simple. I waited in the galley for a reaction, but once again none came. I poured myself a glass of Armagnac and sat there sipping, consoling myself that no news is good news. I closed up the galley and went to sleep.

Saturday was dawning warm, with only a gentle wind under a

light blue sky as we got under way. Under motor power, Patrick steered us out of the harbor and out toward the open sea. As soon as we cleared the breakwater, he called for us to take our positions on deck and raise the sails. It was an awe-inspiring sight as the steady wind filled the sails when they were trimmed for our close-reach point of sail. When Patrick cut the motor, we were sailing westward toward the Var. While Kevin took the helm, *il Dottore,* Michele, and Patrick walked the deck together, *il Dottore* stopping here and there to examine something more closely or to point it out to Patrick. There were some add-on tasks, suggestions from Michele, and some talk about changes to the rigging and the blocks, but my work was waiting for me in the galley, so I left to go down below. With the motor cut out, I could hear the whispered splash of the sea against the hull as we knifed through the Mediterranean. The calming gray noise, along with the gentle rocking, lulled me into a Zen calm as I went about preparing the crew's lunch.

We were able to stay on each tack for long distances, and the light wind didn't heel the boat too much. By keeping just a couple of miles offshore, we had some beautiful sights to our starboard side: the harbor towns of La Napoule and quaint Théoule-sur-Mer, then from Miramar to Cap du Dramont, the sensational coastline of the Corniche de l'Estérel. It made a great backdrop with its dramatic brick-red-colored cliffs, deep green patches of low herbal brush called maquis, and small sandy beaches next to the cobalt blue sea. All of this I could see through the porthole in the galley.

Around eleven, Rick came down to the galley and said that *la Signora* requested a snack of pâté. I was relieved I had remembered her instructions. Rick filled an ice bucket and prepared a champagne service while I worked.

I composed a nice arrangement of pâtés to one side of a large round silver platter. Opposite, I placed a cluster of cornichons in a lettuce leaf cup, then filled another cup with pickled pearl onions, a

third with diced aspic, and then a small porcelain crock of Dijon mustard. I thought it looked smart. I sliced up a crispy baguette and
placed it in a silver bread basket lined with a linen napkin that Rick
had provided. He admired the platter, saying it was "gorgeous."

A few minutes later, I heard footsteps coming down to the galley that were clearly not Rick's. There she was, *la Signora,* platter in
hand, little on it having been touched. If I had any doubts about her
lack of enthusiasm for my selection, they ended when she dropped the
platter on the counter.

"Daveed," she said, using the French version of my name. This
meant trouble. I had the sense that *la Signora* invariably switched into
the French *"Daveed,"* from the Italian *"Davide,"* if she was displeased.

"What is this dog food you sent us?"

For a long few seconds, I didn't say a word. Was there a right answer to her question? Then I started babbling about the high-end
charcuterie I had found, how I had bought their best pâtés.

"Daveed," she said. "Foie gras! Not dog food! When I say pâté, I
mean *foie gras."* With that, she turned and went back up on deck.

Rick came into the galley from the pantry. He had heard it all.
He shrugged and with his arms extended, palms up, tried to offer
some silent sympathy.

"I know," I said. "You were right."

"But I could have been the wrong one," he answered, "and you
the right one."

"Yeah, right . . ."

"Don't worry. You prepare nice dishes for them and she will soon
forget." As he looked over the food on the platter, almost to the point
of salivating, he asked, "Can I make a sandwich with this dog food?"

"It's all yours."

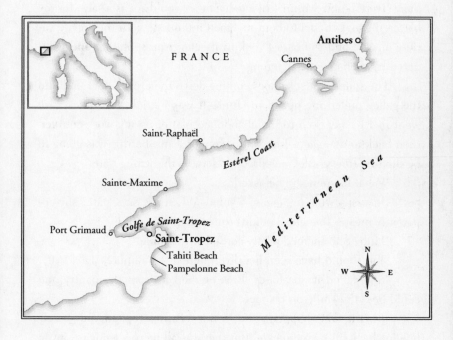

Saint-Tropez

*T*he eerie silence in the galley following *la Signora's* pâté outburst was broken only by the lapping noise of water against *Serenity's* hull as she cut and rocked through the wake of a passing motor yacht. Rick could sense my dismay and gave me some space to deal with it, going off to eat his sandwich in the pantry. I hoped that Saint-Tropez, now within striking distance, would act as a salve for my battered ego. I thought about my good intentions with the soigné variety of pâté and the care I took in its clever presentation and wondered how I had gone so wrong.

The sound of deck shoes coming down the crew ladder and into the galley pulled me out of my funk. It was Patrick. His quick gaze went first to me, then to the abandoned platter on my work counter, then back to me again. I began to wonder if maybe this was going to be the first time a chef was fired for serving the wrong pâté.

"What happened?" he asked.

"It wasn't what *la Signora* wanted. When she says 'pâté,' she apparently means 'foie gras.' I didn't know that."

"Huh? She seemed pretty cordial at the table."

"You should have seen her down here a few minutes ago."

"She called it dog food!" Rick chimed in from the pantry. You could hear the smile on his face.

"I bet it won't happen again, will it?" Patrick replied, only barely holding back his own chuckle. But that was all he was going to say on the subject. It wasn't Patrick's style to talk a problem to death, especially when there was no way to change what had happened. Anyway, he had come down to deal with his agenda, which involved Rick, who by then had stepped back into the galley.

"When we get to Saint-Tropez," he said, now facing Rick, "*la Signora* wants to go shopping, and she wants you to go with her."

"This must be initiation day," Rick said, suggesting he was about to get his.

Patrick turned back to me. "And if you can get the crew lunch set up early, why don't you come with me to Club 55?"

The prospect of having lunch at the famous beach club allowed me to finally let go of the pâté incident. "What's the occasion?"

"The owner of Club 55 is one of the organizers for the Voiles de Saint-Tropez regatta, and I need to speak with him about changing our rating."

I eagerly accepted the invitation, but it wasn't the prospect of fine-tuning my knowledge of regatta handicap formulas that lured me to join him. It was the opportunity to forget about the boat for a couple of hours.

Patrick leaned over to look through the starboard porthole and seeing we were passing the Pointe des Sardinaux, the northern landmark to the gulf of Saint-Tropez, said he needed to get back to the wheel and hurried up the ladder.

About twenty minutes later, while I was assembling the crew's lunch, I heard the sails starting to luff—flopping, dumping wind, and depowering—as the boat was turned toward the wind. We were preparing to go into the marina. I went up on deck to help with dropping the sails and docking.

Up top, while looking at Saint-Tropez from outside the breakwater, I was surprised by its appearance since I was expecting to see a town more in the style of Miami Beach—mid-twentieth-century hotels and apartment buildings with long windows and terraces overlooking the promenade that fronts the coastline. But the postcard view was completely different. In comparison, Saint-Tropez looked quaint, even old in its untouched collage of pastel-colored facades with dark red terra-cotta roofs and light blue shutters, all closed along the upper floors of each edifice.

When we got into the marina and started to back into our spot assigned by the harbor attendant, a crowd of onlookers had gathered on the quay. Boat docking, I would soon learn, is a great spectator sport. People gather around each arriving boat to catch a glimpse of what important person might be walking down the *passerelle* or hanging around on the aft deck. As soon as we made fast and coiled our stern lines, *la Signora,* with Rick in tow, stepped on dry land, the curious onlookers wondering if she was somebody important and if so, who? A few minutes later, Patrick and I went ashore and headed for Club 55. Patrick was armed with a canvas bag full of swag—a bottle of champagne, a large photograph of the boat, and a sweatshirt with the *Serenity* logo.

To get to the taxi stand, we walked along the quay Suffren, which rings the port of Saint-Tropez with a grand line of cafés, restaurants, and shops under multicolored canopies that jut out from the facades of the harbor buildings. Beyond the quay, a sloping urban plan suggested a harbor town bowing to the water. We made our way to the taxi stand, passing the smartly dressed store windows of the chic boutiques and pedestrian-only alleys paved with ancient hand-cut stone.

Saint-Tropez, I had learned, is named after its patron saint, Torpes. History has it that in A.D. 68, a brutal mistral tossed a weather-torn ship onto the coastline, its crew consisting of nothing more than a dog, a cockerel, and a headless man. The body belonged to Torpes, a high official under the Roman emperor Nero. Torpes apparently decided to convert to Christianity, which did not go over well with his boss. Nero became so incensed that one of his most trusted advisers converted he ordered Torpes tortured and beheaded. His body was loaded onto a boat with the animals and sent out to sea. The idea was that the cockerel and dog would eat the body before the boat made landfall. But no such luck. The ways of the sea pushed the boat to the shores of what would become Saint-Tropez. In honor of this poor headless traveler, the village took the name Saint-Torpes, which eventually evolved into Saint-Tropez.

Born a fishing village, it became home to artists and writers who came to refill their well of creativity, and then, eventually, to a certain type of European socialite. It might have remained exclusive had not the director Roger Vadim made the seaside hideaway *the* destination for those who have the need to see movie stars and other celebrities in real-life moments.

"You're going to love it," my father had said during one of my infrequent calls home. "I can still picture the table-dancing scene like it was yesterday." What was he talking about?

In the late 1950s, Vadim saw in this idyllic location the perfect place to introduce the world to his starlet young wife, Brigitte Bardot, in the film *And God Created Woman*. A sensuous location for a new star oozing a new kind of sensuality. But as the film played to sold-out audiences in movie houses throughout Europe and America, the avant-garde backdrop for the film became a star in its own right. Saint-Tropez would never again be anyone's private retreat. My father had seen the movie when it was released, and I think he developed a particular fondness for Brigitte Bardot that lasted well into middle age. He sounded a little jealous that his son, not he, would be walking Saint-Tropez's streets.

It took us about ten minutes to reach Club 55—*Cinquante-cinq*—the best known of the clubs along the Pampelonne beach for the style set. We were led to a table on the terrace nestled among the low branches of tamarisk trees and patches of indigenous bamboo-like reeds called *canisse*. Large white canvas awnings tied off to thick white poles shielded us from the sun. As Patrick ordered a bottle of chilled rosé, I subtly lifted my neck up and to the right to try to catch a glimpse through the thicket of trees of the beauties who were tanning themselves on *matelas* that hovered like *îles flottantes*—floating islands—over the light beige sand. The owner was busy managing the dining area, so Patrick and I ate alone. My lunch of a *salade pêcheur*—a fisherman's seafood salad—and then a *daurade royale*—a regal member of the bream family of fish—grilled and served with braised fennel was perfectly prepared.

Just as we were finishing, the owner came over to our table. From how Patrick spoke of him on the way to the club, I assumed that the two were old friends glad to have crossed paths again, using the occasion to celebrate Patrick's new job as skipper of *Serenity*. Patrick handed him the bag of gifts, and they struck up an animated conversation, catching up on local yacht-world news and *Serenity*'s refit.

It seemed that the end-of-the-season boating races were not just an opportunity to have a little competitive fun. For Patrick, doing well in these races was paramount. The gist of it was getting to the issue of our "rating." To accommodate boats of different specifications within each class, each boat is rated based on a constellation of factors: length, beam, weight, and sail area. The rating then serves to even the field of competitors. When the competitors cross the finish line the elapsed time is "corrected" with the rating in order to place the winners. Because of this system, a smaller boat can beat a larger vessel even though the latter physically crosses the line first.

Patrick had engineered this lunch not to exchange pleasantries with an old buddy, but because he felt the current ratings would give an unfair advantage to his arch nemesis, the sailing yacht *Carina*. On his own, Patrick had calculated the type of rating most beneficial to *Serenity*. Now he was here to solicit the owner's help in getting the race committee to make the change. He saw the gifts as his expression of thanks for whatever could be done in order to help get *Serenity* a fair shake.

Of course, there was another way to look at the gifting. As soon as the owner fully understood what he was being asked to do, the conversation shut down. Not wasting a word, he cut off Patrick's pitch.

"No, it's not possible. The ratings will stay as they are." He was clearly offended by the entire exchange and quickly excused himself from the table, ostensibly to attend to other matters.

It was a silent taxi ride back to the boat. Patrick stared out the window the whole way, his disappointment palpable. I felt sorry for him and a bit embarrassed by the whole experience, but glad I didn't have to make small talk, because my thoughts kept returning to the fantasy lifestyle on the beach. There is a difference between almost there and being there. Suddenly I *really* wanted to be there.

When we got back on board, *il Dottore* was in the chart house talking with Michele, Kevin was sitting up on the foredeck, Ian and Nigel were below taking a kip—a quick nap—while Scott monkeyed around in the engine room. The galley was clean, a nice sight after leaving lunch on the mess table. A short nap seemed like a great idea, but no sooner did I go to lie down than Rick appeared in the mess area with a bunch of shopping bags.

"She had me schlepping all over!" he exclaimed in a tone that revealed hurt pride. Being seen in a town as a rich woman's caddie had been very painful.

I couldn't help but laugh at his resort to Yiddish. "Where did you learn to say that?"

"Remember, I was married to an American!" he responded.

He then handed me a half-kilo tin of beluga caviar and a loaf of *pain au levain*—lightly sour bread—from the famous Senequier bakery.

"*La Signora* would like caviar for lunch," he told me. "With lemon, some butter, and thick slices of the bread lightly toasted. I need to get champagne to them and set up the cockpit *tout de suite*. She told me while we were in town that all they drink in summer is champagne and Chablis."

"That's all they want? Easy enough." A few glasses of rosé at lunch had put me in a very agreeable state, so I quickly thought about reworking what I had earlier prepped for lunch to use for dinner. "Where'd you go?"

"Everywhere! Hermès for soap, Frette for robes, Lalique for all kinds of table ornaments—table ornaments! We're on a boat! I don't know why she needs so many!" he said over his shoulder as he hurriedly went into the pantry to assemble the champagne service. "I still have to go back to Chanel and pick up seven more pairs of shoes. She couldn't have just one. She had to have every color in the line!"

Sunday was a breeze since I was ahead on prep. The plan had been to stay in port for the night after *il Dottore* and *la Signora* left, but Patrick, no doubt wanting to put distance between himself and the failed attempt at Club 55, informed us we'd be leaving soon after their departure. This left Rick a bit unnerved since he had been looking forward to an evening to play in town with no onboard service responsibilities. I kept busy securing the galley for sea until a sharp call from the crew hatchway sent me up on deck. The rest of the crew was standing in a line by the cockpit. Michele pointed me to the spot next to Patrick—in the penultimate position.

"What's going on?" I asked Patrick.

"It's a traditional parting line," he said and left it at that.

The only time I had ever seen this was when I did some work at Regaleali, a large winery estate in Sicily. I had been asked to stay for a few days longer after my recipe-translating assignment in order to help the *monzu*—the estate chef—with a banquet for eighty, the guest of honor being someone quite special. Until I was on the premises, they couldn't tell me who that guest would be. It turned out to be none other than Prince Charles. I had a chance to meet him after the meal as he wanted to give the chef and me his compliments on a job well done. He was very polite and, for the few minutes that we spent with him, gave us his undivided attention. The next day I was invited by my host, herself a countess, to attend his parting ceremony. From the back of the room I watched him give gifts to the line of hosts and others he had met during his stay. At one point, he came up to me and gave thanks for acting as translator when his traveling chef spent some time in the kitchen with us. To me, that was the epitome of etiquette.

On *Serenity,* this same type of farewell ritual, sans gifts, would happen whenever the owners left the boat at the end of a visit. It seemed so quaint, so old-world, so *Upstairs, Downstairs*—so unlike the owners' reputation for being ultramodern in the way they ran their businesses.

The couple emerged and began their farewells with Ian at the far end, shaking hands as they said a few words to each crew member. I caught snippets of conversations, mostly "thank you" and "good job" to my fellow crew members. It was amazing to hear the owners shift from English to French then Italian and back to English without hesitating to find the next thought, comment, or gesture.

When it was my turn, I was nervous. This was my first face-to-face with *la Signora* since the pâté episode. "Davide," she began, her eyes locked onto mine, but with that European graciousness that she had shown at our first interview.

"Next weekend in Monte Carlo will be a very busy weekend for all of us, but especially for you. You remember, yes? When we first talked, I told you that in late May, at Monte Carlo, our yachting season officially begins with the weekend of the Grand Prix car races." She didn't wait for me to answer.

"We will be docked between the sailing yacht *Pegasus,* owned by our friends, to one side and our motor yacht, where the children will stay, on the other. We will arrive on Friday with three other couples, so we will be eight in total. The owners of *Pegasus* will have guests, and all of our four children will be there. You need to be ready for cocktails and a casual dinner for twenty that night. On Saturday," she went on, "a simple lunch—maybe a 'parade' of antipasti," as she put it—"for up to twenty-four, just in case a few more than expected drop by."

Then she dropped the bomb—the bomb that would put me in a near panic.

"On Saturday night, on the eve of the race, you should expect, let's say, about a hundred people for a party that will stretch across the three yachts. Just have large quantities of food available"—"*abbondanza,*" she said.

"The menu can be very simple. Canapés with foie gras. A seafood salad for an antipasto, two pastas—one with a vegetable sauce and the other with shrimp—a fish course—salmon with a light butter sauce—then a meat course—say, *bocconcini* of veal with a red wine sauce—some sort of vegetable or mixed green salad, and for dessert, it is fine if you order a nice assortment of petits fours from a patisserie. Everything should be prepared and brought up to the deck on platters, then served on small plates for eating *in piedi*"—while standing. "Therefore, all of the items need to be fork-friendly—short cut pastas like fusilli or rigatoni, the fish cut into small portions, bite-sized pieces of veal. Petits fours make perfect sense for dessert.

"On Sunday, race day, we will host an informal buffet for up to forty-five, so you should have ready a beautiful assortment of charcuterie, different breads, rolls, and a wonderful display of, I don't know, say thirty cheeses. Why not? We're in France!" she said.

She finished with a question: "*Hai capito?*"—Do you understand?

"*Sì, signora,*" I answered. It was an easy enough question to answer. I had understood every word. I wondered why she was questioning it. So I said nothing. Actually, I didn't know what to say.

"*Allora,*" she said with a slightly squinted look of authority in her eyes, "*fai bene*"—do well—finished with a "See you next weekend," always in Italian, then moved to Patrick and thanked him in English.

The owners walked down the *passerelle* and got into a taxi waiting for them on the quay. Kevin and Rick followed with their bags.

After what had been for me a restless night of sleep, about an hour into our day on Monday morning, Patrick announced that we had to be at the mouth of Monte Carlo's harbor no later than six-thirty the following Thursday morning. Otherwise, we would not get our reserved spot in front of the public pool at the center of the quay. If you want to be able to step off your boat and onto the quay during the Grand Prix—for which there are only a limited number of these coveted spots—arriving when the harbormaster dictates is an absolute must. Missing it means you'll be, at best, in the back of the harbor having to ferry owners and guests through the dense crowd of boats. With *la Signora's* plans for the weekend, Patrick was so concerned about missing the gate that he decided to arrive an hour earlier than our slotted time. That meant we would be leaving Antibes at one or two in the morning, a few days from now. I had a lot to do before then.

As soon as *la Signora* had left, I had gone down to the galley to write down everything I remembered from the parting-line conversation. Then I set my notes aside, figuring I would deal with planning everything the next morning. But instead, all that night, I tossed and turned, asking myself how I was going to pull off a party for a hundred around all of the other entertaining. The schedule and numbers staggered me. At one point, I thought about suggesting we hire a catering company to help, but then I realized I would probably have received an answer like, "What did we hire you for?"

Even Rick, ever so nonchalant, seemed uncharacteristically nervous when I sat down with him to discuss what we needed to do first.

"She's crazy. And this is just the beginning!" he said as he went up on deck to have a cigarette. Both of us knew Monaco would be tough. We just didn't know how tough.

If life is said to give second chances, then Monte Carlo was mine. *La Signora*'s instructions for the Grand Prix weekend had been clear, so clear that I got the sense that there was no margin to deviate. Those feelings were exacerbated when she said "foie gras" instead of "pâté" as she recited the menu. Was she being specific because that was her way, or because she was afraid that if I continued to use my judgment her entire weekend would be ruined? Would a step in the wrong direction in Monte Carlo land me on the beach watching *Serenity* sail away?

For the crew, Monaco would be a long weekend off, just keeping the deck clean and polished, each one taking a turn for watch at night, the rest heading off to one of the English bars near the port. For Rick, it was going to be busy but manageable. For me, it would be the hardest I have ever worked in my life.

How many people one will cook for is *the* most important criterion for all matters relative to delivery. For Monte Carlo, I was nervous because of the vague guest counts. Exactly how many people was I really cooking for? A hundred and fifty? Two hundred? I decided that I should cover myself and plan on cooking meals for two hundred guests over the course of the weekend.

There were some key words from *la Signora,* such as a " 'parade' of antipasti," that kept me wondering exactly what she had in mind for quantity, regardless of how many guests and how much they might eat. How many items constitute a parade in her mind? What about "*abbondanza*"? How does she define abundance? At least I got a break with the petits fours, a course I only had to procure, not prepare. And she had mentioned a display of thirty cheeses. What if it turned out I could fit no more than twenty-six on the table? And I knew the visual aspect had to be right. One chef I worked with liked to say that we taste first with our eyes. It takes a deft hand to attractively present food as well as to prepare it. I never even thought to ask her what kind of garnishing she liked, if any.

After writing the menus for each of the meals, I created the almighty ingredient list and tallied how much of everything I'd need. It was categorized by how I shopped, and it also corresponded to my list of vendors and suppliers: meats and poultry, fish and seafood, fruits and vegetables, dairy and cheeses, bakery and desserts, groceries, and, finally, anything miscellaneous, which was mostly nonfood items like food storage and cleaning supplies. Because of the volume, I also had to preorder certain items and arrange for deliveries to the boat. This would save me time since the purveyors would take care of "picking" the order rather than me spending time in the shops.

At these numbers, the amounts of food that had to be prepared were off the charts given my work space. I looked around the galley and the mess area. Storage was a huge issue, both for perishables and for nonperishables. There was no room. I could see how my efficiency would be slowed as I would spend much time climbing and rummaging through the raw materials, then looking for places and ways to store the prepped items.

Michele came by to check up on us, and I asked him if I would have an opportunity once in Monte Carlo to do any provisioning there. I thought maybe I could stagger my acquisitions through the weekend. He shook his head and explained to me that because of the hordes of spectators in the city, closed streets, and crowds milling about on the quay, getting around was going to be difficult. Plus, I didn't know any vendors or have any sources in Monte Carlo. I would be best served by loading up as much as possible in Antibes and getting bread and breakfast pastries onshore during the weekend.

Since the city was basically cordoned off and the marina would be packed with yachts, the only efficient way out of town was by water, so Michele had hired a cigarette speedboat with a driver to be used as a water taxi. For an emergency this would be the method of choice and also, he explained, would be how the owners and guests would transit from the Nice airport when they arrived. Since I didn't need the petits fours until Saturday night and the cheeses until race day, Michele suggested that I order them from shops in Nice and use the cigarette boat for a delivery rendezvous while in the port.

Rick timed his return to the galley perfectly.

"I know a great patisserie in Nice," he said, "and a cheese shop nearby." Perfect. One worry off my mind. Part of me suspected he really wanted a ride on the cigarette boat and for that reason jumped right in to help. But I didn't care about motives, only that my dessert be taken care of and on board at the right time. "Make sure to include two kinds with chocolate, some small lemon meringues, and an assortment with fruit, and get about"—"*abbondanza*" kept ringing in my head—"360 pieces," I told him. That would be three per person, maybe a little high on average, but I wasn't taking any chances. Then I wrote a list of cheeses that had a nice range of styles, textures, and flavors, all the while considering how they would best be displayed on the table: some I would precut into small pieces, like Beaufort and raw milk Comté; others I would leave in whole form, like round Camembert and square Pont l'Évêque.

"I just hope no one asks for espresso after dessert," Rick volunteered. "If I make one for somebody, suddenly everyone else will decide they need one as well. And then I'm screwed." I knew why. We had only a small, domestic machine on board.

I was determined to make everything from scratch. I was cooking for Italians, most of whom were probably used to eating in great restaurants. When I went over the menus with Rick, he offered to get some of the ingredients on the list, promising he knew exactly where to find them, which in turn lessened some of what I had to acquire.

"Are you sure you have this under control?" I asked as a final confirmation that he now owned the assignment.

"No problem," he assured me. Remembering that he had worked in upscale restaurants, I assumed he knew what I was after.

So I wrote the prep list, considering how much time many of the tasks would take and confirmed what was needed for each of the menus. The Saturday party was the biggest challenge, so I amortized some of the projects over the days ahead, like making the sauces. They'd actually taste better after a day or two in the refrigerator since the flavors would evolve. I saved the butchering tasks until after dinner on Friday—cutting the salmon into small portions and the meat into bite-sized pieces—since keeping fish and meat whole for as long as possible would be better for shelf life and storage.

I placed orders with my short list of vendors for items that had the greatest volume on my menus—the meats, fish and shellfish, fruits and vegetables. Rick and I went over a rental order for china, silver, glasses, and linens. We didn't need much for the "smaller" meals, but for the big party, which was a stand-up occasion, I wanted to be covered for the first three courses. I figured by the fourth course we would have washed enough plates for that course and the momentum would continue throughout the rest of the meal. This meant three hundred small plates. We also ordered three hundred dinner forks instead of salad forks. "It's more elegant," Rick said. Some knives and spoons just in case. A hundred and fifty champagne glasses. A hundred and fifty wineglasses. Water and rocks glasses. Linen cocktail napkins. The rentals were scheduled to arrive on Wednesday. Rick assured me the food items I needed from him would be there, too.

Rick ordered flowers to be delivered to the boat early on Friday morning. Three arrangements for the salon and dining area plus two large ones for the deck. He went to the wine shop in town and bought two huge *salmanazars* of champagne—nine-liter bottles, a case worth in each. As he wrestled the bottles down the hatchway, he proclaimed, "We can't be at the Grand Prix without these!" I had no idea how to find the space in our reefers to chill them. "Don't worry, I'll take care of it," he promised. "I will ask one of the captains of a nearby motor yacht if we can store them in their refrigerators." Some large motor yachts have restaurant-style walk-in refrigerators on board.

On Tuesday afternoon, a van arrived from Italy, arranged by *la Signora*, loaded with provisions for both the upcoming weekend and the summer season: cases of champagne, *premier cru* Chablis, spring water, extra virgin olive oil, sunflower seed oil, canned San Marzano tomatoes, some cases of dried pasta, a case of Arborio rice, a huge restaurant-sized pasta pot and colander, more designer sundries, and other items for the cabins. We used Michele's office as a storehouse, only taking what inventory we thought we would need.

Just as expected, space quickly became a critical concern, and the perishables hadn't even arrived yet. My bilge storage in the galley was fully loaded, especially with Rick's wine, and I began to fill the storage bins under the mess table benches. Scott offered to let me keep the rental dishes in the engine room. "A natural plate warmer," he said, which made total sense, but he was also trying to preserve at least some of our personal space in the fo'c'sle. Patrick borrowed a few coolers from one of the maxi-race-boat teams. They would hold the beverages. But we also needed a few hundred pounds of ice. I had no clue where that would come from. A large quantity of ice is a scarce commodity in Europe. I asked Michele's assistant if he could call the Monaco Yacht Club and see if they might sell us some. The cooking hadn't even started yet.

At dinner that night, I explained my situation to the crew. They could already see that the food and supplies would take over our small living area. Now I asked if they wouldn't mind if I used the fo'c'sle as a makeshift walk-in for the perishables by keeping the portholes closed and cranking up the air-conditioning. Patrick chalked up the high electricity bill that would result as a necessary cost of doing business. He also decided to give the crew a per diem to eat onshore starting Wednesday night. This would also give me the mess area for storage, and not having to cook for the crew would buy me precious time.

Even with the extra space, I still found myself constantly repositioning items in the fridge, those needed first up front or on top, later meals toward the back or bottom. All of my base items—dairy, cheeses, sliced meats, juices, and fresh pantry ingredients like carrots, celery, and lemons—filled a side in one of the reefers. The rest of the fridge space was reserved for the growing inventory of prepped items.

By Wednesday morning, it was time to move into cooking mode, and I began by making the accompaniments for antipasti or entrées like emulsified sauces, such as aioli, and tomato-based sauces. With the addition of fresh herbs, capers, anchovies, garlic, splashes of vinegar, lemon juice or zest, and extra virgin olive oil, or any combination there of, I could top vegetables, fish, and *frutti di mare*—shellfish—with an almost endless list of condiments. This would cover me for the meals outside of the main event on Saturday and give me versatility throughout the weekend.

Time spent in the south of France and Italy also exposed me to accompaniments like black olive tapenade and anchovy-based *anchoïade*—pastes that are blended with other seasonings; an almost mayonnaise-like sauce made with sea urchins called *oursinade;* a pungent green sauce made of parsley, anchovy, caper, a touch of garlic, olive oil, and vinegar called *salsa verde;* and a short list of other *salsine*—sauces—that called for other conserved ingredients out of the pantry like sundried tomatoes, roasted bell peppers, and nuts. This was a great go-to repertoire to keep in the back of my mind as I worked and put meals together. And a copy of J.-B. Reboul's *La cuisinière provençale,* which I had on board, was an indispensable guide to the region's cuisine.

Rick appeared in the galley from his foraging assignments looking pleased. His smile disappeared when he saw the look in my eye after opening the first box.

"Frozen seafood! Why did you get this?" I asked. I was pissed.

"It's good quality," he said.

"I'm trying to make a good impression with the owners and I have to cook with frozen food?" So much for not taking shortcuts.

"With some lemon juice and one of those good olive oils you have they'll never know," Rick replied.

"Did you get the veal stock?"

"Here," he said as he handed me a food-service-sized container of veal base concentrate, a canister of dark brown pasty mass, steps more flavorful than beef bouillon cubes but usually laden with MSG and never able to offer the natural gelatin I needed in order to have a sauce with the shiny and silky viscosity I was after. I wanted refined, rich, and luscious veal stock, the backbone of the sauce maker's craft.

"You have to be kidding me. I'm not using this."

"Why not?" Rick asked. He couldn't understand why I wasn't grateful.

"When you said you knew where to get stock, I saw five gallons of beautiful *fond de veau* arriving at the boat. I assumed you had a connection or friend that worked in a restaurant around here."

Suddenly it was Rick who was pissed. He walked out of the pantry and into the salon.

I wanted complete quality control in an effort to deliver flavor, and proper stock was the essence of the red wine sauce I needed to make. That afternoon I bolted to one of the larger butchers in town and rallied about thirty pounds of veal bones cut into small pieces. I would roast the bones that night in order to get them nice and caramelized for good color in the stock and, more important, the deep, roasted meat flavor I was looking for in my sauce. A sauce like this would be the perfect condiment to the seared pieces of veal *bocconcini* that would go into it just before service. By Friday I'd be ready for the final steps to make the sauce.

Five

Spaghettoni

Monte Carlo

$\mathcal{W}$e left Antibes at precisely one-thirty in the morning. While the crew stayed up for the ride, it was my only chance to get some sleep. I had no difficulty passing out until the pounding racket of the anchor chain being let out through the pipes in the fo'c'sle pulled me out of my dream state five hours later. We were backing into our spot in the port of Monte Carlo.

The marina was like a big open piazza on the water, much wider than most harbors, and apart from a couple of boats it was beautifully empty when we arrived. We were guided just off of center and tied up to the quay. From the aft deck I got the first view of the city. Right beyond the quay, the streets around the public pool in the middle were transformed into the racetrack that worked its way around the entire city. Spectator grandstands were constructed on either side and adorned with billboards and international flags. I could see that the temporary overpasses above the track were close to being fully operational. Already, the public-address system wired throughout the city broadcast an endless stream of announcements, interviews, and commentary in three languages. For the Formula 1 Grand Prix weekend, the elegant city of Monte Carlo was transformed from its polished and pristine self into an arena and host to one of the most famous sporting events in the world.

I did not come up for air again until mid-afternoon, and by then boats were anchored, three, four, five deep, behind our reserved front-row seat. Crews were hopping from one boat to another in their dinghies to shoot the breeze with old shipmates.

The quays were mobbed as well, and Ian had taken it upon himself to search for celebrities after spotting Mick Jagger walking past earlier that morning. The report came down to me that Simon Le Bon of the rock band Duran Duran was on the aft deck, talking with the owners' children. Later Rick would fill me in about the Italian paparazzi trying to get their subjects to pose while darting compliments at them—"*Bellissima! Stupendo! Encora!*"—until the Monte Carlo police shooed them away. I was too busy down in the galley to enjoy any of this firsthand.

I had to finish up everything I would need for the Saturday party. I had made peace with the limitations of my marine stove for everyday cooking. But there was no getting around the fact that it could not meet the demands of this kind of volume production. But I wasn't going to let anything get in the way of making this weekend work.

The fo'c'sle was transformed into a faux refrigerator. Portholes stayed closed. I even opened the chain lockers in the floor to try coaxing coolness out of the sea under the steel hull. But I wasn't done. Because the anchor was laid for our stern-to parking, one of the chain lockers sat vacant. This could be a perfect place to store the cheeses. The conditions were basement-like—just what we needed. I lined the inside of the locker with garbage bags, and then carefully stacked the cheeses inside. I put the cases of vegetables as far forward as possible near the forepeak. Those crew members who slept near the chain locker were going to get a mixed smell of garlic, onions, and cheeses as they shivered through the night. Late Friday morning, eight large pastry boxes of petits fours took the entire surface of the vacant eighth bunk. Whoever packed them wrote "Serenity" on each to designate our order. How ironic I thought. The weekend was shaping up to be the furthest thing from serene I had ever experienced. I put "Don't Touch!" signs on each.

By Friday afternoon, the race-car drivers had started their practice runs through the city streets. The high-pitched revving of their 800-horsepower engines reverberated off the modern high-rise apartment buildings, back into the harbor, through *Serenity*'s hull, and would not stop until the moment when the checkered flags were waved and the race finished on Sunday. This only added to my stress. Nor did it help when Patrick came down below to post some all-area pit passes that Michele had arranged for the crew. "If you have time, you should check it out," he said, and left them pinned to our little message board. What a tease. I asked Kevin to get them out of my sight.

It was now early Friday evening. "Showtime," Rick announced when the owners and guests arrived. I quickly went into my cabin to change into my uniform. Rick was readying a tray with flutes of champagne to offer as a welcoming start to the weekend. I could hear muffled compliments in Italian as *la Signora* gave her guests the multimillion-dollar version of a "nickel tour" around the interior of *Serenity*. It was getting louder and clearer as they made their way toward the pantry.

"*Ciao, Davide!*" *la Signora* greeted me as she introduced a few of her friends. Minutes later, *il Dottore* stuck his head in the pantry to greet me with a big smile. They were ready for a big weekend. They didn't come forward to the galley, probably for good measure. It wasn't a sight I was proud to share. Even if it hadn't been so full of food, something happened to the decorating when it came time to do the galley. Gone was the classy nautical feel apparent throughout the rest of the yacht. The galley decor looked only one step up from that of the engine room.

Several minutes later, now alone, *la Signora* came back to the galley to review the plan. She wanted assurances that her orders were going to be fulfilled. I wanted some small sign that she trusted me.

Dinner that night was fine, easier than expected. Only fourteen people. A simple plate-and-serve-type menu: small shrimp salads with porcini mayonnaise that was divine, baked sea bass with a *tian* of potatoes and zucchini, crispy *tuile* "cups" filled with crème fraîche and berries. The whole sequence of dishes went well with Rick's nonstop pouring of champagne. One meal down, only three more to go. Kevin came down after dinner and offered to help. It seemed this was typical of him, always thinking of the next person. "I think I'll need all hands for the big party" was my only request. Once dinner was over and I had cleaned everything up, I went back to cooking. By one o'clock, after some further reorganizing, restacking, reshuffling, repositioning, and the disposal of lots of garbage, I went to sleep.

Going to the bakery in the morning for bread and breakfast pastries was my only opportunity to get off the boat for a little while to see the world and gather my thoughts. Beyond that, Rick was my link to the outside, giving me constant news of activity on deck or on the quay. "Incredible women all over," he'd report. Just what I needed to hear. Then Patrick came into the galley with his camera to change film at the mess table and tell me what great shots he got of the race cars coming around the S-turn near our berthing during their practice runs.

I could have done without the Saturday lunch since it got in the way of valuable prep time, but my "parade" of five antipasti was easy enough to serve, even if it took the whole morning to prepare: asparagus with Parmigiano-Reggiano, lemon, and olive oil; leeks vinaigrette with green peppercorns; goat cheese medallions with olives and crushed fennel seeds; toasts with *oursinade*—topped with minced celery hearts and spring onions; and the very mild French garlic salami, *saucisse du l'ail*, thinly sliced and topped with batons of pickled bell peppers and a drizzle of extra virgin olive oil. Throughout the afternoon, there were occasional momentum busters, such as when one of the owners' kids wanted a snack *panino*. Fatigue weighed me down, and I began to feel like I was having an out-of-body experience. And things were just warming up.

The real show—at least for me—wouldn't begin until late Saturday afternoon. I took a break on deck with some of my crewmates earlier that day.

Ian spoke up first: "How are you going to be able to do this in that little galley?"

Nigel piled on: "That's a small stove for a hundred, mate."

Even Rick couldn't resist: *"C'est bête"*—basically, this is mad. "How does she expect all of this food to come out of here?"

By early evening I could see Rick feeling the pinch, too. He flipped his umpteenth Marlboro over the side as large bags of ice arrived. Between the ice and the rental glasses, the pantry became virtually impassable. Rick and I quickly huddled to work out how we would organize service. Passed canapés as the guests arrived. This would go on for an hour or so. We worked out the dinner timing once *la Signora* gave her fifteen-minute warning. Each course would be put on platters in the galley, then go to a table on deck, where Rick would serve individual portions on small plates. This would be an elegant way to do service while at the same time keeping the guests from completely assaulting the buffet table. In theory this all seemed to make sense.

Patrick put on his formal attire—a dark blue captain's blazer complete with epaulets, brass buttons, and the *Serenity* logo embroidered on the breast pocket to be worn with white pants. He came into the galley, looked around at the masses of food and rentals stacked everywhere, and with a "glad it's not me" grin asked if we were ready, before heading up to the deck.

Kevin offered to help with any last-minute prep, so I put him at the mess table with a toaster to start making croutons for the canapés out of France's great white bread for toast, *pain de mie*.

Nigel volunteered to help with the dishes, so I explained how I planned on recycling the early-course plates. We fired up the dishwasher for the first time—and hoped its three-minute cycle would be a strong ally. Ian, seeing the others pitch in, sheepishly admitted to having worked as a waiter for a caterer one summer, so we immediately shanghaied him to be a food runner between the galley and Rick.

He would also be the busboy, charged with bringing down all the used plates and silver. "Should I wear white gloves?" he asked with a little sarcasm. I certainly appreciated the last-minute volunteerism, but these guys had never worn the shoes of a banquet chef who was about to be "in the weeds," as they say in the restaurant business. They couldn't predict the intensity of the next few hours.

Things began heating up in the galley. I arranged a few trays of canapés and showed Kevin how to do it. Then he took over from me. Rick came down to pick up the first tray. "Prince Rainier is on board," he declared, fixing himself one last time before going topside. He smiled wide and said, "Here we go, flat stick!" "Flat stick" is a speed-boat driver's term meaning "full speed." That evening he accelerated like one of the freshly tuned engines that screamed from the race team garage area, a background noise that continued through the night.

I set up the antipasto in the pantry. Meanwhile, the large pasta pot took all four burners to get the water to a boil. I had to prepare two different kinds of pastas with only one pot, so the fusilli would get scooped out into a colander. The pot would then be temporarily moved to the counter, while at the stove I tossed the pasta with the still simmering sauce until I had two platters' worth. Now it was time to return the pot to the stove for the second pasta. There was no way I would have blanched the pasta ahead of time—a practiced but lame shortcut—especially when cooking for a large group of affluent Italians.

It took only two courses to discover my system of plate washing was a bust. The dishwasher couldn't keep up, plus the process of load-ing trays, rinsing them, placing them in the machine, then looking for a place to dry the prior load competed for the same space that I needed to cook and plate the food. Kevin began to hand wash, a valiant but futile effort. Ian had to manage finding places to put down stacks of dirty dishes, while I needed him to quickly take the platters up to the deck. This wasn't working, and suddenly piles of plates were everywhere.

"Ian, bring the plates forward. Scott, can you take the plates and scrape them into a garbage can on deck, then hand them down the crew hatch? Nigel, use the shower in the head for the pre-rinse. We'll take them from there and send them clean to the pantry." Not perfect but better. Finally there would be a wash system that flowed somewhat in the manner of a proper restaurant kitchen.

"This is mad! Absolutely mad!" Rick said as he ran into the pantry to grab more plates and give the call for the next course. "I can't believe how fast these people eat!"

"What's going on up there?" I asked.

"*Che meraviglia*"—what a marvel—"everyone says, and they grab the plates as soon as I can get them served. It's impossible to stay ahead! Then *la Signora* wants me to keep pouring champagne!"

"And Ian is scrambling to keep up with the busing," I said.

"Just keep sending me food and plates. Don't worry about timing. You decide when to change courses. At this point it doesn't matter," Rick said as he disappeared behind the pantry door to the salon. His hair began to take on the look of a mad professor.

Kevin started to laugh at the insanity in the galley. "Do you think they'll invite us to join them?" he said, adding another note of dry humor.

I could hear Ian on deck giving Scott the heads-up that more plates and platters were coming his way. There was a constant clatter of empty wine and water bottles being dropped into the bin on deck. By now, filled garbage bags were piling up in the crew quarters as Scott and Nigel worked in tandem from the deck to below. The oversplash from rinsing the masses of plates in the head had most of the floor in the crew area drenched. Pasta, sauce, and soaked pieces of bread blocked the drain. This couldn't be dealt with until after the party tide was out. Nigel filled the sink with the flatware, which needed to be sorted before washing.

"Shit! The cheeses in the chain locker. They can't get wet!" I exclaimed. I broke from the stove to go forward. Nigel helped me move the mounds of garbage so I could open the chain locker. Thank goodness, I had put garbage bags on top of the cheese to act as a cover.

"David, *la Signora* is asking for the *vitello*"—the veal. "How long?"

"Three minutes," I said, the standard restaurant line cook answer that gives something the waiter wants to hear when you are not quite ready. I was now wet with rinse water and sweat. The floor was getting slippery. The humidity from the stove and dishwasher made the galley feel like a steam bath.

Kevin tried his best to keep up and stay out of my way, at the same time agreeing with Rick about how crazy this all was. Nigel delivered stacks of plates and as much flatware as he could carry by hand. "The sooner we get it out, the sooner it will be over," he kept assuring me.

When the fourth platter of the meat course went up on deck, I knew we were close to the end. All I had to do was arrange the petits fours on platters, get them to the buffet table, then make the galley somewhat presentable so that I'd be in decent shape for race day. The sight forward was pretty scary. Our world had been turned upside down—*distrutto*—destroyed. It would take all of us to put the fo'c'sle back in order. We had our work cut out for us the next morning before the guests got up to have breakfast on deck. Garbage had to go out, the head had to be washed, rentals had to be put back in the crates, and some form of order had to be restored below while at the same time the deck had to be cleaned and all of the brass polished. I suddenly realized that Patrick had never come below to offer a hand.

For dessert, I could have sworn there were three boxes of chocolate petits fours. As I looked through all of them, a bit puzzled, I heard Ian say, "Uh-oh," while he took a break at the mess table.

"What's up?" I asked. I could see a look of embarrassment on Kevin's face as he turned away.

"Well, we had a little problem last night," Kevin said. "I seemed to have caught the edge of the box and felt icing squirting through my toes when I tried to climb up to my bunk. I can't believe you didn't hear us laughing when I hopped on one foot to the head to wash my foot off."

My chocolate petits fours. I thought for a second about the efforts and skill of the *chef pâtissier* making these little gems. And then I thought about what I was going to do to make things right. But after my third nineteen-hour day, I had no energy left for either yelling or crying. We arranged the others on platters, and no one went home hungry. The meal had ended.

By midnight, we were cleaned up enough below for me to go on deck and get some fresh air. I stayed on the foredeck to check out the scene. The cool air—or what seemed cool compared with the galley—refreshed me. Gipsy Kings music blasted from the yacht next door, the Latin rhythms starting to lull me into a trance broken by the music from other parties on neighboring yachts. I watched small groups of guests chatting and laughing on *Serenity,* while attractive Italian women danced barefoot to the music in their little summer dresses on *Pegasus* with the night lights of the city behind them. I wondered what a hundred pairs of designer shoes looked like on the quay.

Another night I might have stayed up and watched the show, but I was so tired that I quickly went down and crawled into my bunk. I passed out after the second breath and went into a deep, comfortable sleep. Then the racket awakened me. A group of guests were stomping on the deck above me and banging on the hatch-cover glass, repeating in unison: *"Davide, Davide, abbiamo fa-me, abbiamo fa-me!"*—Da-vid,

Da-vid, we have hun-ger, we have hun-ger! The words were coming out louder and louder, faster and faster.

Rick came into the cabin.

"David, *la Signora* wants pasta for everyone. Penne with spicy tomato sauce." I looked at my alarm clock—it was two-thirty in the morning. *Damn it.*

"That's what they're saying," I said, still in a daze.

"They're nuts! It just won't stop!" he said as he went to get the service wares together.

"How many people are out there?" I asked when I went into the galley.

"Maybe thirty or forty, mostly friends of the kids."

I was in no mood to cook. It would take almost an hour to boil the water, plus I had to make the sauce. Then it came to me. This was why the cases of pasta and the big pot had been delivered. After a long and challenging few days, I learned firsthand the meaning of the Italian party tradition after a late night called the *spaghettoni*. An hour later, eight pounds of pasta with spicy tomato sauce were being portioned on deck, and just short of nauseous I made my way back to the bunk and finally to sleep.

I awakened to Ian handing garbage bags up to Scott through the crew way. Rick was still sleeping. I went above to see what was going on, the clear and bright morning landing hard on my eyes. Kevin and Nigel were hosing and brushing the deck. On the quay, I saw two of the owners' twenty-something-year-old kids jump out of a taxi. Ties loosened and collars opened. I got the sense that they were returning from a night at the casinos and wanted to board their boat before their parents awakened and saw that they had been out all night. Still sorely lacking sleep, I edged my way onto the pier and sleepwalked to the bakery. Thankfully, only one stop today.

I should have felt good. Every meal had been a success so far, but I was so tired and so cooked out that even though this was the day of the Grand Prix, I couldn't generate any excitement. At least lunch would be easy—sliced cured meats on platters, an arrangement of cheeses, and a big basket of *panini* were all anyone would get for lunch.

As I walked through town, I had to acknowledge that *la Signora*'s menu plan for the weekend had actually been well thought out, clearly a result of having done this before. She had put together a doable menu for the numbers even in a space and facility not equipped to handle the volume. But in a proper kitchen with a couple of other cooks, prep time would have been halved. On the front end, our decision to rent lots of service wares to make the occasion casual yet elegant was not only smart but necessary. I just wished we had a little more than four days' notice to provide all of it. The guests must have been invited in advance to plan their schedules, so why wait to tell the staff that would be doing the procurement?

Rick's contributions to the ingredient list, I realized, were also good ones. I shouldn't have snapped when he returned with frozen seafood and concentrated veal stock base. They were quality items in their own right. Did I really want to clean twenty pounds of baby octopus and twenty-five pounds of shrimp? I probably could have been smarter and gotten away with a little cheat on the red wine sauce. I made the sauce in the traditional, time-consuming manner. Roast the bones, make a rich stock, do a wine reduction, make a sauce base, pass through a sieve, then simmer to clean the sauce and reduce, finally passing again through a *chinois* for a clean, clear consistency. Even in a proper kitchen, this can be a thirty-hour process.

The few gallons I needed for the party could have been made with a nice red wine reduction blended with a double concentrate of the veal base then thickened with some cornstarch. With a final flavoring from a jolt of red wine to bring up the acidity and some herbs and seasoning, it would have been finished in a fraction of the time. Plus, that late in the evening, no one would have noticed the difference if the flavors were on.

Rick had been around this block before. I realized I was the neophyte. When I returned to the boat later that morning, I apologized to him for snapping.

"Don't worry about it," he responded. "You're a perfectionist. Now you know for the next time."

Race time began an hour after lunch. My responsibilities were over. I climbed the ratlines to the spreaders near the top of the mast to watch my first Grand Prix with Kevin and Ian. *La Signora* told me to be careful going up and didn't think it was a great idea. She knew I was exhausted. I went up anyway and attached a lifeline around my waist. As the race began, all eyes were on the serpentine racecourse. I watched for a while but found myself pulled by another view. I looked east, down the coast toward San Remo and Portofino, toward Italy, toward a place I felt comfortable enough to call home. Not even the loud pops of downshifts and cheers from the massive crowd could break my gaze. Italy was only a week away.

Portofino and the Italian Riviera

Our cruising schedule was determined, in part, by long-standing yachting superstition. *Il Dottore* did not want any departures on Fridays, and so we were ready to leave for Portofino late Thursday evening, an hour before midnight. By hedging the consequences of maritime lore, we would keep out of harm's way.

At a quarter to eleven, four days later in base port, we were all on deck ready to perform the parting procedures we had been assigned. A few late-night strollers on the quay watched, and friends from neighboring yachts stopped by to wish us well. For the next three and a half months, we'd be cruising along the western shore of Italy, and I had that unmistakable sensation of change, that the life I had carved out for myself here in Antibes, a triumph from my years abroad, might become a part of my past.

The portholes below were latched shut; the marine band radio, radar, and navigation lights were turned on. Even the temperate and breezeless weather of the night added to the sensation of going away. Patrick started *Serenity*'s growling engine. I was on the aft deck when he made the call: "Everyone ready . . . stern lines off!" They were taken off the bollards by yacht club attendants onshore as Nigel and I pulled them on board. As soon as Patrick engaged the engine into forward, Kevin started to bring in the anchor while Ian packed the chain in the lockers below.

As we slowly and carefully started pulling out of our slip, we heard from the other sailors on the quay, *"Bon séjour!"* "Good luck!" "See you in September."

Once we had cleared the marina breakwater, Patrick called everyone to the cockpit to explain the watch schedule. "I want two of you on deck at all times, with a change occurring every hour, on the hour." Given that there were seven of us, this meant two hours on, five hours off, regardless of the time of day, until we arrived at our destination. For the trip to Portofino, we would all be needed for one rotation. We chose the order for the passage. Rick proudly volunteered for one of the graveyard shifts from two to four. "At this hour, what's the point in going to bed when I'm not even tired and we will be in Portofino by six or seven? I'm pulling an all-nighter!"

I liked the responsibility of watch duty. It made me more than a below-deck crew member. One of us would drive the boat, keeping it on course by following the predetermined compass headings. The other watched for traffic at sea and, when sighting another vessel, made an assessment, based on the arrangement of red, green, and white lights mounted on its masts and decks, of what type it was and, most important, what direction it was headed. Then its course was tracked in order for us to proceed with prudence. At the same time, we were both expected to eye the sails, monitor the radio, and make the required log entries recording any events or course changes. On deck, the only illumination was the dim map light in the chart house just forward of the cockpit and the compass light inside the binnacle. The cockpit took on the comfortable feeling of a late-night, darkened cocktail lounge. For those couple of hours on watch, I was not just the cook on board. I was a sailor, sharing responsibility for the welfare of the boat and helping in the safe passage to a destination.

But time on watch was also a time for conversation. While in Antibes, at the end of the workday on the boat, everyone would go back to his life onshore. Except for Rick, I didn't get a chance to get to know the rest of my crewmates very well. But standing under the stars, bound together for two hours in shared responsibility, acting as captains of our ship, with little to do other than keep the boat on course and stay alert to some adverse occurrence, we would be silent. Eventually we'd begin to speak of things that revealed who we were.

"Have you ever been to Italy before?" I asked Scott after getting settled into driving the boat on the heading that Kevin told me, upon relieving him, would keep us on a straight shot to our destination.

"No, never," he said while looking into the dark void of the night beyond the rail. It seemed like I had interrupted his thoughts.

"You'll love it," I said.

"If we were going on our terms, possibly. But since we are going by virtue of our employers, I see this as work, not as a holiday." He spoke as if wherever we'd go, it wouldn't much matter to him.

"But if you've never been, here's a paid opportunity to go there. You don't have to be on a vacation to get something out of a place you've been."

"True, but Italy just hasn't been on my list of must-see destinations."

On this topic, it seemed we had nothing in common. I figured it best to change the subject.

"I noticed you brought a lot of books on board."

"I'll be able to catch up on my reading when the owners are on board."

"No repairs or maintenance then, right?"

"Something like that," he said.

I got the sense he knew a lot. All kinds of things. Which was appropriate for a marine engineer. He *had* to know a lot. We spent the rest of the hour in our own wandering thoughts, which were occasionally broken by matters relating to our course and heading.

When Nigel came up for my second hour, he was interested in how long I had been moving from one restaurant to the next. As he was on a round-the-world tour, we talked about the challenges of living out of duffel bags and backpacks.

His tour was a time to see as much as he could and possibly find ways to put enough money away so that when he got home, he could pursue his dream and settle down.

"All I want to do is make enough money to support my diving habit, mate," he told me.

Not long after sunrise, I was awakened after a few hours of sleep by the change in engine noise, going from cruising RPM to quiet idle speed, meaning we were approaching our destination. I put the jumbo espresso pot on the stove for the crew coffee, and then went up on deck to see that we were just outside the inlet to the marina of Portofino.

Patrick brought the boat to the mouth of the harbor. From this vantage point, the huddled harbor buildings, some with roof terraces adorned with large terra-cotta pots filled with vibrant flowers, were fronted by rows of small colorful boats on moors and backed by lush greenery blanketing the steep terrain that went up to the sky. I was taken by the almost surreal beauty of this protected marina. I wondered what it must have been like centuries past when Portofino was a working harbor, built to service those that worked the vessels that went out to sea.

For now, *Serenity* needed to be seen by Antonio, the harbormaster who lived and operated his business from a little sailboat tied up at the middle of the quay. Antonio watched over this popular marina where there were only a few spaces that could take a boat as large as *Serenity.* When I saw Patrick coming over to me with a bottle of whiskey and a handheld radio, I knew what he wanted. The whiskey was for Antonio, and I was sent to shore in the launch.

Antonio, a true salt, slightly graying and fit, loved *Serenity* and didn't hide his pleasure at having her call on his port. I received a big *"buon giorno!"* from him when I arrived at his boat. I handed him the bottle, and for a few minutes we chatted away about which yachts were cruising the Mediterranean and which had been in port thus far. I then asked him if we could bring *Serenity* in. "Of course," he said, beaming. He assigned us a berth next to the ferry dock for the weekend, telling me it would be no problem as long as we were out by seven o'clock Monday morning. I called Patrick, and he slowly backed the boat along the narrow stretch to the quay. It never occurred to me what would have happened if Antonio said no. The owners expected to step onto their boat that afternoon.

After helping to clean the deck and dry the varnished wood with a chamois, I headed to Panificio Canale, the bakery at the center of town, to get some freshly made focaccia, the pride of Ligurian bread making. The tiny shop was busy, locals shuffling in to get first dibs on the second bake of the morning. The smell reminded me of a pizzeria—hot, yeasty bread, olive oil, tomato sauce, but without the cheese.

"*Ciao, marinaio!*" was how Mary, the woman behind the counter, acknowledged me, her voice sailing over the crowd as soon as I walked in. Amazingly, she remembered me from my last visit. I had been here when I worked at Cà Peo, a restaurant tucked in the hills behind Chiavari just down the coast. "The *americano!*" she shouted out, blowing any plans I might have had to pass as a native. "What boat did you come in with?" It seemed that she had a special thing for sailors and would give them a little extra attention—the way local bartenders give special treatment to home port fishermen.

"*Serenity.* We'll be here for the weekend," I replied loud enough for her to hear me at the other end of the shop.

"*Fantastico!* What can I get for you?" she asked, as she worked her way down the counter to hand me a piece of warm focaccia she had cut with a scissors from a large sheet. "Try this, *caro*, it's the best!" She reintroduced herself as Mary instead of Maria, but I told her I remembered. This pleased her.

The focaccia was delicious—thin with a slightly crispy outside and spongy inside, olive oil filling the dimples on top and sea salt crystals crunching in my mouth at the first bite. All I needed was some soft and tangy *stracchino* cheese spread over the top, and my preference for savory over sweet in the morning would be satisfied.

I made an executive decision that the crew should experience a taste of local flavor our first day here. Mary convinced me to buy a full sheet of plain focaccia, and then another with a thin layer of tomato sauce that had black olives strewn on top. Both were cut into quarters, wrapped in white paper, and then tied with string as they do in cake shops. Immediately, the oil started to show through the paper that had been warmed by the bread. I honored some of the other crew requests with some *cornetti*—croissants—filled with marmalade for those that craved sweet. As soon as I turned to leave, Mary greeted her next customer without missing a beat: "*Ciao, bellissima!*"

The rest of the crew were deep into maintenance or polishing tasks when I got back to the boat. Our day was under way, and there was an aura of stress on the crew members' faces as they seemed to work a little faster than normal. I assumed it was because this was our first weekend with the owners on board in Italy. Nigel and Kevin were the only ones who seemed interested in the focaccia, grabbing a couple pieces from the platter I left on the mess table and taking them back up on deck. The rest didn't seem to care, and even though I put another pot of coffee on the stove, I had the sense that my effort was good, only late in delivery.

I sat at the table to pull some ideas together for the weekend's menu. This area reminded me of fish, seafood, and lots of great vegetables. After reviewing my notes from the restaurants where I worked in Liguria and Lombardy, I looked through my Italian regional cookbook and other great resources, Alan Davidson's *Mediterranean Seafood* and Pellegrino Artusi's *L'arte di mangiar bene.* I was inspired to make poached or baked fish with a classic condiment of the region, *salsa genovese,* a green homogeneous blend of parsley, garlic, capers, anchovies, a few olives, olive oil, a touch of vinegar, and a cooked egg yolk or two making it different from *salsa verde*; seafood salads; the purple-tipped artichokes from the region; crêpes with the same wild-greens filling and walnut sauce as traditionally used in a pasta called *pansotti;* and an almost flourless chocolate cake that would go perfectly with a light and fluffy *crema di mascarpone*—mascarpone cream—both of which I learned from my friend Franco at Albergo del Sole. For this one, I'd exchange the rum in the *crema* recipe for espresso. I already had all the dessert ingredients in the yacht's stores save the mascarpone, which would be easy to find in any *latteria. La Signora* had suggested when in Portofino to keep an eye out for *bianchetti*—tiny fish that are deep-fried whole and served to her preference with lemon on the side. And I thought of pesto, that simple amalgam of basil, garlic, pine nuts, and oil, admiring how classic and important it had become to the history of Italian cuisine. Christopher Columbus carried it on his voyages from Genoa and so would *Serenity.*

Santa Margherita Ligure is a nostalgic but manicured resort town, a small city by the sea not far down the coast from Portofino and only two hours due south of Milan. It is considered by many to be the crown jewel of the Italian Riviera. Long ago, some creative soul, no doubt in a cost-saving gesture, chose to paint the decorative architectural detailing onto its buildings rather than carve it out of stone or wood. Now it is the Italian Riviera's signature feature, and only the most skilled of craftsmen continue the tradition that had such humble beginnings. Manicured palm trees, expertly cut shrubs, and clusters of flowers brighten the boulevards, traffic islands, and coastal walkways.

I arrived at Santa Margherita's open-air food market just as the nine o'clock church bells rang. At this hour only the regulars were doing their shopping. By ten, they knew that throngs of visitors would descend on the market, taking up lots of room at the stalls, looking but not buying. I, too, wanted to complete my shopping before the tourists arrived. I also would have loved to follow up a morning of shopping with a leisurely lunch with wine, as I did in Provence, but today there would be no time for leisure. By late afternoon, the owners and their guests would be arriving.

I learned in the market that it was already too late in the season for any of the *primizie*—first of the season—tender vegetables and greens long awaited by the locals after the winter months. But an amazing bounty was still available—piles of artichokes, fava beans, peas, different varieties of zucchini, three colors of asparagus, leeks, and a veritable garden of greens and herbs. I could get Italian *salumi,* cheeses, and groceries in any number of shops nearby. This was also a good chance to find a few bottles of small-production Ligurian olive oil, preferable for its light and almost fruity flavor, and some of the area's great black olive paste, which would make a nice addition to the pantry. The small but meaty local olives, with their subtle brininess, lend themselves well to mixing with mayonnaise as a condiment, or to blending with the juices left in the pan after baking fish to make a simple sauce.

The fish market was only a few minutes away, but it appeared that *la Signora* wasn't the only one with a taste for the tiny *bianchetti.* By the time I arrived, only one vendor had any to sell, and even he had only a few pounds. I cleaned him out. If *la Signora* arrived with a full boat of guests, I would serve *bianchetti* as a dinner first course. Fewer guests, and they would be the lucky ones to have it as a luncheon main course.

At another vendor, I spotted a large bright red center-cut piece of tuna. The meat was glistening and showed a very thin fat line, that dark, useless part of the meat that runs along its spine. I had to get some. Long before I set sail, I read somewhere that in Liguria, a traditional method of cooking fish is to set it on a thick piece of hot slate called a *ciappa,* a method essentially the same as cooking on a griddle. I asked the fish vendor where I could find one. He pointed me in the direction of a housewares store in the harbor area just down from the fish market. I should try this, I thought. So I bought enough tuna for a full boat—eight guests and seven crew. It would be tuna steaks from the *ciappa,* smeared with that olive paste, topped with a cluster of *à la minute* chopped parsley, and served with roasted potatoes on the side.

Around eleven, I made my way back to the dock, catching the little coastal ferry that would bring me back to Portofino. During the short ride, it was my turn for stress. I could feel the tension rising in me. I knew it had to do with our being in Italy, essentially in *la Signora's* backyard. She knew the difference between good versus very good and truly authentic Italian cooking, and I worried about my cooking passing the test of her highly refined palate.

Rick greeted me on my return, and then joined me down below.

"Make sure there is enough for a second passing," he said as we rummaged through the silver closet looking for which platters would be best to use that night.

"Seconds?" I gasped. I had planned on a multicourse meal, but had calculated amounts based on one pass for each course.

"*C'est normal,*" he responded, as if I should have known this already. "Plus, you never know how much someone will take the first time, so it is proper to offer a second pass."

I didn't know this—in fact, I hadn't even considered it. And I wasn't sure what "seconds" actually meant to them. Is the second-round portion the same size as the first? Would it come off as wasteful if I sent full platters the second time, and there were no takers? I settled on a 50 percent solution. If I was cooking for eight, I would make enough for twelve, the second passing made up of smaller portions.

La Signora had gone over with Rick how she wanted the meals served, and now it was Rick's turn to explain this to me. He'd present the first platter for each course to *la Signora,* then move counterclockwise to each of the other women, but because of the banquette he couldn't serve from the left, so he'd have to find a place to extend over the table to get to those on the other side. He'd finish the women with *la Signora,* then move on to the men in the same direction, ending at *il Dottore.* The platter would come back to the galley, never being left on the table. I would then rework and arrange a second platter for the next pass. Dessert, I suggested, should be plated, at least sometimes, because soft and creamy items like *panna cotta,* that delicate, custard-like Italian classic, needed to be portioned, as it would not fare well if served on a platter. Others, like cakes and tarts, could be offered as per our new, standard method of service. Unless otherwise directed, we seemed to have our system for the remainder of the season.

The owners arrived on schedule, circling the area in their helicopter in what seemed like their signature greeting, then landing nearby at a private airport. It must have made them proud to see the boat from above, sitting in the middle of the quay, stretching farther than any other in the marina. Two other couples came on board with them.

Not long after, I could hear the owners and guests coming below, chatting with the clipped energy of holidaymakers. *Il Dottore*—relaxed in what appeared to be his weekday uniform, slacks and a button-down shirt with an open collar and rolled sleeves that had the sharp look of custom tailoring—stuck his head in the galley with a big smile and said, "*Ciao, Davide,* how are you?" while he looked around, taking in every detail of his yacht. Then Rick came into the pantry with a "here we go" look, suggesting to me that even he was a little nervous now that he had to be on full-time good behavior. All of a sudden, it became a whirling dervish of activity.

A few minutes later *la Signora* came into the galley to say hello and get an overview of the weekend's menu. Her colorful printed blouses seemed to be a trademark. I had mentioned that to Rick when we were in Monte Carlo. "Haute couture is what she's about," he said.

"*Ciao, Davide.* What good things are there to eat this weekend?"

she asked with a slight edge in her voice. I told her how good the food shopping had been that morning and that I had found the *bianchetti* she requested. She appeared happy to hear this. Then I briefly explained some of the items I planned on serving and how they would be prepared. I couldn't help but feel as if she were testing me, making sure I stuck to her dictates and wasn't going to surprise her or her guests with anything other than the food she wanted. I told myself that perhaps she just wanted to know—and she did seem genuinely interested in food—but I could not shake the feeling of having to toe the line rather than use my own judgment.

While *la Signora* was grilling me, I could hear Rick in the pantry, no doubt preparing the cocktails. Hoping to impress *la Signora* with something I had done on my own initiative, I happily reported that I had saved 10 percent on the food shopping. I wanted to show her, a little too eagerly maybe, that she could be confident I was spending her money wisely.

"Davide. After eight *miliardi*"—about five million dollars—"to buy this boat and another three for the first refit, do you think we are concerned about saving 10 percent on the grocery bill?" she said with a smirk, as if holding back a laugh. She looked at Rick, and I followed her look to him. It was clear that even though he couldn't understand Italian, he, too, had caught her point and was holding back a laugh. Then she continued, "It's okay, Davide, you can take the summer off. You don't have to concern yourself with trimming the budget."

A few minutes later I decided to go topside for a breath of air. Patrick, Kevin, and Ian were helping *il Dottore* raise two proud new additions to *Serenity*—the European Union flag and the Italian tricolor. It was official. *Serenity* was now registered as an Italian sailing vessel, governed by Italian maritime law, after decades of cruising under British registry. The guests cheered as *il Dottore* looked up at this symbol of his heritage with unmistakable pride in his eyes.

I returned to the galley to begin Friday night dinner, determined to get an early start to make sure I had enough time to cook. I looked at the pile of fresh artichokes I had bought earlier in the day. They looked fabulous. I decided to make them the way I was taught when I worked in Milan at the magnificent specialty and prepared-food store Gastronomia Peck. During the cookery I had to work fast since one of the tricks was to not let them oxidize too much while I trimmed their tough outer leaves. Once I got to the hearts with the lighter-colored tender leaves still intact, I coated each with a little fresh lemon juice. And because of their smallish size, the fibrous flower inside the artichoke was a nonissue. Putting them in acidulated water—water mixed with lemon juice—was forbidden in the Peck kitchen since it would result in their flavor becoming just that, acidulated water, and their texture would get mealy. Also, any water on them when added to hot oil would flare up, creating spitting oil, burned edges, and a resulting gaseous flavor.

Once the artichokes were ready for the final step before cooking, I heated a large fry pan with a few lightly crushed cloves of garlic in some olive oil. While the garlic began to sizzle and release its essential oils, I halved, then thinly sliced, each choke lengthwise. When the oil was perfumed and the cloves were light brown, the artichokes went in the pan and I sautéed them over high heat. In the process, I added a little lemon juice to keep the artichokes green, or "to keep color," as they say, and also to add a little acidity to their flavor along with a seasoning of salt and pepper. Fresh herbs could go in at this point like a touch of fresh oregano in spring-summer or thyme in autumn-winter. When they were just beginning to become tender, I removed them to a side platter. Prepared in this way, *carciofi saltati*—sautéed artichokes—offered versatility in the many ways they could be served: with pastas, in risotto, baked fish, seafood, roasted meats, and poultry. That night, they went perfectly with baked fillets of *branzino*—the long, slender, and esteemed Mediterranean sea bass—the only adornment being a touch of chopped oregano and a drizzle of local extra virgin olive oil to finish.

The entrée rolled off my hands as if well rehearsed, and rightfully so since I remembered well the Peck kitchen during artichoke season, working at the large table with the owners and chef, taking jabs all afternoon as to when I'd finally be able to clean an artichoke correctly and quickly, case after case, to their level of satisfaction. I guessed the training worked since Rick said that dinner went well. With a start of asparagus *tricolore*—three colors—under shaved Parmigiano-Reggiano and *panna cotta* covered with crushed strawberries for dessert, I felt pretty good about the menu.

Peck had made its mark, and getting in that kitchen was a coup. It started with a great referral, took much convincing during the interview, and required a lot of permit gathering. Foreigners in their kitchen were few and far between. But once in, I knew every day would leave a lasting impression, and it turned out to be one of the most inspiring places I ever worked. A few weeks after starting, I wrote in my journal, "An intense situation. A hard work ethic and discipline maintained. A tough chef. Sixty cooks. Volume, consistency, perfection. Everyone is bravo. The Peck system works very well."

The four brothers who owned the operation—Angelo, Mario, Remo, and Lino Stoppani—held fast to one credo that worked its way throughout the ranks of chefs, cooks, pot washers, counter personnel, and me, the lone intern: if you start every day with a dedication to being the best, then greatness will be achieved and maintained over time. That dedication to perfection was relentless and they constantly reminded me where I was working. When I was there, Peck was already a century old and had grown throughout the neighborhood with a *gastronomia, rosticceria,* cheese store, pork store, one-star restaurant, high-end cafeteria, and wine bar.

Saturday offered a light-wind morning. I awakened at six-fifteen, early enough for a quick workout before I headed to town to do any last-minute provisioning. The crew could take care of their own breakfast, and Rick would see to the owners' *colazione*—breakfast—nothing more than a simple "continental." By nine, when I returned, most of the crew already polished the brass. There was plenty of brass to be polished, varnished wood to be dried from the morning dew, and a harem's inventory of cushions and pillows to arrange in the cockpit. Rick, I could detect, was already attending to the owners' and guests' cabins. I went down below to stow the provisioning I'd brought back and to check out my new *ciappa*. Scott, who had been assigned deck watch for the day, came down to ask me if there were dishes to be washed, and that's when I learned that from now on, whoever was on watch would also be responsible for helping with the washing up and cleaning the crew head. Patrick stuck his head in to say we'd be pulling up the lines by ten to go for a sail, and then head to Sestri Levante, a short distance down the coast, where we would anchor for lunch and take a siesta.

In the hour I still had left before we sailed, I was motivated to get some extra projects started. First, I decided to make a large quantity of marinara—mariner's—sauce since it was going to be a staple in the *Serenity* repertoire. In lieu of peeling a lot of fresh tomatoes, I would make do with the canned whole peeled tomatoes I had on board since they were from San Marzano in southern Italy. I'd make a base sauce with a little onion, anchovy, dried oregano, and some hot red pepper flakes. This "mother" sauce would be used when making pasta for the crew, finishing pan sauces for baked fish, as a component in dressings for seafood, or to add a hearty layer of flavor to vegetable dishes like eggplant caponata and bell pepper *peperonata*.

The trick, I learned, to making a sauce that could be used in many different ways was to balance the seasonings, anchovy being one of them, with the tomato to attain a harmonious result. By constantly tasting during the cookery, the end result could be achieved while the flavors became more concentrated. Subtle additions of seasonings or aromatics like dried oregano would build flavor. Too much of any one element and the sauce would taste one-dimensional. Therefore, any additions were made little by little, gently, or, as the Italians say, *piano piano.* But with a nice, even base, I could always take the sauce in a new direction by adding something like torn basil leaves just before serving to freshen it.

The sauce needed to simmer for at least an hour. I attached the rails of the pot-holding apparatus around the edges of the stove, and then affixed the guards to secure the saucepan. Even though the wind was light and we wouldn't heel much, I wanted to test the system. Satisfied that the pot would hold, I went on deck to help take us out of port. I decided to stay up there after the sails were up to enjoy the day for a little while. It was good to get outside after the confinement of the galley.

The pungent smell of tomato sauce began to rise to the fore-deck. The only noise I could hear was the calming swish of the bow wake as *Serenity* gently glided through the water. The smell of the sauce was making everyone hungry. I went below to stir it and taste for seasoning.

We were still an hour away from Sestri, where we would drop anchor and have lunch, so I went on deck again. I was surprised to see other boats come fairly close to us, often altering their speed to match ours. They showed their admiration by blowing their horns and waving. One fancy fifty-something-foot motor yacht, a Riva, made circles around us with the guests yelling, "*Bravissimo! Bravissimo! Che bella!*" It didn't take long for the Riva's wake to begin rocking us, slowly at first but then with increased regularity. This enrages sailors, and I could see our crew getting annoyed. In the light wind, the motorboat was making our sails luff, which in turn dumped what precious wind they were trimmed to catch. This slowed us down from the already gentle pace *Serenity* was making. I got so involved with what was happening to the sails that I forgot about the sauce. Eventually, the sweet smell of simmering tomatoes changed to a powerful scent of over-caramelized sauce approaching burn.

I bolted down the crew ladder to the galley, afraid of what I would find. A large pool of sauce was boiling on the surface of the stove, its burning edge the only thing keeping it from spreading. Because the whole stove was made out of thin metal, the top got pretty hot. There was sauce all over the side of the pot and the burner plate. Plus, not having been stirred, the tomato solids clustered on a hot spot right over the flame and burned on the bottom of the pot. The whole batch was ruined. And cleaning up would be a hassle.

Finally, after I mopped up the sauce, I went back up to help drop and stow the sails, and after finding a good hold on the anchor, the crew broke to have lunch. I stayed on deck and saw that we weren't far offshore and alone in the anchorage. Sestri made a beautiful backdrop, and the coastal terrain of the Italian Riviera cascading in the distance would flank the guests while they dined under a large canopy rigged over the table on deck. *Il Dottore* and his buddies had gone for a swim. I had to go below and get ready to serve them.

What a great way to entertain, I thought. Arrive in Portofino on a private helicopter. Cruise on a classic sailing yacht. Swim in a quiet anchorage with gorgeous surroundings. Enjoy a graciously served lunch of crispy fried *bianchetti,* augmented with seasonal market vegetables, fresh fruits, and white burgundy. Finish with a nap or idle chat with friends on deck. It didn't get any better than this.

By three in the afternoon, sails went up again, and I went back down to the galley to start dinner prep. In order to be available for maneuvers, I constantly listened to the activity on deck so I could time my tasks to those needs. From time to time, I went up top to take a look, ask Kevin what was happening with the sail, and catch some fresh air. We were back at the marina by six, and now my work was cut

out for me: cocktails and canapés *subito*—immediately—for the owners and guests, crew dinner at seven, owner dinner at nine, clean up
by eleven-thirty. I figured I would be lucky to *hit the rack*—go to bed—
by midnight. Life in the galley, I started to see, would become a constant juggle of diligence, productivity, organization, and cleanliness.

I had built the dinner menu around the *ciappa* since it was such
a unique method of cooking that I thought would be interesting for
the guests. It didn't come with any instructions for use, so I took a
guess at how to prepare it for its debut in the *Serenity* galley. I gave it
a wash with only a little dish soap and warm water, and then at-
tempted to season it with a thin coat of oil. I heated it on a burner of
the stove, which created a lot of smoke and in turn set off a screech-
ing alarm. Scott dashed into the galley and was relieved to find nothing serious had happened, only a false alarm from what I considered
a standard kitchen procedure. I could see Patrick, Kevin, and *il
Dottore* through the hatch above me, and I explained through the window that there was no reason for concern. Harmless, yes, but I was a
little embarrassed nonetheless.

I must have missed something along the way preparing the stone
because the end result for the tuna steaks was only satisfactory at
best. I couldn't get the sear and browning on the outside of the fish
that I wanted. It was probably a result of not having the stone hot
enough. I figured the stove burners were not powerful enough to do it
justice, even at full. My solution the next time would be to keep it in
the oven at 500°F and use it like a pizza stone. With the heat hitting
it on all sides, the *ciappa,* I hoped, would yield better results. Or
maybe it just needed more use in order to get it properly seasoned.
Regardless of my ultimate disappointment in the searing, the finished
platter looked nice, with thick steaks of tuna cooked to medium-rare,
each topped with a small mound of oily olive paste and a cluster of
roughly chopped parsley then garnished with soigné trimmed and
seedless lemon wedges.

Rick came into the galley with an empty dessert platter. "Your dinner was a big hit," he said. "*La Signora* wants to see you in the salon."

I walked into the salon, not sure what to expect. "Davide," *la Signora* said, "tell everyone what you cooked the tuna on. I have never seen that!" Even though I was less than pleased with the result, I launched into a discourse on how I came to use the *ciappa*. *La Signora* looked very pleased—a good way to end, I thought—and then, changing gears, she pointed to her dessert plate. An empty disk of china that had shadows of chocolate near the rim. *La Signora* said to me, "And this, *stupenda*."

The almost flourless chocolate cake with espresso *crema di mascarpone* was the finish to the meal. I had cut it into ten portions, and since there were only six at the table, I figured some had seconds. I could only imagine what it must have tasted like because I had never paired those recipes before—two different textures and a mocha-like flavor that was flavorful but not heavy and overpowering. Thankfully, mascarpone has pretty good shelf life, so I would keep it on hand from now on. It was nice to get some positive feedback, and it inspired me to prepare the next meal.

Sunday found us slowly cruising along the northern end of the Cinque Terre, a rugged high-terrain region that stretches along eighteen miles of the coast where five quaint seaside villages stand, hence the name, Five Lands. I remembered that there was a local train and boat services that stop at each, as well as the famous hiking path that connects all of them called La Via dell'Amore—Love Street. From sea level, the sense of scale next to the steep and fertile coastline behind them was a magnificent vista, a hazy silhouette as it continued to the distant south. Rows of vineyards tracked in parallel lines along the high coastline like a topographic map. It amazed me that people could grow and harvest grapes and make wine on this rugged terrain with funny names like Pigato and Sciacchetrà. I thought about the increasing migration to the larger cities by the children of the *contadini* that worked the land, looking for more action, and wondered how this humble and isolated lifestyle would survive successive generations.

In the market the prior morning, I had seen avocados for the first time in my years in Italy, revealing a supply line of Israeli agricultural exports from the eastern Mediterranean to the west. I thought it would be interesting for the owners to have something unique, so I had brought some back to the boat. My idea was to serve them as an antipasto with sliced Prosciutto di Parma *dolce. Dolce* refers to a style of curing the ham that uses less salt, rendering a moister texture and "sweeter" flavor than other methods of curing. The combination made sense to me.

When the first course was served, I had to go to the chart house to talk to Patrick. I noticed that the owners and their guests were eating with surprisingly little talk at the table amidships. This was unusual. Lunch was usually boisterous, before the afternoon heat and Chablis slowed down everyone's pace. As I passed the table, *il Dottore* stopped eating and looked up at me.

"Davide, what are these green things on the platter?" he asked.

"Avocados," I answered. I decided to explain myself. "I had never seen them in Italy before. They were in the market the other day, so I couldn't resist," I politely responded. Then everyone else stopped eating to hear the conversation.

"Why did you serve them?" he pressed.

"I thought they would be great with the prosciutto."

"I don't like these. They're too strange," he said as he uncharacteristically pulled up his lip in a look of disgust.

"*Amore,* it's okay," *la Signora* said from the other side of the table. "It's typical cuisine from California. They also grow them in the Mediterranean. Try something new."

Il Dottore cut her off and started to argue with her: "But they're not *cucina italiana."* The guests were caught in the crossfire, but judging from their plates, everyone was doing just fine. He carried on about traditional food versus experimental food and how on a classic yacht there was nothing new or experimental about the way the boat was being sailed.

I realized that I still had to fine-tune my understanding of the owners' likes, dislikes, and preferences and how far I could experiment. I took responsibility for my choice, politely saying as the Italians do, *"Colpo mio"*—it's like saying "my bad"—an honorable admission.

"It's all right, it's all right," *il Dottore* said and closed it with a look on his face like "get my drift?"

I would never have thought an avocado could stir up such controversy. It's true the Italians are passionate about what they eat, and this confirmed for me that I should not stray from the familiar. It also confirmed that although *la Signora* drove the service agenda, *il Dottore* had a major say in how the boat would be run, both at the helm and in the galley.

That evening, upon our return to Portofino, we were greeted by a very large and elegant motor yacht called *Debutante* that sat at anchor near the mouth of the harbor. Kevin had worked on her the previous summer and viewed her like a long-lost friend. A few of the crew appeared on *Debutante's* foredeck as we slowly passed across her bow.

"Congratulations! She looks great," *Debutante's* captain said from the rail.

"Che bella barca"—what a beautiful boat—*la Signora* politely said while admiring the sleek white yacht.

"Hey, Patrick, you guys got our spot!" the captain said half joking, but acknowledged the first-come, first-served rule of getting into Portofino. "The harbormaster said you'd be coming back in tonight."

"Maybe 'cause you need two spots!" Patrick shouted back, ribbing the other captain about *Debutante's* much wider width.

Kevin stood straight up on the foredeck. "There's a stewardess on board I wouldn't mind getting to know," he said to me out of the side of his mouth. That night, after the owners and guests left until the next weekend, he passed off his watch duties to Ian and darted off in the launch to visit his alma mater.

Because of an early-morning departure time, I skipped my workout and went to the bakery to get some more focaccia for the ride. Mary, the friendly clerk, handed me a fresh sample no more than a half hour out of the oven and wished me well with my work: "*Buon lavoro!*" We were heading to Lerici, a small port town near the regional border where Liguria meets Tuscany, in an area called the Gulf of Poets.

Everyone's friend Antonio the harbormaster untied us from the dock. I liked him. He represented the special way some Italians do business—cordial, genuine, and eager to please—and his methods ensured my desire to return. *Debutante* was gone, off to the next stop on their cruise. Soon, Portofino was hidden behind the terrain that protects it so well. Santa Margherita and Rapallo also faded into the distance. Then I saw Chiavari, where, high up in the hills behind, in a small locality called Leivi, the nine-table restaurant Cà Peo could be found.

Cà Peo was where I got my introduction to the vegetable-laden cuisine of Liguria. Franco and Melly Solari earned a Michelin star by building a menu and wine list that exploited an artisanal touch to the local ingredients they used. Melly made her signature pesto in a *mortaio*—mortar—every day, which I'd tried, but I wasn't able to achieve the bright green color and smooth, pasty texture like hers. She told me the basil of the region was special. From offshore, you can see the long rows of greenhouses along the coastline where it is grown.

But pesto was half the story. Melly told me that during the Second World War, the occupying Germans took all the wheat out of the country and her mother was forced to make pasta out of chestnut flour. "It was the only farina that we had." People came to the restaurant for her *trenette* or *lasagnette* chestnut flour noodles tossed with that pungent and herbaceous pesto. And with this, she practiced the value of preserving local necessity through her menus by remaining true to traditional methods.

We passed the Cinque Terre again, and the five towns that make up this famous stretch of coastline: Monterosso al Mare, Vernazza, Corniglia, Manarola, and Riomaggiore.

Scott pumped out the tanks and charged the batteries from the generator while Rick stripped the guest cabins and heads. Once we got to Lerici, we'd wash down the boat, get laundry out to a service, and do a massive cleaning inside and out. Then we'd take a two-day weekend, and *Serenity* would become "our boat."

"Hey, David, check it out!" Rick came into the pantry with an armload of empty jewelry boxes.

"What's all that?" I asked.

"They were in the cabins. It's incredible. Host gifts."

I didn't even know what a host gift was until Rick explained to me that it was good etiquette to bring a token of appreciation for being one's guest. There were velvet-covered boxes from Bulgari, Buccellati, and others I had never heard of like Chantecler in Capri, which was thoughtful given that at some point during the summer we'd be there.

"Also, it's probably because this is the first season with the boat," Rick concluded. He put the boxes in the galley garbage bin under the sink and went back to work while practicing his growing Italian vocabulary picked up from listening to the owners and guests: "*Buonasera, Grazie, Prego . . .*"

Suddenly I heard a violent popping sound and noticed the rancid smell of burning electric. Black smoke quickly filled the engine room, galley, and crew quarters. Alarms in the engine room went off. It was a sailor's worst nightmare—a fire at sea. Scott, Kevin, and

Patrick raced below to contain the flames. Thankfully, the fire in the electrical panel was put out quickly, but for extra precaution Scott covered the panel with a fireproof safety blanket. Fortunately, we would soon be close to La Spezia, a major harbor where parts could be found. For me, I had a major refrigeration challenge on my hands. At least this didn't occur at the start of a weekend with reefers full of perishables.

Patrick opted for Lerici instead of the commercial and naval port of La Spezia for its good shelter, but also to put us in a quieter, less congested marina. It was still early enough in the season that the mass of visiting pleasure craft hadn't arrived yet. The town itself was noticeably different from all the other ports along the Ligurian coast south of Genoa. The multicolor buildings ceased after Portovenere, and even there, gone were the ornate painted architectural details so characteristic of the Riviera. It was as if the craftsmen kept themselves in the Gulf of Genoa, and the geographical expanse of the rugged Cinque Terre acted as a natural border to this gateway on the Tuscan coast. It seemed like a nice enough place, almost like a hideaway off the beaten track of popular tourist destinations, and it turned out to be very good for provisioning. And just south we would discover beautiful small coves and bays where we could beach the tender and hang around.

Scott asked me to go with him to find a chandler—a mariner's hardware store—in La Spezia to act as translator. In the taxi on the way over, he surprised me by showing a little knowledge of our whereabouts.

"You know why this is called the Bay of Poets?" he asked.

"No, I've never heard of it before," I said.

"It's because the poets Shelley, Keats, and Lord Byron lived here."

I wondered why a guy who had a cold attitude toward Italy stored this bit of information—until he said, "All British you know."

While we were in La Spezia, I contacted one of the deckhands on the sailing yacht *Pegasus* that had co-hosted the party with us in Monte Carlo. The yacht's home port was there, and my new friend Corrado, who grew up in the area, told me about the local *frutti di mare,* most notably the coveted *datteri di mare*—sea date mussels. They are so named because their light brown shells resemble dates. There is only one way to get them, however, and that's not from the local fishmonger. We would have to free dive for them. Fortunately, Corrado clued me into a good spot to find them, just offshore in Portovenere.

The next morning, just after sunrise, Nigel and I boarded the tender and set out for the spot where, as Corrado had put it, "the mussels cling to the rocks and seawalls just outside of the town." We stopped the boat where we thought might be the spot, but questioned whether we'd need a permit to do this since I remembered hearing from somewhere that they were regulated. But without too much hesitation or worry we donned fins and masks, and then dove in like a couple of escaped convicts—fast and quietly. Once our eyes were accustomed to the murky light underwater, we scanned the seawall. Sure enough, they were there, just as Corrado had said they would be.

"It's only Wednesday," I said to Nigel once we pulled ourselves back in the tender with a bucketful of the rare mollusks. "The owners won't return until Friday night, and these are highly perishable."

Nigel thought about it for a moment before stating the obvious, "I guess we'll have to eat them ourselves for lunch."

"And now I remember *la Signora* told me no mussels," I said.

And what a lunch it was. We set our portable table over the windlass and under a canopy on the foredeck. Al dente linguine tossed with sea dates steamed with only a touch of white wine, olive oil, garlic, fresh-chopped Italian parsley, and hot red pepper flakes; thick slices of large, pungent tomatoes dressed with a little Dijon vinaigrette, which by unanimous decision by the crew became our "house" dressing; stove-top-grilled bread, thickly sliced and drizzled with olive oil; and an arugula salad. Rick augmented the meal with some crisp and dry Chablis. It was alfresco dining at its best.

No one said anything, but I could tell by their faces that they were enjoying the food and the time spent together. We relaxed and took kips on deck for an hour. While lying along the lower jib sail that was folded like a paper fan and tied to the bowsprit, the long spruce extension from the bow, I felt transported to another life—I was the Italian lounging in *my* backyard on the Italian coast. Soon enough it would be back to work and the punishing schedule that was my real life. But for this brief moment, among new friends, I experienced the other side.

"Hey, Kevin," I asked after a short while, "what does the 'S/Y' I sometimes see before *Serenity* mean?"

He was lying down near the anchor hoist. "Sailing yacht," he called back.

"Then 'M/Y' must mean motor yacht," I concluded.

"That's correct. And 'SS' is steamship, 'USS' is United States ship . . ."

"And 'HMS' is Her Majesty's ship," Scott cut in.

"But for *il Dottore,* it's 'TMY,' " Ian added.

"What's that?" Kevin asked, looking over at him as if what Ian just said was ridiculous.

"That's my yacht!" Ian said with a big smile.

It wasn't long before Patrick snapped us out of our banter. He cut in, disregarding our break to discuss business. No one really wanted to talk about work, but we listened anyway.

"After this next weekend," he said, "let's use some of our downtime to sail and practice."

"Practice what?" Kevin asked. For the first time, I detected a note of cynicism in his voice. Patrick ignored the question.

Patrick gave a quick review of our sailing performance and his desire to see the crew get better and faster while under way. He didn't think we were performing up to the capabilities of the boat.

"I want to see us get a little more efficient, a little tighter, pick up some more speed," he said.

For me, that was the captain's prerogative, and going out to practice would be a blast. What better way to spend a day off than to go sailing? Kevin didn't say much after that. Rick, who could care less, drifted off and went below. Ian and Nigel were up for anything, but I could tell their minds were already cataloging lost opportunities on-shore. Soon enough the talk returned to the more standard-issue crew topics of bars, money, and women. But I realized at that moment another fire was smoldering. And one look at Kevin told me that unlike the engine room fire, the smolder between him and Patrick would not be extinguished quite so easily.

Seven

Why Is the Risotto Black?

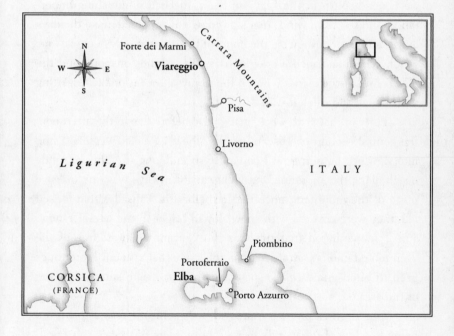

Viareggio, Forte dei Marmi, and Elba

*S*ix weeks into the summer, as we were making our way down the coast from Lerici, a calming rhythm had taken hold on board. None of the frustrations or noise of daily life—no traffic to sit in, no crowds to work through, no whining scooters cutting in and out of tight city streets—interrupted our peaceful offshore existence. As we headed south in the Ligurian Sea, time had diminishing importance, and the calm winds that slowed us down helped make the days longer and hotter. Knowing the hours of the day was only necessary for watch schedules, accurate log entries, siesta times onshore, and the next arrival of the owners. I even found myself occasionally forgetting what day of the week it was.

Early in that sixth week, just a little before five in the afternoon, the central section of Tuscany's coast, the area called Versilia, came into view off the port bow. I could see several long stretches of sandy beach along the shoreline, but what caught my eye was one massive piece of the mountain range not far behind it. Palisades that looked like they were covered with snow shined bright in the late-afternoon sun. I remembered that this was the Carrara valley, source of the even more famous Carrara marble, the stone that affluent Florentines used to build grand *caffès*, spas, and the resort-like summer homes of the area.

Our destination was Viareggio, a beachfront resort town and home to a few of the world's best yacht builders. Viareggio was familiar to me because I had worked at a great little Michelin one-star restaurant there called Romano. It was so close to the marina I could walk to it. I had been there in winter, when most of the shops and *caffès* along the long, wide *strada piedi*—walking street—that ran parallel to the beach were closed for the off-season. Now it was in full swing, and Viareggio's grand hotels, beach clubs, and cabanas preserved a lingering aura of its creation as a popular summer retreat at the turn of the twentieth century.

Friends in Florence had told me about summers at the coast, and that during the high season, *per bene*—privileged—socialites relocate to the more exclusive Forte dei Marmi, just a little farther north. Not surprisingly, Rick took aim for where the style set hung out and announced that the second we hit land, he would be off to check it out. I decided once we got settled in to reward myself by going to Romano for lunch. I also had an ulterior motive.

After the avocado incident a couple weeks back, I realized that the owners were not inclined to try anything new or different. Romano Franceschini's style was their style. It would be a match. Romano's menu featured simple preparations of super-fresh local seafood, and he had an extensive cellar of Italian wines. In the kitchen, Franca, his wife and the chef of the restaurant, had mastered using as few ingredients as possible so as to highlight the flavors of the fish rather than do anything to mask them. This inspiration perfectly suited what I could cook on board, so I intended to put their methods into practice and, as a compliment, attempt to reproduce some of their authentic offerings. I was also hoping that Romano would give me some leads to the best places to purchase fish, the kinds of seafood his restaurant had made its reputation serving.

I walked into the restaurant without a reservation, remembering that it wouldn't be too difficult to get a table on the early side of a weekday lunch. The servers I had worked with were all there, and Romano, surprised to see me, was as warm and wonderful as I remembered him. He immediately went to the kitchen to get Franca. After I explained why I was in Viareggio, they were very impressed. I was led to a table and never saw a menu. At the end of my extravagant two-hour fish lunch, Romano took a seat at my table and inquired as to my whereabouts since I had left the restaurant and how I had ended up on board *Serenity.*

When I asked him where he got his seafood, he immediately revealed his source, a small storefront near the harbor. I had seen the *pescheria*—fish shop—when we first arrived. I had even taken a moment to step inside. I have to say, I wasn't impressed. The place appeared barren and lifeless. But when I returned to the shop with regards from Romano, I learned why. I was taken to the back of the store, where I saw the catch that never made it out front. The shopkeeper said that the fish had just arrived a few hours prior, during the late morning, when the day boats returned. The fish were still firm from rigor mortis—the stiffening of the body that occurs within hours of death—a clue to freshness. I arranged to come back at the end of the week, when my bosses would be returning.

The next day Patrick again suggested that instead of remaining in port, we take the boat out for some crew-only day sailing. "You know, we'll take her out and stretch her legs. Plus," he explained to all of us, "I already told the boss that we'd get in some good practice runs."

It seemed like a good enough idea to me, and none of the crew expressed any reservations. The winds were light, so hauling wouldn't be that bad, and it was a little cooler offshore.

Patrick seemed to have a plan. At first, we'd go out for long stretches, doing the occasional maneuver but really focusing on sail trim and sail changes. With so many sails in *Serenity*'s wardrobe, even the basic suit could be dressed up with many different accessories— where and how to attach blocks, lines, new hanks, and other marine rigging. Patrick and Kevin were forever huddled together, trying to figure out things like how close we could sail to the wind while not sacrificing the speed we'd built up. It did get a little laborious. I would soon learn that I had been wrong about lighter wind meaning less hauling. It actually meant more work, constantly changing and raising the huge light-wind sails to find the right mix for increased performance. But on crew-only sailing days, cooking took a backseat to sailing, and it was great to be outside and part of the team.

Slowly, we all began to notice that Patrick was taking these afternoon sailing exercises much more seriously than the rest of us. He would bark out orders, or berate one of us for not having done something the way he wanted it done. Other than that, he didn't say much, except for sharply phrased questions about how we were doing something. No casual conversation or praise. But despite his sour temperament, even I could see that his serious attitude was producing results—from a tighter rig to smoother runs of the lines and more perfectly trimmed sails.

As line cooks to this operation, Rick and I mostly did a lot of pulling. In between the next set of instructions, Rick took a break to supply the crew with cold beverages. But I could see that his head wasn't into this. He was probably on a beach somewhere imagining himself nodding graciously to a beautiful woman.

But even Rick could not totally ignore what was happening on deck. As the practice runs became more intense and demanding, Kevin began to give voice to the concerns we were all feeling—that lurking beneath Patrick's aggressive agenda was something more than a desire to put together a team that would not embarrass the owners in the season-ending regatta. As this or that maneuver was called into question, the conversations between Kevin and Patrick became terser. To me it still seemed like they were arguing over murky philosophical differences in how best to sail a boat. But then Kevin escalated his response.

In a gesture that could be construed as showing disrespect to his captain, he walked up to the foredeck, as far away from Patrick as the boat would allow, and anchored himself there for each practice sail.

Later that day, Ian leaned into me and observed, "Kevin's not calling back to confirm Patrick's orders." I knew this was a bad sign. Sometimes it was better to stay below.

Nigel was the first of the crew to gather around the mess table that night. "Why is the risotto black?" he asked. His scrunched-up nose suggested he was put off. Or was his nose merely registering the smell in the galley, an odor redolent of the deep sea.

The answer was cuttlefish. More accurately, the black ink they carry in the precious sac so hard to extract from deep inside their bodies. As we moved down the coast, I began to experiment more and more with local specialties, such as this evening's fare, *risotto con seppia nero*—risotto with cuttlefish ink. Nigel was aimlessly pushing the blackened kernels of risotto toward the rim of the dish, his way of avoiding a direct confrontation, but I took it personally and became determined to get him to give it a try.

"Come on," I said.

He smiled and said, "Okay, okay." He tasted the risotto in small bites and, after a long pause, pronounced judgment: "This is really good, mate." Scott, on the other hand, wasn't shy about declaring, "The start to this meal is vile." He pushed the dish away untouched.

Now, of course, I had to concede that I had been serving the crew lots of pasta and risotto, maybe more carbohydrates than they were accustomed to. But no one seemed to be putting on a gut. Our lives were just too active for that, especially now that the crew-only practice sails had been added to our daily routine. And I had to think, these guys were living pretty well. Some of the food served to the staff at restaurants where I had worked was, as the Italians say when reserving comment, *interessante*. Then again, some *was* interesting. I knew it wouldn't take long for my crewmates to agree.

In the early afternoons, I'd have the mess area to myself to write letters home and leaf through my journals to look at the recipes I'd written down from my various *stages* and turn to the books I had brought along—most notably the regional cookbook that Nadia gave me and *Mediterranean Seafood*—to plan out my menus and generate shopping lists for the weekend. It was important to stay ahead and have some idea of a plan, but in the back of my mind I tried to remain flexible. Everything was subject to change as a result of what might be found in the markets. Plus, I could only hold about two days' worth of food for both guests and crew, so keeping abreast of what I had on hand was good practice.

After the morning food-shopping trips, I'd come back and spend a good deal of time putting everything away, with cheeses in one place, other dairy in another, proteins below, fruits on top, bread wherever it fit. Invariably, there would be a trip to the storage area in the bilge to stash shelf-stable ingredients and, in the same trip, pull what I needed to start my prep. I'd return with my hands and arms full of provisions only to realize—after I climbed back up, scraping my arms along the way—there was something I forgot or something I should have stored. Back down to the bilge, yet again.

Scott came below to ask if he could make his late-morning cup of tea. I found it hilarious that he could want a cup of hot tea in the rising heat of the day. It was the end of June, and it was beginning to feel like we were closing in on the tropics.

"Scott," I said, "the rest of the world is drinking iced tea at this time of year. So are the rest of your compatriots. Why don't you have yours the way the Italians drink theirs—flavored with peach juice? You know, cool, refreshing, and no steam!"

Scott knew where I was really headed. In addition to steaming up my galley with his boiling water, he also had the habit of wedging the engine room door open, which raised the galley temperature fifteen degrees. Worse, the diesel fumes from the engine now had a direct path to everything sitting in the galley.

"My food smells like it has been infused with motor lubricants," I complained, halfheartedly.

"I need to ventilate, mate," Scott said.

"But do you have to do it now? It's going to make the fish smell like they were pulled off an oil rig," I pleaded.

"You have your crosses to bear; I have mine. Sorry, mate." He moved deeper into the engine room and started inspecting some clear tubes filled with some kind of white material mounted on the wall in a very elaborate mechanical apparatus.

"What are those?" I asked, trying to make nice, but I was genuinely curious.

"Filters for the water maker. We might need to use it sometime. Luckily, we're in port so much that our tanks can always be topped off," he said.

I'd never thought about the concept of literally making water. I was intrigued. Scott explained that the water maker was a desalinating system made up of pumps and filters to rid seawater of salt and other impurities, and then purify it.

"Is homemade water any good?" I asked.

"Some say it's better than tap water," he said.

"How neat would it be to make pasta in a pot of homemade water?" The irony was lost on me that by desalinating salt water to make freshwater, I would be adding salt back to the water to make the pasta.

"And how neat would it be to have a proper breakfast?" Scott answered with a left-field comment.

"Depends on what constitutes 'proper,' " I countered. Scott had been hinting about eggs and bacon since we left Antibes.

"It's a matter of upbringing," he answered.

"Okay," I surrendered, but wasn't completely sure why. "I'll make you a deal. Empty a tank, fill it with homemade water, and I'll make your favorite breakfast, as long as you don't mind pancetta instead of bacon."

"Like a true Yank," he said, smiling, "ending with a covenant."

A spotty wind followed us the next weekend as the owners filled the boat with three other couples. We raised sails on the first morning, *la Signora* watching with her friends, cheering us on as we heaved and hauled. "*Vai, vai*"—go, go—she bellowed with the enthusiasm of a coach exhorting her team. The other ladies followed with "*Che bella!*"—how beautiful—while looking up at the gigantic concave triangles of white sails as they took shape. Between *la Signora*'s cheerleading and Rick's lowbrow commentary at the base of the mast, it was hard to concentrate. At the same time, *il Dottore* coaxed his friends to jump in, "Come on, guys, don't just stand there!" His friends had the slightly embarrassed look of being upstaged by the crew. We got the sails up, then moved forward to let them have their boat back.

It didn't take long for the wind to pick up once we headed out to sea, and the boat started to heel considerably. We probably carried too much sail, but *il Dottore* seemed excited playing tactician and wanted to push his boat a bit. I had gone below to prep lunch in what was fast becoming the greatest sail I'd never see. I could hear excitement on deck as the crew raced around, hauling and trimming, loads increasing in the lines and masts, winches grinding—sounds that reverberated through the deck planks above me. We heeled even more, and I positioned myself against the rake so I could stay perpendicular to the horizon. I called Kevin through the crew way to ask him how long we'd be on this point of sail and to ask that he give me fair warning if we were going to tack. Changing the point of sail, which in turn changed the side from which the wind hit us, would shift the angle of my work surface. It was like doing my tasks—chopping, dicing, and filleting—while standing on the lower side of a playground seesaw. But if I knew when the shifts were coming, I could reposition my prep station before everything went flying all over the galley.

Good thing the sea was fairly calm and I was contending only with the wind and the heel. Bouncing in a short swell would likely have closed me down. As it was, I made sure to work only with small quantities, and I left very little if anything on the counter. I timed opening cabinets and the refrigerator so that the pitch didn't spill or empty the contents all over me. And I improvised. The large sink became my most valuable holding pen.

Cutting and chopping uphill was one thing—gravity kept the pieces out of the way while I worked. Cutting downhill became a whole other story, and gravity was my foe. Everything rolled, rested against, or got in the way of the knife blade when slicing anything round. Zucchini became my worst enemy.

Then there was my ongoing nemesis, the marine stove with no gimbals. The custom rail system built to hold the cookware on the burners proved a bust because it had been designed without regard to pot sizes. With increasing heel, it was useless. Hot liquid spills were more than an inconvenience, especially since I cooked in shorts and didn't wear shoes. In Italian, the word is *un casino*—a general term for anything chaotic. Under way like this, things instantaneously became *un grande casino*.

Rick came into the pantry to grab another bottle of champagne.

"This is beautiful" is all he said while tearing the foil off the bottle top before bolting back up to the aft deck, moving with a slight jolt against the heel of the boat.

"We might tack in a couple of minutes," Kevin reported a few seconds later through the open hatch above me.

"Who's driving?" I asked.

"*Il Dottore* took the helm."

I could picture the boss, standing at the wheel in the cockpit, steering with one hand, a cocktail in the other.

"Can you share with Patrick that I'm down here trying to make lunch?" I asked, knowing that the message might be conveyed to Patrick but that he would never forward it to *il Dottore*.

I could see through the porthole that we were making our way back up the coast toward Forte dei Marmi. The beaches looked crowded with hordes of black dots at the shoreline backed by rows of colorful beach umbrellas and blue-roofed cabanas. One beach club lined up after another, with the white marble cascades and mountains framing the scene from behind. But this was no time to enjoy the view. I needed to have the crew meal on the mess table as soon as we stopped, then a half hour or so after that, right into lunch for the owners and guests.

The boat started to level off, and I could hear the headsails above me luff. We were tacking! I didn't hear the call, and no one gave me the heads-up. I was right in the middle of cutting fruits for a *macedonia*—a mix of precious stone fruits that I carefully carried back from the market so as not to bruise. I scrambled to get the fruits to the other side of the guarded counter edge so they didn't roll on their own. Right then, Kevin stuck his head through the hatch.

"We're tacking," he sheepishly declared, suspecting the damage had already been done.

"I caught it on the luff." I didn't hold it against him. I knew he meant well. By then, I had gotten used to listening for things around the boat, especially on deck when we were under way. It was the same as training your ear to the sounds of cooking—different pitches of sizzles with changes in heat and the varying sounds of boils and simmers as the density of liquid changes.

Rick came into the pantry to take a quick break. He made himself an espresso, correcting it with a shot of cognac.

"Nice stuff," he said, downing his pick-me-up in one swallow. "Don't worry. I bet we'll be off the wind soon. *La Signora* is getting a little queasy."

He looked through the leftover breakfast pastries in the pantry, fishing for a snack. "Too sweet," he said, and then made himself a cheese sandwich.

"What are you making for lunch?" he asked while chewing.

"Ours or theirs?"

"The owners', of course." His look suggested that I had asked a ridiculous question.

It took me a while to catch on to why Rick had been so adamant since Portofino on a "second passing" for each course. It meant there would be enough left for him. I had the feeling that some of the other directives he laid down for me were also coming from him, rather than *la Signora*. But the couple of times I questioned him, he held his ground, repeating the order *"La Signora* insists." Rick knew I was much too insecure around her to question it.

For lunch that day, I had decided to create two Tuscan classics. The antipasto was one of my favorites—fresh shrimp with white beans, tomatoes, and basil. With the hot weather, I served it at room temperature, not warm as is the custom. The short list of ingredients lost nothing in taste appeal with the change in serving temperature. Dressed and seasoned with a great olive oil and large crystal sea salt, this layered combination was a true example of the "one dish, one flavor" mantra of my friend Franco, the proprietor of Albergo del Sole.

My only concern was the word to use to describe the shrimp. While I was working in the States, I came to realize that on the East Coast, the correct word was always "shrimp" and on the West Coast it was "prawns." However, in the Italian American restaurant close to my parents' house, shrimp were listed on the menu as "shrimp scampi," and I didn't discover until living in Italy that "scampi" is not a reference to how shrimp are cooked. Scampi are a different crustacean altogether, resembling something in size between a crawfish and a very small lobster. The French call shrimp *gambas* and smaller ones *crevettes*. In Italian, I was first led to believe that shrimp are *gamberi*, small ones being *gamberetti* and large ones being *gamberoni*. But as I moved down the Italian coast, shrimp took on different names. In Tuscany, they were *spannocchi*. Yet in the fish shop in Viareggio, the vendor sold them as *mazzancolle*. Then there are the variations in these words that come about as a result of local dialects.

"Hey, David," Rick asked from the pantry when he came to grab another bottle of wine, "how much in dollars is twenty-five *miliardi*"—billion—"of lire?"

"I'd say fifteen or sixteen million," I replied, based on the exchange I had been getting. "Why?"

"Because whatever they're talking about, that's what it costs."

It wasn't our business to know what transpired across their dinner table, but it would have been interesting to know what cost fifteen million bucks.

The *secondo*—the entrée—was *cacciucco livornese,* the great dish from the commercial port of Livorno (spelled "Leghorn" on most English-language maps) that is Tuscany's contribution to the repertoire of Italian fish stews. The dish requires five varieties of fish, one for each *c* in the word *cacciucco,* and preparing it correctly is an exercise in orchestrating the different cooking times for each one.

The best way to describe making *cacciucco* would be a stove-top braise. The liquid for the "moist heat" method of cookery needed to have enough seasoning to augment but not overpower the flavor of the fish. This base sauce would be kept at a steady simmer as I added the succession of fish that I used—in this case, clams, monkfish, swordfish, sea bass, and a wonderful flaky Mediterranean fish called *scorfano* in Italian, scorpion fish in English. As they cooked in the simmering base, each added to what would become a very flavorful sauce. The smell of coastal Italian cooking coming out of the galley was sure to raise the guests' anticipation of the meal.

I could have used *Serenity*'s marinara sauce as a base, but instead, because of the season, chose a light and simple fresh tomato sauce made with very ripe tomatoes, a small amount of onion, salt, pepper, and sugar, in a manner chefs like to call "clean." This would let the flavors of the different fish speak for themselves. Some hot red pepper flakes to spice it up, according to the owners' preference, and grilled bread on the side made this a wonderful dish for *pranzo*— lunch. It is also a good item for entertaining, as it holds well. If the fish is cooked halfway the first time, it can finish with a gentle reheat.

Earlier, when I was talking to the cooks in Romano's kitchen, one offered his suggestion for making *cacciucco,* saying I should use "bellies and jowls." No doubt this would make for a soulful concoction preferred by many a local, but with my top-shelf owners, I didn't use the fishmonger's reserve. Using fillets cut into nice chunks proved to be the right move.

When an Italian wants to show satisfaction after a dining event, he'll lightly press a pointed index finger into his cheek and turn it once or twice without saying a word. Both index fingers to both cheeks and it was even better. After lunch *il Dottore* came down to the galley and gave me the official hand signal for when something is really good, maybe the best thing one could have in one's life—*buonissimo*—by rolling his hands and fingers over both cheeks as if turning doorknobs.

Back in port, I went to see Romano to thank him for helping me. He was gracious and even gave me a bottle of his own olive oil from the family groves north of Lucca. I greedily decided to keep it for myself so I could drizzle it on a piece of grilled bread with a swipe of garlic—the Tuscan snack known as *fettunta.* The oil was so concentrated and distinct it left an impression of place through flavor. I almost felt as if I were eating a part of Tuscany.

I had hit a home run with my *cacciucco,* and it felt good to get some positive feedback.

Rick said to me after the meal, "Hey, David, we should do a whole fish so I can do some table-side service in the salon. They'd love it."

"It would certainly be different." My thoughts leaned toward the practical. We didn't have a side table or cart.

"This is not a restaurant but one big house party. I need to give them some flair!" he proclaimed.

"It would make you look good in front of the boss," I said, teasing him.

"*C'est normal,*" he insisted. Whenever Rick wanted something, he'd cloak it in a shroud of normalcy, as if that alone entitled him to whatever it was he wanted at the moment.

I thought that afternoon about Rick's definition of the job. He spoke the truth—this job did have the feel of a house party, and a rather exclusive one at that. *Serenity,* one of three boats in the owners' stable, was earmarked as their floating summer home. What a great way to live. Two or three days each week sailing offshore and dipping into little coves and marinas must have been a great release from their workweek. Or did they really work? It was hard to tell. I had the feeling *la Signora* stayed pretty active, and I knew *il Dottore* ran a major conglomerate. But I still found it hard to imagine them in high-stress situations.

I became increasingly curious about the rest of their lives as well. Each week they arrived on the family helicopter or jet, had a car service bring them to the boat, happily walked up the *passerelle,* came on board for the weekend, then reversed the sequence for the return trip. No public transit for them. I wondered who did all of the coordination, arranged the private air travel, scheduled the different car services, pinpointed the location of the boat. Michele told me back in Antibes that the owners maintained dedicated staff for their nine homes, three yachts, two jets, helicopters, and numerous cars. I made a rough count and figured it ran somewhere in the neighborhood of forty or fifty personal service staff. And that didn't include the battery of employees who worked in the gardens and on the ranches. I was just a small part of their world, but they exhibited a quality found in so many powerful and successful people: when they spoke to me, I felt as if I were the only person in their employ. I also knew being a good cook satisfied only one requirement of my job. We need not become friends, but the owners had to like me.

In that regard, I did understand my job was ultimately the same as Rick's job. Both were about keeping the owners happy. Cooking for them in a private setting was very different from having them as customers in a restaurant, where other customers would be competing for the attention of the kitchen and dining room staff. In the situation I was in, the owners' needs, their schedule, their whims, became my own.

Because *Serenity* was their weekend residence, the feedback was different. The restaurant chef, influenced and informed, is the decisive palate behind the menu. A dissatisfied customer simply won't come back. In private, it is the owners' desires that mandate the cooking. And here, communication was up close and personal. As I learned, the owners were not shy about letting me know when something wasn't right. Even though we were two months into the season, I had not worked for them long enough to be entirely sure if my cooking had yet made the grade. But I did start to get a sense, the more I prepared meals for them, watched their patterns, and took feedback, that I knew how to approach the food when the cooking began. Something as simple as knowing their preference for spiciness paid off with *il Dottore*'s two-handed doorknobs.

I arranged the canapés in concentric circles on the silver tray we always used for cocktail service. I wanted the small, handmade savory pastries to suggest the artisanal effort by virtue of a neat, symmetrical presentation. Aesthetically, it worked beautifully and fortified my edict that making the first selection visually pleasing also made it more desirable to eat.

La Signora came into the pantry while winding her watch,

dressed up in a casual elegance I had not seen before—dark blue slacks and a crisp white blouse, her open collar giving way to a large pearl necklace. She seemed to be wearing a little more makeup than usual, that is, if she ever wore any. A gold lamé headband kept her long dark hair behind her ears so the matching pearl earrings could show.

"We are going to dine onshore tonight, so no need to cook," she said as she put her watch on.

"Very good," I responded, trying not to show surprise or disappointment. But when she left, I threw my hand towel into the sink with a frustrated snap.

Why couldn't I have been told sooner? She knew I worked all afternoon getting their dinner prepped and ready. Not even a mention of how good it smelled in the galley or an acknowledgment of seeing the components of the main course—my *mise en place*—out and ready for service.

Now what do I do with all of the food? Obviously, my time in planning, shopping, and prepping and the cost of goods didn't matter. I could hold some for the next day, like the *calamaretti farciti*—tiny calamari stuffed with Romano's wonderful shrimp-and-vegetable filling, a signature of his restaurant. But I really looked forward to serving the incredibly plump *rombo*—turbot—just caught, gently baked with zucchini and a splash of wine. The rest would go into the crew menu, but I already had that meal ready, too. I made enough of the filling for the *calamaretti* to stuff pasta for baked cannelloni. Oh well, I thought, it's their boat, their life, their money.

"As soon as I serve the ladies their tisane before they go to bed," Rick told me upon hearing the news, "I'm outta here." *La Signora* had provided us with her custom tisane mix of dried herbs, flower petals, and roots blended at her local *erborista,* a concoction prepared like tea that apparently made for better, restful sleep and was a cure for all that ails you.

"Where are you going?" I asked.

"Back up to Forte dei Marmi! The harbormaster gave me the names of some clubs to hit. Time to play with the Florentine girls!"

"By the way," I asked him, "what were you doing at the harbor office?"

"Making a telephone call. I can't stand calling long-distance with phone cards," he said with a flip of his hand. Rick's use of stock French gestures always made me laugh.

"You just go in and ask to use the phone?" I said incredulously.

"I have it charged back to the boat," he explained. "I'll pay the boat back if Patrick asks. Just don't tell the rest of the crew."

Monday morning, the owners were gone, and we threw ourselves into a massive group effort to get the boat washed down and clean. Scott, as if programmed, opened the engine room door first thing and kept it that way for the better part of the next few days. Rick got the laundry out and brought the flowers, at least those still in good shape, to the harbormaster's office, knowing what he had to do to keep those phone lines open. He left *Serenity* more than slightly hungover, complaining in French, "*C'est con,*" which in Rick's vernacular roughly translated into: "These stupid tasks are a complete bummer and are taking away from my leisure time." It was amazing how many large, stuffed laundry bags came out of the aft part of the boat. Much more than the crew. Patrick disappeared, only to return in time for lunch. Interesting, since I'd been on board, I had never seen him clean, paint, or varnish a thing.

To some degree, we all wanted *our* lives back. Ian set up the folding table that fit over the anchor windlass while Nigel rigged the canopy above. Instantly, the foredeck again became our version of a summer porch. It was actually a better place to hang around than the cockpit. The perk of being parked stern-to put our bow a hundred-plus feet from the quay. So not only did we have a jury-rigged summer porch; we had a private one as well.

The weather channel on the ship-to-shore radio, *canale* 68, crackled from the cockpit and reported clear skies and fair wind for the next few days as a high-pressure zone steadied itself over the central Mediterranean. Hearing this, Patrick said we should go for afternoon practice sails. "Glitches in maneuver speed" was how he put it. I had gotten used to these practice runs and never minded the fresh air. But others didn't see it that way.

By Tuesday evening, Kevin's building frustrations that had started in Lerici could be detected in his eyes and his manner. I asked what the problem was, and he admitted it was over Patrick, who seemed to show a Jekyll-and-Hyde personality. Onshore, sharing a drink with us in the bars, Patrick was one of the guys, relaxed and friendly. But back on board, he became short-tempered, demanding, and inflexible.

Kevin was clearly not used to being spoken to that way. And something else was bothering him. Patrick had begun to pull rank to ensure that there was only one way to do things—his way. Invariably, after Kevin finished a job on deck, Patrick wanted it done over, his way. I remembered when Chef Forgione in New York used to tell his cooks, "There's the right way, the wrong way, and then there's my way." I've always looked forward to the time when I would have "my way." Clearly, so did Kevin.

An hour later, Kevin's aggravation added to the gristmill of shipboard gossip.

"They're at it again," Ian told me, taking a break at the mess table to get away from the argument on deck.

"Who?"

"Kevin and the skipper."

"What happened?" I asked.

"Something about the blocks on deck and the way the lines are running. Kevin was concerned about chafing the varnish on the rail."

"Varnishing is a lot of work. What's wrong with looking after it?" I asked.

"But Patrick says the new leads hinder our performance because they don't shape the sails as best as they could be."

These contretemps flared up with daily regularity. Under way, Kevin continued to stay up front while Patrick drove and kept to the aft deck. Problems began when they met in the middle. I was generally sympathetic to Kevin in these disputes, though, truthfully, not because I had fairly examined the arguments of both sides but because Kevin was great to work with. If he found me struggling, no matter how much he had to do on his own, he always found a way to give me a hand.

Over time Patrick and Kevin began feuding over more than boat maintenance or sailing techniques. Kevin had his sights set on becoming a captain one day, he told me one afternoon. By the time he joined the crew of *Serenity*, he had already become a highly accomplished sailor, having completed two full circumnavigations of the globe. But he didn't have enough hours on the books to qualify to take the captain's test. That's why he was sailing on *Serenity*—to log hours. But when he caught on that Patrick's weekday training runs were about his desire to compete successfully in the end-of-the-season regatta, he felt the captain was abusing his authority. Kevin could be persuasive, and soon the rest of the crew began to suspect that our practicing was less about pleasing the owners and more about Patrick's wanting to beat the sailing yacht *Carina* in the Saint-Tropez regatta. Soon the mess table scuttlebutt led us to unanimously decide that Patrick's desire had slid into obsession and that he was pursuing his obsession on our backs. "It's a damn yacht, not an America's Cup racer," I heard Kevin say under his breath the next day after another sharp exchange.

Patrick continued to press hard, pushing the crew to haul lines faster while he steered more deliberately and monitored the instruments even more closely. The more Patrick barked, the quieter Kevin became. Kevin disappeared one day in port, and I became concerned. He later admitted that he had gone to the Perini Navi yacht-building yard.

"Why?" I asked.

"I wanted to see when the new yachts rolling off will be sailing," he answered straightforwardly.

Now I worried that Kevin might jump ship mid-cruise, right before the owners boarded for the entire month of August. Everything had been going so well. Why couldn't Patrick just back off and let us have a happy cruise? I suspected this was only the beginning of the problems. Catching Rick in an unguarded moment confirmed this suspicion.

Rick had not been himself the last few days and was becoming more somber and preoccupied. At first, I attributed it to the open tension between Kevin and Patrick, which was getting to all of us. But one afternoon while we were sitting at the mess table, the real reason came tumbling out. Rick's divorce had not been amicable, and he was particularly upset about the limited visitation he had been awarded with his son, reduced even more as a result of a court action filed by his ex-wife's parents. Under that bon vivant persona, Rick actually was a devoted and guilt-ridden father. He began to withdraw.

Rick had let me into a part of his world that he kept hidden from everyone else. And he stowed this other side of himself once we hit dockside. As if he regretted having shown me his true self, the wild Rick emerged with a vengeance. He was all over the party and bar scene, so much so that when I saw him one night at a club in Forte dei Marmi, he was running on psychic speed, sending champagne to every woman he fancied and befriending their jealous boyfriends by buying them drinks as well. But now I knew he wasn't just a party boy—he had real responsibilities and disappointments that increasingly wore him down.

———

The next weekend we met the owners at Portoferraio, Elba, the largest island of seven landmasses in the Tuscan archipelago—or, as they are commonly called, the "seven sisters." Legend has it, according to the *Italian Waters Pilot,* the seafarer's bible of port, sea, and weather information I found in the chart house, the archipelago was formed when a necklace fell from Venus, goddess of beauty and love, and splashed into the waters of the Tyrrhenian Sea, thus creating the islands.

A good-sized town surrounded the harbor on three sides, the buildings capped with almost flat terra-cotta roofs that cascaded up the hill to the citadel on top. This is the main harbor where ferries from the mainland, mostly Piombino, bring visitors, cars, and the delivery trucks that supply the island. I had to assume they were from Piombino since that was the name of the ferry in whose wake we trailed upon our arrival. We didn't stay long and headed to the other side of the island, along the way passing beautiful views of rolling hills spotted with vineyards and, on the shoreline, what looked to be many places only accessible by boat.

Our weekend stay in quaint Porto Azzurro kept us from Portoferraio on the other side. It suited me, at least visually, since it offered the feeling of being in a remote island location. But this was both a curse and a blessing—a curse because if I had to do any major last-minute food shopping, the better resources were on the other side of the island; a blessing because our anchorages during the weekend gave meaning to the boat's namesake, serenity, by shielding us from the crowded little beaches in the secluded bays of the islands. Although I had enough in the yacht's stores to put together serviceable meals, *la Signora* told me upon arrival that she and her guests would be going onshore to dine one night at a friend's summer home just up the hills. I began to wonder if she had seen a bit of my annoyance from the previous week and she understood I needed to be kept abreast of her schedule.

On a lazy Sunday, we had a guest at the mess table. *Il Dottore* came below to spend some time with the help—and to satisfy a basic need. He had, on other occasions, demonstrated an ability to carry himself with an easy grace when he came forward to spend some time chatting with his crew. But on this day, it was the aroma of simmering tomato sauce wafting up to the deck and carried downwind to the cockpit that prompted the visit. This reawakened his dormant desire for a pasta fix. As part of an effort to control his weight, *la Signora* was adamant about how often pasta would be served to the owners and their guests—never, unless she specifically requested it. But boys will be boys, and while *la Signora* was napping on deck, *il Dottore* tiptoed down the crew ladder to sneak a bowl with the crew. Rick offered to set him up with better china, but he refused. Everyone was a little nervous at the table, but the boss made easy small talk. Ian and Nigel looked like schoolboys in front of the principal, guarding their every move, while Kevin was proud to host him in the forward section of the yacht.

As he left the table, *il Dottore* gave some compliments, saying how fortunate the crew was to have pasta *fate bene*—made well—with the right amount of sauce, heat from the chiles, and cooked al dente. I especially noted what he considered al dente, since preferences differ and it is completely subjective. Then *il Dottore* enlisted us in his conspiracy. While climbing up the crew ladder, with a wink through his glasses, he declared, "No need to trouble *la Signora* over this."

The amber glow of the island as the sun was setting was a magnificent sight, one of the many unique pictures one catches only at sea. It was the end of the weekend, and my only regret was not having had a chance to visit the house where Napoleon served his first exile. Scrawled on one of the walls in his own hand, said the pilot book, were the words: "Napoleon is happy everywhere."

We were heading back to the anchorage in front of Porto Azzurro. As he drove, Patrick scanned the horizon, the way an experienced sailor checks virtual latitude. Suddenly he called for the binoculars. *Il Dottore* quickly handed them to him from the chart house. This could mean something important, the boss obliging in respect to the watch of his skipper. Patrick saw her, far off in the distance, like a seagoing apparition. Yes, it was *Carina,* sailing proud with all her sails perfectly trimmed. Patrick's nemesis was under way a few miles off our quarter stern. He took it as an unintentional taunt and remained quiet. We saw her as a thing of beauty.

Eight

The Battle of the Fishes

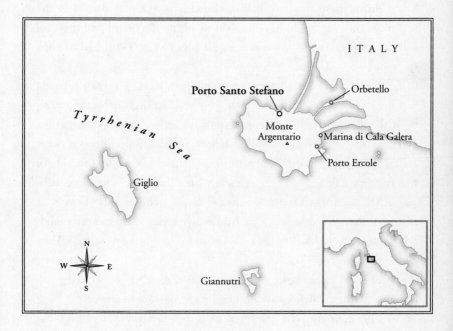

Porto Santo Stefano and the Argentario Coast

I was exhausted. After three sixteen-hour days, I wasn't in a rush to go anywhere. A quiet Monday at anchor would have been perfect in this beautiful part of the world. The owners quickly left when we got back to the anchorage and even skipped the parting line. Something about having to take off in their jet before dark. While Kevin drove them to shore in the launch, Patrick announced to the rest of us that we would have a leisurely dinner on board and then set sail that night. "Leisurely" was easy for him to say; I still had to cook the meal.

The weather fax showed an excellent forecast—no sea or wind warnings for the next few days. We'd be heading slightly southeast, almost paralleling the Italian coast, until we arrived at the two harbors of Porto Santo Stefano, huddled below an island-like block of land called Monte Argentario. A unique geographical feature on this side of the regional border between Tuscany and Lazio are the three isthmuses that connect Monte Argentario to the mainland. If all went as planned, Patrick explained, this would give us an early-morning landfall. Rick, who unlike me was always itchy to move on, asked, "Why don't we leave now?"

As I was cleaning up the galley after dinner before we were under way, I asked Patrick why he liked night passages so much.

"Fuel economy," he answered matter-of-factly. I didn't think that was the entire answer.

"And to get a better berth at the marina. The harbormasters, but more important, the customs officers like the early arrivals. They're less suspicious of boats that arrive at the top of their day," he said. In the first-come, first-served world of private boating, the early boat really did get the best berth at the dock. "Also, we don't lose a day in order to make repairs, get parts, or do any provisioning," he added.

But I knew that even the most seasoned, hardened sailor has this thing for sailing under a blackened sky, lit only by the moon and stars.

That night, close to midnight, with our bearings set for a direct course toward Porto Santo Stefano, we were destined for a great seven-hour passage. The weather was perfect for sailing—only a moderate breeze—and because of the downwind point of sail, any chop in the water would not be uncomfortable. *Serenity* would almost be able to surf as she moved in the direction of the waves. We began to glide through the water at a comfortable six knots, the same speed we would have maintained had we gone under power. With the wind blowing over our starboard side, we also had the right-of-way over both sail and power vessels. Together, the favorable conditions were a rarity in this part of the Mediterranean, and a cruise like this was a perk of the job.

I volunteered for the fourth watch, which would have me on deck from four to six in the morning. I came up to the cockpit and looked out in all directions. It felt a little eerie, as if we were the only vessel on the sea. The few sounds breaking the stillness of the night were those coming from the gentle simmer of the wake just behind us, the occasional splash of a small wave against the hull, or the creaking of the lines stretching and the wooden masts bending. As the boat made way, she slowly rolled from side to side, maybe a degree or two. I couldn't see more than a few yards off the rail, but it was enough to stare at the surface of the water, which reflected the ambient glow from the navigation lights, red on the left side to port and green on the right, starboard side.

A starry night in a near-silent sea, it was incredible how many luminous stars filled the night sky. What could be more seductive? The astral storyboard above that was laden with mythology and astronomy made me wish I knew more about the constellations aside from the two Dippers.

The stellar ceiling also made me think of a scene I witnessed while I was having an after-service drink in the bar at one of the restaurants, La Contea, where I had worked. The owner was escorting an American couple to the door after their dinner. He didn't speak English and they didn't speak Italian, but that didn't stop them from complimenting the meal. Judging from their smiles, he knew they were happy, so he kept saying, "*Grazie, grazie.*"

"But how come no Michelin stars?" the wife asked just as they were approaching the door.

The owner understood "Michelin" and remarkably found a small reserve of English words to make his point. "Stars?" he asked. "Come with me."

He took them just outside the front door of the restaurant and pointed up to the night sky.

"Look up," he said in broken English. "I have all the stars I need!"

Midway through my watch, about five in the morning, Ian came up on deck. He took the helm from me while I grabbed the binoculars to watch for ships. We were making small talk about Antibes, chuckling about the daily ritual of sailors in the bars, when I finally asked him what he had been doing before coming to the Côte d'Azur.

"I was a manager at a company that makes reproductive prostheses for breeding racehorses. Kind of a niche business."

I held back the impulse to laugh. He assured me that his company was one of the best in the business. I was glad I hadn't laughed because it was clear that he took his job seriously.

"But I was bored," he said.

Right then, the wind got shifty and the sails started to luff.

Serenity started to slow down. Ian stayed on the wheel as I went forward to deal with the flopping foresail. As I began to take the slack out of the line that controlled the sail's trim, I had only one wrap on the deck cleat, not thinking in the dying wind that I might need two. All of a sudden irregular gusts made the sail luff with more vigor. I started to haul faster to get control of the sail, but the wind increased, and in no time the rogue line came off the cleat and in its violent shake caught my head in its path. Within a fraction of a second, it wrapped itself twice around my neck like a boa constrictor. I remember the next few seconds only as a blur of terror. *I'm going to die* I thought.

I knew enough about the power of the wind and sails that any more tension in the line and I'd be strangled or left with a broken neck. My body went limp, no doubt an involuntary reaction to the fear. I don't know how, but I pulled up from deep within me my high school training as a lifeguard—in the event of a lunging victim, one can escape by pulling the victim underwater, then push up from under. I knew if I could relax my neck and shoulders, I could get my hands between the rope and my skin. I needed to move fast, and with the next shake of the line that gave any semblance of slack, I grabbed both wraps and pushed up. The rope coils rubbed and chafed my nose and ears along the way. Pain meant nothing to me. With every inch upward, I could think only of the moment when the rope would be fully off my head and I would be out of danger.

When it was finally off, I crumpled to the deck. I fought off the urge to faint by staying focused on tightening the line and securing it to the cleat. Once that was done, for the next few seconds all I could think about was how close I had come to an early death.

When I got back to the cockpit, I explained to Ian what had happened. During the gust, he had his hands full dealing with the mainsheet and didn't hear or see anything.

"Good thing I stayed on course, mate," he said. Good thing indeed. The wind trued itself and saved my life that night. A few minutes later, we changed the topic to what kinds of giant sea creatures lurked in our path.

I woke up about two hours later to my anchor chain alarm clock, the rapid-fire noise of the large steel links banging against the pipe as the hook was dropped. Realizing we were in port, I went up on deck to help the crew back *Serenity* into her new temporary base. I wanted to know more about Monte Argentario, so I checked the pilot book to get a general sense of what was going on in this part of Italy and to locate our whereabouts on the harbor map. I also asked my crewmates if they knew about the region.

This luscious area of secluded anchorages, beaches, and clear water encompasses two main harbor villages—Porto Santo Stefano on the north side and chic Porto Ercole on the south, both having been protected from invasion by the mainland town of Orbetello. Throughout this southwest section of Tuscany the fertile areas of the Bolgheri and the Maremma produce prized Sangiovese and Merlot grapes in what has become one of Italy's most important wine regions. Long stretches of the protected coastline thwarted any development, giving way to national parks and nature preserves. Off the coast and within sight lie the lower islands of the Tuscan archipelago—the scuba-diving haven Giglio and its little sister island Giannutri.

After lunch I decided to go for a walk around town to survey the shops and markets to see where everything was and what ingredients I could find for upcoming meals.

Of the two marinas in Porto Santo Stefano, we parked in the one that seemed farthest from anything, and with *Serenity*'s length and the amount of water depth she needed because of her keel, we were far out on the quay. That translated into a long walk on foot carrying heavy bags of food. Before we left Antibes, Patrick asked if I wanted to convert one of the refrigerators into a freezer so that I could stock up once and just defrost food as I needed it. This meant I could carry more and shop for less. I declined, opting to use only fresh ingredients, especially since so much was available in the markets and shops. Plus, I believed that everyone on board—owners, guests, *and* crew—should benefit from my foraging onshore.

Now, as I walked down the quay passing gift shops and *caffès* but no markets, I wondered how far I would have to go to find what I needed. I strolled over the curved incline that separated our marina from the next, and to my surprise I found an empty harbor. There were old metal sheds and piles of worn nets on the cobblestoned quay, service vehicles parked around, a *cantiere*—shipyard—and the smell of fish, signs of an active fishing economy. I knew I was getting closer. Finally I spotted a few fish stalls across the street from the main quay. I was surprised that they were open during the afternoon siesta and excited to see what each had to offer, but disappointed in what I found. There wasn't much on the ice tables, and the messy condition of the stalls was far from inviting. Strange, I thought. This is a wealthy area. Maybe picky shoppers had come in the morning, and with the volume of business it was hard to keep up with the housekeeping. I figured I was seeing all that was left until the fleet's new catch came in.

I ventured away from the harbor and into town. It appeared as though every Italian town has a Caffè Sport, and here I found one. A pick-me-up after the night passage was in order, the heat of the afternoon quenched with a cappuccino *ghiacciato*—iced. After engaging the barista in a little chat, I asked if there was an open-air market. There was, daily, I was told, except for Sunday, some days better than the others. On my way back to the boat, following a different path, I finally found the shops I was looking for. Signs over gated and shut bakeries, a *latteria* for dairy, butchers, and grocery shops were everywhere.

"David, we're over here!" Patrick's voice called out from under a *caffè* awning as I reemerged on the quay. Most of the crew sat around an outdoor table. I could see from their flushed faces and happy manner that Ian and Nigel had already downed multiple beers. Patrick offered me a drink, but I knew that even one beer would put me to sleep. Ian, slightly slurring his consonants, declared that the *caffè* would be the "official extension of the crew quarters," a pronouncement Nigel quickly seconded. The guys had been at sea long enough that they yearned for a shore-based rally point. The establishment was called Il Grottino—the Little Grotto—an apt name for a little hideaway almost directly across from our *passerelle*. The guys had already acquainted themselves with Salvatore, who owned the *caffè* with his brother, the two also being the afternoon and evening staff.

There are conflicting stories as to how Monte Argentario—Silver Mountain—got its name: one held that it was named for the silver trade practiced by a Roman banking family that owned the land centuries ago; another claimed that it had been named for the many silver mines in the area. I leaned toward believing the former until Pina, Salvatore's mother, who ran the *caffè* in the morning, told me the mountain was named for the glistening, silvery sea in front of it and the argent color of the olive trees that covered its sides. Pina's matriarchal attitude and wise manner won the day.

Rome is only an hour and a half away, which explained why there were so many cars tagged with "Roma" license plates parked along the streets. Salvatore mentioned that near Porto Ercole was the ultra-chic and exclusive hotel Pellicano. Then he warned me about running into any redheads on the island of Giglio, just west of Monte Argentario, by reciting the proverb *"Attenzione, la rosa e pericolosa!"*—Watch out, the redhead can be dangerous! He told me that among the locals, the accepted view was that all redheads on the island were direct descendants of Barbarossa—Red Beard—the pirate. I assured him that when on Giglio, I would not forget his warning

It is said that a cook's job is the hardest on a boat. I was beginning to think that it wasn't so easy onshore, either. It was odd to me that across the street from a fishing harbor, the fish market wasn't laden with fresh catch all along the ice tables. Instead, the fishmongers were aggressively trying to hook me into buying what they knew and I could see was of inferior quality. The eyes of the sea breams were gray and cloudy, not clear; the snappers looked limp instead of firm and shiny; and when I took a peek at the gills on most of them, their color was graying instead of bright reddish pink—all of these telltale visual signs of waning freshness.

Fish going south have that smell we call fishy. And when the fish really go downhill, they start to have a faint aroma that resembles ammonia. Conversely, truly fresh fish smell like the sea. The plump and firm anchovies I bought that day probably landed the prior evening since they smelled as if they had just jumped out of the Mediterranean, and their freshness would make them easier to debone.

My mind went to work as I walked the stalls, looking and searching, determined to find something else I could cook that weekend. I started to think that just because *Serenity*'s money flowed as freely as Rick's *premier cru* Chablis, being spendthrift in the market and buying only the most expensive ingredients might miss the point of true Italian cooking. Then I thought back to the *cacciucco*—the fish stew I made earlier in the month—and how I had chosen to use prime fillets instead of the recommended bellies and jowls, argued by "fishionados" to be the best parts. Maybe I should look beyond the familiar, I thought, because some of the most-sought-after dishes are made from the humblest of beginnings, and "specialties" are often composed of uncommon finds.

Out of necessity, the Italian food culture adapted to using flavor and technique in order to make just about anything delicious from what is available. And this weekend, I decided, so would I. The weekend's menu was built around what looked best: large calamari and tiny ones—*calamaretti*—slightly different from those found in Viareggio, huge *seppie*—cuttlefish—very small octopus called *moscardini,* and my fresh anchovies. In some circles, these are all considered bait; in others, they are delicacies. On *Serenity,* they would become the latter.

The owners came down that first weekend in Monte Argentario with just one other couple at what was becoming their regular arrival time, Friday evening cocktail hour. After quickly settling into their accommodations, they were ready for welcome drinks and canapés on deck, then right onto dinner in the salon.

Over the course of the previous weekends, I noticed *la Signora* had displayed a bias toward crispy food—marmalade and crackers with her caffe latte in the morning, crusty breads and *grissini,* and fried fish. Pattern recognition helped me choose my first course for the weekend. I decided to make the little calamari *fritti*—fried. I had the right oil on board with a high smoking point that was perfect for frying. *La Signora* had sent sunflower seed oil to the boat the week before Monte Carlo, so I kept a few extra cans in the stores. I gathered from my time abroad that this was Europe's oil of choice for high-heat cooking. Since it imparts very little flavor when something is fried in it, the flavor of the main ingredient comes through. For small, delicate items like *calamaretti,* shrimp, or anything that is going to be cooked only a few minutes in hot oil, this is critical so that with the end result you taste the food, not the oil it was cooked in.

It took a while to clean those thumb-sized *frutti di mare* of their eyes, beaks, and innards. I was glad they were for only four people. Two passes for a full boat of eight guests would have been a lot of fish to clean. I could have asked my friends at the fish stalls to clean them for me and now wondered why I didn't. Certain fish vendors will offer the service outright, but I learned it should never be a problem to ask for fish to be scaled, gutted, and filleted; or shrimp peeled and deveined; or cephalopods like calamari, octopus, and cuttlefish "cleaned."

I dredged the *calamaretti* in flour seasoned with salt and pepper, making sure they were completely coated and dry—dryness being an important part of frying throughout the process—and then fried them in small batches in the hot oil. Too many at once would have cooled the oil down, leaving the *calamaretti* soggy. When they were golden brown and crisp after swimming in the hot oil, I skimmed them out onto what I like to call a landing pad—a tray or dish with absorbent towels to catch residual oil. After a little seasoning of salt and pepper, I quickly arranged them in a nice pile, not too high, on a platter garnished with lemon wedges and parsley sprigs, then served them *subito* while still hot and crispy. If they were piled too high, steam from the pieces inside would be trapped and make them soggy.

For the *moscardini,* instead of stewing them in a tomato-based sauce, I simmered them in an aromatic broth—a little onion, celery, parsley sprigs, a bay leaf, a pinch of hot red pepper flakes—that had tomatoes in it. And since it was high season for peas, they would become the accompaniment to the small octopus. In Liguria, a classic method for making *pasta col pesto* is to put a small peeled potato—the size of an egg—in the pasta water, letting it cook until it falls apart, which in turn puts more starch in the water to eventually help the finished sauce adhere to the pasta. I applied this same trick for cooking the peas, letting a few small potatoes break up in just enough water so the peas floated just over the base of the pot. Since they would only need minutes to cook, the liquid had thickened enough to be a perfect base for the octopus. Just before sending the platter to the table, I added a drizzle of extra virgin olive oil and a *gremolata*—a fresh accompaniment of parsley chopped with a little fresh garlic and some lemon zest. *Basta.* We had a nice entrée from humble beginnings, light enough for summer, and another method by which to preserve the delicate flavor of the main ingredients.

On Saturday, I brought out my journals to see which version of the marinated *alici*—anchovies—I should make. Flipping through the pages, I was grateful for having taken extensive notes at my various *stages*. At the time, it seemed as if I would never get enough down on paper. But for everything I wrote, there were undoubtedly countless things I missed. That day, my journals provided a treasure trove of information to inspire me for that evening's dinner. Those years abroad as a *viaggiatore dei cucine*—a kitchen traveler—exposed me to such an amazing variety of food and preparations that I wondered how much I missed during those first two years when I lived silently, not able to speak Italian.

I grew up shy of tough, oily anchovies in little tins that were impossible to open. Their strong, salty, and unsatisfying fishy flavor obliterated everything they touched. But living abroad changed all that. I discovered that a good-quality cured anchovy is completely different—plump, meaty, tender, not overpowering, and, when used sparingly, a great addition to many dishes. And I hadn't tasted anything made from fresh anchovies until arriving in Italy.

I found three recipes in my journals for anchovies. They were called *alici* when fresh and *acciughe* when packed in salt or oil. I was already using them as a seasoning by adding small amounts in the beginning stages of cookery to boost the flavor of a sauce. One recipe I found was a pantry staple at La Contea, the restaurant in Piedmont where I worked. Tonino, the owner and himself a very passionate cook, would clean salt-packed anchovy fillets under cold water, dry them well, and then repack them in an abundant amount of olive oil with various seasonings. Pepino, the appetizer chef at Peck who was Calabrese, liked to chop oil-cured fillets and blend them with chile peppers to create a loose paste to use in dressings and sauces. Then there was my Tuscan friend Massimo. He took the fresh fillets, used two methods of marinating—first in vinegar to "cook" them, then in olive oil with other seasonings to flavor them—and later served them as an antipasto with grilled pieces of bread. I went with Massimo's recipe since it was the preparation that used fresh anchovies, *alici,* that I was after.

I immersed boneless anchovy fillets in champagne vinegar for a few hours, basically the same method as making a seviche, replacing the lemon and lime juice in the classic Latin American method with the vinegar. When the fillets turned opaque and were essentially "cooked," I took them out, washed the vinegar off under cold water, patted them dry on a landing pad, and lined them up in a baking dish. I added minced garlic, hot red pepper flakes, and chopped parsley over the entire surface, then covered them in olive oil. These could keep up to a few days in the refrigerator, but for my immediate needs a couple of hours at room temperature would be sufficient for the aromatics to perfume the oil and flavor the fish.

But which oil to use? One of the proudest food icons of *la cucina italiana* is extra virgin olive oil, an ingredient that plays as much a role in the beginning of cookery as the drizzle does at the end. Cold-pressed is the purest and most delicate. Too much light will render it rancid, so the better oils are found in dark green bottles. Its low smoking point makes it bitter when too much heat is applied, so I cook with it *leggermente*—lightly—as my friend Enzo, the olive oil producer, suggested, using low heat when simmering so as to not diminish its flavor. Gently cooking aromatics—onions, celery, carrots, garlic, citrus zest, herbs, chiles, anchovies—in an abundant amount of oil will release their flavor and permeate the oil, which in turn creates a layer of flavor that will remain throughout the cookery. A final step before a dish goes to the table is the addition of *un filo d'olio*—a line of oil—that shiny and supple enhancement to whatever it is drizzled on. As Enzo put it, a drizzle added to a dish makes your food taste better.

Like wine, extra virgin olive oil is directly related to a particular area, characteristic of a growing season, method of cultivation, and hand of the producer. So I began to consider pairing the right oil with the right dish. Lighter-style oils like those from Liguria, Sicily, or the southern region of Apulia could be teamed with vegetables or tender fish; heartier oils from Tuscany and Umbria with meats, pastas, soups, and big-game fish like tuna or swordfish. The fruitier style of olive oil from the south of France, completely different from Italian oils, lends itself better to cooking with orange zest, fennel, and saffron. For the anchovies, I chose a Tuscan oil to keep with the theme of regional cooking.

That evening, to make the presentation of the anchovies a little more interesting than just a flat arrangement of little fish on a platter, I came up with an *à la minute* creation from things I already had on board. I took inner leaves of Bibb lettuce as a base and filled each with a chopped salad made with celery hearts, diced tomato, pitted green olives, cucumber, and roughly chopped parsley—all tossed with a touch of the oil the anchovies were marinated in and finished with a splash of red wine vinegar. On the top of each pile, I placed a couple of the anchovies and added a pinch of coarse sea salt. I made enough for two per person. It was almost like a soigné Greek salad except the anchovies replaced feta cheese, and with a little attention to knife work the colors of the salad were beautiful.

"They loved it," Rick said when he came back into the galley. "Look, the platter is empty."

"Good to know because this weekend has been tough."

"You seem to have figured it out," he said with a note of understanding sincerity.

"It's making me cook a little out of the ordinary."

"Isn't that what *la Signora* is looking for?" Rick asked.

"I guess. But then there's the other side." He knew I meant *il Dottore.*

"This reminds me of seeing only snails and eels at the riverside fish stands where I grew up," Rick said as he loaded the platter with seconds. "When it's all you can find, you make the best of it." He was referring to the Gironde River that fronts the famous Left Bank vineyards of Bordeaux, a place he spoke of often. "So what's the next course?" he asked.

"Cuttlefish *al forno*"—baked—"with a sauce of the pan juices, a little marinara, and basil."

"If we were on the Atlantic coast, I'd say to use butter and wine!" Rick was showing a little hometown culinary pride.

"Red or white?"

"It all depends," he said as he left the pantry with the second round of the anchovies.

I began preparing the cuttlefish entrée and thought ahead one course to dessert. It was a good thing stone fruits were in season— peaches, nectarines, plums of all colors, apricots, and cherries—a natural way to finish any meal. At the market, they were everywhere. After a couple of visits to the same vendors, I felt like a regular, and they would offer to set aside the best they had providing I came back to them the next day. The fruits were so flawless, so ripe, so unblemished that I made my long treks back to the boat very cautiously.

One of the best parts of traveling is to taste something that is truly local. I realized my job required more than just adhering to *la Signora*'s dietary rules set forth during my initial interview. Rather, as we cruised down the coast, I had to inspire a sense of place with the food and use the best of what a location had to offer *at that moment*. *La Signora*'s reaction to the anchovies and cuttlefish brought this home. "David, this meal was just right. This is what I want," she said to me in passing later that evening. Rick also reinforced this, sadly mentioning that little or none was left for him to eat.

I loved Sunday evening. The owners were gone, the pace quieted down, the boat was once again under our sole watch. I always slept better the first night after the owners left—whether from sheer work fatigue or from the knowledge that we had survived another weekend, it didn't matter. It was also when working on *Serenity* lived up to her name.

The next morning *Serenity*'s maintenance routine began again in earnest. Nigel was walking around with his can of brass polish, Ian hosed down the deck, Rick collected all the dirty linen, Kevin worked on the chart house roof, Scott buried himself in the engine room, and Patrick was barking directions to anyone within earshot. Chores on a yacht adopt a certain sameness as the crew fights an unending and repetitive battle against the harsh effects of salt water and the structural stresses of a vessel in constant motion. But this Monday started the week off differently—with a fight.

"I can't believe I just finished varnishing the roof of the chart house, and now he wants me to re-sand and re-varnish again," Kevin sputtered between sips of fresh iced tea in the galley after lunch. He was clearly angry, but in his steely, controlled way I could tell he was keeping a lot in reserve.

The "varnish wars" that had been brewing between Kevin and Patrick seemed to be going from skirmishes and sorties to all-out confrontations. Ostensibly, the two sides were arguing over which kind of varnish to use on the mahogany. But by then, we all knew there was much more to it.

We were supposed to have the afternoon off, but Patrick had a long list of other projects he wanted to get done.

"I don't even have enough time as it is," Kevin vented, talking not to me but to himself, as if reexamining what had just happened to help him figure out what he missed the first time.

"And what about the money we're spending?" he said, calculating aloud the cost of hiring a few extra day workers from the *cantiere*—shipyard—in town.

"This is just crazy," he said to me, but he was still talking to himself. He finished his tea, washed and dried the glass, and replaced it in the pantry. Like everything else he did, Kevin was thorough.

"Patrick's nothing but a wart," we heard Rick say from the pantry, eavesdropping as usual.

We were all operating in high gear those final weeks in July, knowing that at the beginning of August, the owners would be on board for the entire month. For me, their arrival meant daily nonstop heavy loads—multicourse meals, snacks, crew meals, nothing on the menu repeated, and deck duties. For Rick, it meant the entire interior to take care of and service for each meal. For Kevin and the deck-hands, it meant keeping the yacht in pristine condition every minute of the day. Kevin did not need Patrick's make-work projects right now.

A few hours later, Kevin and Patrick's battle surfaced on deck. Ian came below and, while passing through the galley, reported, "Oh boy, it's getting good now."

"What's going on up there?" I asked.

"The tiff is on the surface now, mate. They're sniping at each other pretty openly," he said, then headed up the crew ladder and went back to work.

I wanted to get off the boat and catch some clear air. When I saw the fishing boats returning as they did every afternoon at five, I headed over to the other harbor to check out the scene. Low-flying seagulls squawked behind each vessel looking for a free meal. These were working boats, nothing fancy, a couple of sizes in the fleet, each painted with a different-color trim that signified its ownership. They quickly backed into their spaces and were tied up by a small troop of dockhands who worked their way down the quay as the boats arrived. Within minutes, service vehicles pulled up to each boat to receive the Styrofoam crates of sorted fish passed fireman style by the deckhands onto the trucks. I didn't see anyone carting even one box to the fish markets across the street. The trucks left, and soon after, the dock-workers and boat hands sorted through the nets and lines on the quay, fixing, sewing, coiling, and preparing for the next day's run.

That night, over dinner at the mess table, Patrick asked us if we wanted to invite some of our new friends from Il Grottino for a day sail midweek. I immediately became suspicious of this seemingly gracious gesture and wondered if he was trying to pull us to his side in the conflict with Kevin. I also hoped this wasn't another Club 55 gifted proposal for support. I didn't really know. But we decided to take him up on his offer to sail for a few hours and then anchor for lunch in a small bay at Giglio.

It turned out to be a great day, our friends from the *caffè* ecstatic at having been invited for a ride on *Serenity*, a very generous effort on Patrick's part and not typical of visiting yachts. I made a buffet lunch for twenty of sliced prosciutto with room-temperature baked zucchini, penne with shrimp and fresh tomato sauce, a platter of bruschetta— grilled pieces of bread swiped with garlic, then topped with diced tomatoes marinated in olive oil—and an arugula salad with minced celery hearts, shaved Parmesan cheese, and toasted pine nuts. Rick, ever the consummate host, made sure the food was served on silver and porcelain and that glasses were never empty.

One of our guests, Danilo, seemed very knowledgeable about food, and we had a great conversation about local dishes. It turned out that his family owned a restaurant just outside town, and he had spent many a Saturday night in the kitchen while growing up. I asked him why shiny and firm fresh fish were so hard to find, even in a busy, thriving fishing port like Porto Santo Stefano. "Most of the seafood goes directly to Milan and other large markets, like Rungis in Paris. The better the fish, the more money the fishermen will get for their catch. And in the local market, even though you have money to throw around," he explained, "you are a *straniero*"—an outsider. "Once you've made your little purchase and left, the vendor may never see you again. He needs to take care of his repeat customers."

So there it was, the dynamic of supply and demand in the local fish business. Danilo paused, then added, "I'll do something for you. Let me know what you need, and I'll introduce you to the guy that sells to our restaurant. With my word, he'll serve you well."

The next day I called Danilo to take him up on his offer for the upcoming weekend. That evening I was to go to a certain boat and give the fisherman my order. I did as told, and the man said he would deliver the items to *Serenity* on Saturday morning. I was a little nervous about leaving it to a stranger to deliver food on the day I needed it, but I put my trust in Danilo that this fisherman would deal honestly with me.

On Saturday morning, as we were getting ready to go sailing, the *pescatore*—fisherman—arrived on the quay with two Styrofoam boxes. I went down the *passerelle* to greet him. *Il Dottore* came with me. I wasn't expecting him to join me, nor was the fisherman.

I asked how much and pulled out a wad of 100K lira notes, starting to pay without looking in the boxes. *Il Dottore* asked to see the contents. I was caught off guard by this, realizing that if the contents were bad, *il Dottore*'s trust in me as someone authorized to spend his money would be shaken. He was doing what I should have done—a quality check—before I started peeling off bills.

The fisherman cut the tape on the boxes. *Ecco!* I could smell the sea. In the first box were three kilos of firm, shiny vermilion *triglie*—red mullet—perfectly lined up like soldiers, and in the second box were five kilos of beautiful orange and white scampi, both caught, the fisherman assured us, a day earlier. You could see the pride in his eyes. Thank goodness, I thought to myself. I looked at *il Dottore* with a smile, and he complimented the fisherman on bringing us such a beautiful catch, although he did not walk away without adding, "*Però costoso*"—Although costly.

Il Dottore came into the galley later that morning. I thought for sure he was going to mention something about my little faux pas on the dock.

"*Ciao, Davide,*" he said.

"*Buon giorno, capo,*" I answered, using the familiar word for boss as if it were our first meeting of the day.

"Do you have any mortadella and a little bread?" he asked.

"Sure." I went to get it from the pantry. I got him a couple of *panini*—small breads just larger than rolls that I kept on board for snack sandwiches—a knife, and a plate and put everything together on a small cutting board.

"*Grazie,*" he said in his very calm tone. He made himself a sandwich and ate it over the sink. I wanted to strike up a conversation, but I had no idea what to talk about. I was still a little timid around him following the avocado incident in Portofino, but I decided to take a shot anyway.

"How was everything at the office this week?"

"*Pieno, molto pieno*"—full, very full—he said between bites. "You know, Davide," he continued while looking out the porthole above the sink, "you're fortunate. You can have this anytime. I think about this sandwich all week."

I wasn't sure how he'd take it if I asked him if he'd want to trade places for a day. I kept on with my tasks and let him have his moment alone. He finished his snack, asked where everything went, put most of it away, thanked me, and headed back up top.

Unlike *la Signora,* who maintained a clear, bright line between the upper and the lower decks, *il Dottore* seemed to enjoy spending time down below, if only to sneak the food that his significant other wanted him to avoid.

Dinner that night started with an Arborio rice salad made with a copious amount of tender peas, arugula, and extra virgin olive oil from Danilo's family. I had been using a lot of peas and other shelling beans, even for crew meals. Shucking peas, favas, fresh cannellini, or magenta-and-white-husked beans I only knew in French as *coco rouge* was an easy kitchen task I passed to my crewmates to stave off boredom while we were at anchor. And they got pretty good at it. As a matter of fact, they were getting more and more interested in food.

The salad was placed in the center of the platter and surrounded with the scampi tails that were broiled and finished with a squeeze of lemon and a drizzle of the same oil. For the entrée, I cut the small red mullet into precious fillets, gently panfried them, and served them with a simple coulis of fresh tomato with a hint of hot pepper and basil. I offered a side dish of steamed green beans tossed in *olio-limone*—oil and lemon—then finished the meal with a very rich *panna cotta*—cooked cream—made with mascarpone cheese and served with apricots quickly roasted with a splash of champagne, sugar, and a few pieces of orange peel. Amaretti cookies on the side were an appropriate accompaniment since their *amaro*—bitter—flavor is the result of flour made from the kernels in apricot pits.

Kevin stayed in the galley throughout the service, avoiding Patrick. He asked a lot of questions about the cookery, and I in turn asked him about his background. He was an officer in the British army, he told me, and started his military career at Sandhurst, famous to most Americans as the military college where Winston Churchill trained for his military career. At twenty-seven, Kevin wanted to become a licensed captain. He was taking a master's course—something like a homeschooling program—on navigation, seamanship, safety, and engineering, but in order to be certified, he also had to spend a certain number of hours at sea. After two journeys to the South Pacific, this summer on *Serenity* would fulfill that requirement.

Kevin brought one other valuable talent to the job. The guys liked working for him and with him because he set a good example. If start time was eight in the morning, he'd be ready to go at a quarter of.

Rick and I hoped that over time, Patrick and Kevin would come to some compromise. Or one of them would lose interest in continuing the fight. After all, they always seemed to be arguing over things no one else cared about. But we both knew it wasn't the little things that were at the heart of their conflict. It was about one big thing—Kevin's feeling that Patrick was applying racing boat tactics to a pleasure craft fit for recreational use. That night, Kevin tried to explain his position to Ian, Rick, and me, wanting us to understand that he was not mutinous, just annoyed and rightly so.

"He sails by gauge technique—fixes and formulas, not the wind," Kevin said. "He talks in yacht-racing terms: 'Our VMG—velocity made good—is optimum,' he'll report.

"That's fine," Kevin went on, trying to justify his case, "but what about the wind?" A difference in seafaring philosophy wedged a fundamental gap between the two men.

None of us realized it then, but Kevin was talking to us about the problem because he had come to a decision. He was not the type to come to a decision quickly, but once he did, his resolve was unshakable. Although he didn't mention it to any of us that night, Kevin had already called Michele, the yacht manager, from the phone in Il Grottino and told him there was a problem that he needed to deal with. He wanted Patrick removed as captain. Michele agreed to drive to the boat in a couple of days. Knowing he'd be coming anyway, I made a follow-up call to Michele, asking him to bring some jars of backup pâté to the boat for August, knowing I probably wouldn't find foie gras in southern Italy.

When Michele arrived, he didn't waste any time summoning us all to the salon. Everyone was a little uncomfortable sitting on the owners' furniture. We had never done this before. After some small talk Michele acknowledged the elephant in the room.

"I heard there is a problem between the captain and the crew," he said. There was silence. Nobody wanted to stick his neck out.

"All right, is anyone going to say anything?" Michele asked, then began, "Ian, how is everything for you on board? Do you have any problems with Patrick?"

"I'm okay," Ian answered sheepishly, but then added, "It can be a little frustrating and maybe that's part of the job, so I'll just work around it."

Michele turned next to Scott. "I'm okay as well," Scott volunteered. "But I don't like this hanging out at night with Patrick as if we are all buddy-buddy and during the day we're spoken to in a different way."

"And you, Richard?" Michele asked, turning to Rick.

"Everything is okay," Rick responded. "I'm fine." His mind was elsewhere.

In frustration, Michele turned to me: "David, what is going on?"

It was a tough spot to be in. There was no question where my sympathies lay, but could I trust there would be no retaliation?

"I sort of hear everything that is going on," I said, and added candidly, "but I'm going to play Switzerland. I know there have been some problems, but Patrick has left me and the galley alone."

Michele turned to Kevin. "So, Kevin, tell me, what's going on?" he said very quietly.

Kevin paused, and I could sense his mind logically piecing together his argument. He turned and looked directly at Patrick, man-to-man.

"I can't understand how you expect me to keep the boat and the rig in order and managed when you're so inconsistent. You wait for me to finish something, and then tell me it's not the way you want it. Why can't you tell me before? Also, it's very hard for me to be a filter if you're going to the guys behind my back. It undermines me. You tell the crew to do something the way you want it, and I go to the guys and complain about the way they're doing it, and they point their fingers back at you, saying that's the way you told them. It's ridiculous."

Kevin looked around, first at Michele and then at each of us in the salon. Patrick locked into Kevin's face, never wavering in his stare. He was clearly furious.

Michele nodded his head, looking from person to person, and then asked, "What's the solution here? Are we going to vote the captain off the boat, or is there a better way to work this out? The owners are very proud of this crew, and they love this boat, and I'd really hate to have to tell them what's going on and that there's going to be some kind of a major change at this point."

Patrick finally spoke up. "I didn't understand that the way I am is such a problem. I know Kevin and I haven't gotten along, and I know that we don't meet on the same wavelength. I just didn't realize that it had such an effect on everyone else. The last thing I want is to try to run a boat with a crew that has no respect for me."

Michele was a pro at dispute resolution. He gave Patrick's conciliatory words a chance to sink in. After a long pause, he asked, "Well, then, guys, is it too late? Is your respect totally gone? Or are we going to try to fix this?"

He threw the decision over to the crew. Another long silence. I looked at Kevin, wondering if he would take the opportunity to rally the crew for a no-confidence vote on Patrick.

It was Kevin who broke the silence and, in doing so, communicated something fine about himself. He was interested more in fairness than in winning. "I have no problem with Patrick staying as long as things change. We just need to get on the same page and be consistent."

I suspect Kevin knew in his gut that the owners would not want to go looking for a captain mid-season, and that if Patrick were put out, they would look to Kevin first, giving him an opportunity to become captain. But I also suspected that he wasn't the kind of person to promote himself at someone else's expense. His turn would come. And it would come honorably. We ended the meeting with Kevin saying, "I guess it's not about voting Patrick out. It's about getting to a consensus here."

"Then it's settled," Michele said. "Bon voyage."

August Ferie

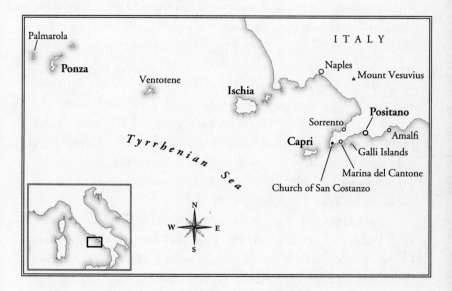

Ischia, Ponza, Capri, and the Amalfi Coast

*E*arly one morning a few days later, while smoking his breakfast cigarette and dangling his legs over the rail at the bow, Rick tried to explain to me how dire our future would be. "For the next thirty days . . . a whole month," he said, emphasizing each word to be sure I didn't underestimate the length of time he was describing, "we will be working flat stick." It was only seven-thirty in the morning and already the heat was building. Since our arrival at the southern Italian island of Ischia, it felt as though the humidity crept up on us earlier and earlier each day.

"A full boat for a month, David. Do you understand what this will mean? They"—meaning the owners and the three couples who would be their guests—"will be on board *every day*. You have no idea how trapped you will feel. It will be like a submarine—no place to go, only here on the foredeck or down below, that's it. *C'est dingue*"—French slang for "This will be crazy." "Our summer is over," he pronounced, ending on a dramatic note.

"It won't be that bad," I assured him with my ignorance-induced confidence. Ever the practical one, I was thinking only in terms of my kitchen needs. "I'll need to find more space to hold the stores, and I've decided to turn one of the fridges into a freezer, but once we get into a rhythm, it'll be a bunt. Plus, look on the bright side. No more practice sails."

Rick barely looked at me as he flicked his smoldering butt into Ischia's bustling, ferry-filled harbor. "I will have to do laundry for fifteen people. I'll be like a migrant worker. *Vraiment*"—truly—"*dingue*."

Rick was in a funk. But it wasn't only about the owners. The old Rick would have breezed his way through that problem. Beneath that devil-may-care exterior was a devoted father terrified of losing contact with his beloved son. The farther south we sailed, the more difficulty he was having getting his ex-wife on the phone, and she of course controlled his access to their child. He began to express the idea that his ex-wife was deliberately keeping his son from speaking to him.

With Ischia as our base, the early itinerary included calls at the volcano-crest island of Ponza and then on to beautiful Capri. We were to continue around the Sorrento Peninsula to the Amalfi coast for a stop at Positano, then we would go on to Sardinia. I hoped that once in the Amalfi area, I would have time to visit my friends at the Michelin two-star Ristorante Don Alfonso, where I had done one of my favorite *stages*. So much had happened since I walked through their doors I wanted to brag a little bit, to show everyone how far I had come.

I replayed in my mind that first bus ride from the train station to Don Alfonso as the bus climbed and swung around countless hairpin curves in a channel-like road cut out of the steep terrain behind Sorrento. Clusters of wildflowers poured over the stone walls that flanked the roadsides and looked as if they had been laid block by stone-cut block by the strong arms of determined Romans. I later learned that this was exactly how they were built.

As the bus got closer to the summit, I looked down to the shimmering ripples of the Mediterranean, the island of Capri in the distance. My first breathtaking views of the Provençal countryside were magnificent. But the sea is different. I found its open horizon liberating. My eyes were seduced by the deep blue of the water—the Bay of Naples to the north and the Gulf of Salerno to the south. On the other side of the road the blur of lush green and yellow washed across acre upon acre of trellised lemon trees. That is where I told myself I wanted to have the Mediterranean sun bronze my arms into those of an Italian chef.

Ristorante Don Alfonso rested majestically at the top of the peninsula in a town named after its place between the two gulfs,

Sant'Agata sui Due Golfi, a plaster-lathed building painted rose, like the potted flowers that adorn it. After I met Alfonso and his wife, Livia, I was escorted upstairs to an apartment on the top floor—very clean, very white, and sparsely decorated but well appointed. The final reward came in the form of a spiral staircase up to a rooftop deck with its own sweeping view of the sea.

The island of Ischia is only an hour by ferry from Naples and the largest in the gulf, but it had a different feel from *Serenity's* previous stops—a little funky and raucous, especially after the tranquillity of the Argentario coast. As we approached Porto d'Ischia, I was surprised to see so crowded a harbor, filled with small speedboats darting back and forth while dodging the ferries' wakes. Even from a distance, I could see that the entire quay teemed with people. I later learned why. Porto d'Ischia not only is one of the most popular ports in Italy used by small-craft sailors but also served as the terminus for ferries and hydrofoils packed with holidaymakers from Naples.

Once we docked and went ashore, disco music blasted from quayside *caffés*, cars honked along the narrow streets in town, sidewalks were mobbed, and the subtle smell of diesel fuel belied the area's reputation as a spot for skin cleansing and rejuvenation in its legendary hot-water mineral springs. The place was packed.

I should not have been surprised. After all, it was August, and like many European countries, Italy shuts down for the August *ferie,* and now it appeared to me that anyone who could afford to made his or her way to the southern Italian coast. It also explained why no crew members were Italian. What greater display of class insensitivity could there be than to deny a workingman his holiday month so that an elite family could have theirs? In relying on non-Italians, the owners had a win-win situation: they didn't have to feel they were depriving a fellow countryman of his traditional vacation month, and by hiring someone like me, they could keep to the dictates of regional

Italian cuisine as opposed to having one man's homebred regional
food bias.

The four couples boarded Serenity, and it took the better part of
the morning for everyone to get settled. I could hear *la Signora's* on-
slaught of requests and directives to Rick while he ran around trying to
keep everyone happy. The owners also brought their black Labrador,
Alessandro, who would be joining us for the month. He was a well-
behaved and perfectly groomed large dog, but an unexpected addition
to the guest list. Who was going to take care of him? Of course, *la
Signora* had "Alex's" feeding schedule worked out. There was dry food,
"but he likes just about everything," she said over her shoulder when she
came in the galley to say hello, a not-so-subtle hint that she expected
me to rustle up "people food" on a regular basis. I also noticed she didn't
have a bowl for him. Should I use the everyday porcelain or something
from the crew set? One of my mixing bowls would have to suffice.

We spent the first week cruising and anchoring along the island's
coast in the general vicinity of Porto d'Ischia because of what I assumed were practical reasons. Since we were going to be in remote locations and at anchor a lot during the ensuing weeks, this may have
been a last chance for any repairs and major provisioning.

The food shopping was pretty good in town, and the menus immediately reflected the spirited cuisine of Naples—tomatoes everywhere, especially the little sun-ripened *pomodorini* packed with flavor
that I used with reckless abandon, zucchini, eggplants, bell peppers,
and southern Italian *peperoncini*—chile peppers. We found a great
shop, maybe better described as an emporium of Neapolitan pastries
and gelato, called Calise that got regular business from us. It was a
very popular destination for nightlife, or so I heard after Ian and
Nigel's late-night forays into town.

As a gesture to his hosts, one of the guests got into the habit of always bringing back a large *treccia*—soft, milk white, handmade braids of fresh mozzarella from his excursions onshore. There was always more than enough for everyone. As delicious as it was—with a little coarse sea salt and extra virgin olive oil; under marinated *pomodorini*; with hot red pepper flakes, anchovies, olives; in griddled Parmesan-cheese-and-egg-coated sandwiches called *mozzarella in carrozza*—there was only so much one could take, and after a couple of days, even Kevin wasn't shy about voicing a preference for change. Regardless, I was having fun with the food since this region's cuisine is the one most recognized in the States as Italian American.

The guests on board began to relax as I tried to condition myself to the fact that no longer was it only two or three days of full service then a break. Service was daily, the end already feeling a millennium away. With a total of fifteen people plus a dog on board, it didn't take long for all of us in the crew to feel cramped up forward. Our long lunch hours lounging around our collapsible deck table became a thing of the past. Rick's "flat stick" description of August didn't even begin to describe the pace, heat, and building fatigue. Plus, the residual tension between Patrick and Kevin continually wore on everyone.

One of the guests eventually struck Rick as a problem. "This guy will be no good," he said to me one evening.

"Why?" I asked.

"I don't know. He just looks like trouble." His instincts proved right when a couple days later the guest, whom we tagged Dennis—as in the Menace—ordered an American-style breakfast. His desire for a truck-stop menu, with farm-fresh eggs, strips of crispy bacon, and golden hash browns, wreaked havoc on my schedule while Rick had to break his housekeeping routine to play waiter. Day to day, we never knew when Dennis would forgo the standard continental offering and summon us to provide his road-stop fare. Worse, it started giving Scott, Ian, and Nigel ideas about what to have for their breakfast.

"Maybe I'll get my proper breakfast now," Scott would say in my direction—just loud enough to be heard.

More and more, the galley became the hub of all kinds of activities. Now that the crew had gone native at the table, and begun to respect my mantra that a Mediterranean diet is both 'good and good for you,' I had to be flexible about other things they cared about. For example, music. Seven different guys with seven different tastes kept our stereo in constant rotation. It would never fail that when I yearned for some peace and quiet, someone put a CD in the player. At least Rick's up-tempo disco dance choices kept our energy flowing through the day.

At night, there was the issue of Scott's snoring. Patrick and I never heard it, but according to Kevin and Ian it was a regular occurrence. Their method of silencing it was to bombard him with pillows. Nigel was on the ready for backup if needed. With Kevin, Ian, and Nigel's bunks above Scott's, hitting the target was easy.

We were anchored near Castello d'Ischia, an old fortress that encompassed the better half of the island it sat on and connected to the main island by a narrow causeway. Without much to do one afternoon, Nigel went free diving and came back with a large octopus and more sea urchins than I knew what to do with. As he unloaded his haul on deck, the octopus wrapped its legs around his forearm, refusing to let go. *La Signora,* ignoring Nigel's plight, was ecstatic, *"Guarda che belli!"*—Look how beautiful!—she said to her guests. The octopus, when finally pried loose from Nigel, provided some entertainment and was returned to the water. Part of me wanted to make *insalata di polpo*—octopus salad—but since this creature was a regular in the markets, I could easily add it to the menu at any time.

After examining the sea urchins, *la Signora* asked that they be served as soon as possible, as a first course that night. Then she explained how they should be cut open. I had never dealt with fresh sea urchins before, so I was eager to learn. "Carefully hold them in the palm of your hand, then with a scissors cut them from the valve to halfway up the shell in order to cut around them like the equator. Rinse the half shells under cold water to clean them, but be careful to leave the roe intact." Since the sharp spines can make for a nasty sting, her method made sense. That night I would serve them on the half shell with lemon and crusty bread. Small pieces of torn crust would be used to scoop out the urchins' briny roe.

It must have been quite a sight that evening—a polished sailing yacht parked by itself in one part of the marina, two crew members in their uniforms standing on the old stone quay next to the *passerelle,* rinsing and cutting sea urchins in bare hands with scissors. Nigel and I were going through them, culling for the biggest ones, when a man came up to see the catch.

"Where are they from?" he asked in raspy Italian.

When I told him, he acknowledged that was good water for them but suggested another spot he believed to be better. Then he asked how we were serving them.

"You should toss them with spaghetti," he came back.

"That sounds pretty good," I said. Nigel had no idea what we were talking about as he carried on the task at hand. I continued our food talk. "How do you make yours?"

"Scoop the roe from the shells and toss with spaghetti, chili flakes, and parsley over a very low flame. Add the pasta water little by little until the urchins melt and coat the pasta—almost like making a carbonara. It's the best way to eat them."

The mention of carbonara, a Roman dish, surprised me, because he appeared to be the kind of guy who didn't venture higher up the boot than Naples. But what he said made complete sense. The use of gentle heat and small additions of pasta water to work the main ingredient, in both cases eggs, into a thick and creamy sauce was the same method. Having learned the technique at a small winery estate, Colle Picchione, just outside Rome, I was inspired to try his recipe that night.

I saved a bunch of urchins to make a small plate for Rick, Nigel, and me to try after dinner service. It turned out to be one of the most delicious *primi* I had ever tasted, and the satisfaction displayed by my co-workers was unanimous. I now had a new front-runner in my all-time favorite foods repertoire, a recipe provided unsolicited by a passerby on the Porto d'Ischia quay.

Nigel, a quick eater by nature, disappeared up the ladder as Rick and I finished our plates. Now that we were sated and mellow, the subject meandered to the question of "what next?"

"What are you doing after the season? Staying here or maybe going home?" Rick asked as he lay supine on the mess table bench.

"I don't know yet," I answered. I hadn't even thought about returning home since I arrived in France more than four years earlier.

"Maybe it's time."

He had a point. Maybe it was time for me to start thinking about returning home and trying to put together a stateside career.

Rick planted a seed in my mind that needed no watering. Before, when I tried to picture myself back in America, I found the scene intimidating. I had grown to like the simpler lifestyle in Italy—not so many choices about things like food or even mineral water. I thought of a grocery store in the States and the overwhelming variety of products it offered. And there was always time in Italy to go into a *caffè* and enjoy a perfectly made coffee served in a ceramic cup and saucer.

I found Italy easier on a human-interaction level, too. Now that I had my *carta d'identità*, I could work legally and reside as long as I wanted. With it I could receive medical coverage, college tuition, pension, mandatory five-weeks-a-year paid vacation, *tutto*. Four years ago, I had crept into Italy as a clandestine worker—now I could live in the country without the risk of being deported.

Then there was the freedom issue. In Italy, much more so than at home, a good day was about balancing work with life's other needs—family, friends, home, community. In the restaurants where I had worked, the rule was a busy but steady pace, centered on keeping the guests relaxed and happy. During meal breaks, restaurant owners wanted the staff to sit and eat. If they had a question when they saw you eating, they waited until you were finished. And you didn't have to create a way to busy yourself at the stove or risk being criticized if you weren't.

While at anchor one day on the other side of the island and just outside the breakwater of a small marina and village called Sant'Angelo, Rick and I were getting the day together down below when we heard a crack of laughter, applause, and heavy footfalls on deck that began to make their way down below. Moments later, in front of me stood a dripping wet, burly middle-aged man in shorty dive gear holding a speargun in one hand and a magnificent *cernia*—a grouper—in the other.

"*Buon giorno!*" he said with a big smile on his face. "So you are the chef *americano*?" He told me his name was Gianni.

"Where did you come from?" I asked. I could see from the speargun that he either was or fancied himself to be an expert fisherman, but beyond that I had no idea how this guy had found our boat or what he was doing in the galley. He certainly could not have been a friend of the owners, at least not in my mind.

"I'm a friend of Fabrizio's. I live on this side of the island," he explained. Fabrizio was Dennis the Menace's real name. The picture was beginning to fill in.

"Fabrizio asked me to try to catch some fish for the owners. When I caught this beauty, I brought it over, and everyone requested it to be made for lunch. What do you think? How are you going to cook it?" His tone clearly implied that he didn't want some hack American making hamburger out of his catch.

"I could make it in *acqua pazza*," I suggested.

"You know how to make it that way?" He looked shocked.

"Sure," I said.

"How come?" he pressed.

"I learned to make it at a restaurant above Sorrento. *Sono bravi*"—they know what's going on.

"Okay chef," he said in English with a half smile and a look like I had better deliver on the promise.

This fish was perfect for *acqua pazza*. The gentle method of cookery had gotten its name from using something as fresh as this, fortified with tomato, a hint of caper, and parsley and cooked in a miraculous, aromatic bath resembling the purest seawater. With steamed potatoes on the side, the preparation would be optimum.

And this was exactly how I learned it at Don Alfonso.

"Come here," Beppe, the *chef de cuisine* at the restaurant, said one day as he was plating a lunch entrée. "You have to see this. It's called *pesce in acqua pazza*."

"Fish in crazy water?" I asked, not sure if I had translated correctly.

"*Sì, sì, sì*. You'll understand soon," he replied. Alfonso was in the kitchen, too, and he told me that it could be made only in late spring and through the summer, when the tomatoes were ripening on the vine and full of sun, when they were their boldest. It didn't matter which fish you used, he told me, as long as it was flaky and very fresh.

"We serve this with poached new potatoes from our garden," Alfonso continued. "I will show you the garden later," he added. I could see by the way he presented a pot of perfectly pared and poached potatoes that the garden was very special to him.

Local olive oil, the fish, diced tomatoes, capers, chopped parsley, salt, pepper, and the potatoes. That's it.

"The tomatoes," Alfonso started to explain, "must cook down while the fish releases some of its water to create a simple sauce, highlighted with parsley to give it an herbal edge. Then you season lightly with the capers. Once done, the overall flavor will resemble the sea, only better." I thought to myself, that's the trick to using capers— as a seasoning. Over the years I had mixed feelings about capers. Every time they had been used in a dish, their briny taste overpowered every other flavor. But how to avoid that? The villain was the brine. Alfonso showed me the capers that they used. *Capperi sotto sale*. Packed in sea salt, they were larger and plumper than any I had ever seen. The salt was rinsed off, and then the capers were finely chopped. In this way, they could be added like a seasoning to the desired taste. Just enough adds a subtle back flavor of a caper berry, not the brine.

I began to fillet Gianni's fish and took note of the glistening of its firm white flesh. Once I had it broken down and the short list of ingredients prepped, I could feel it would come out well, one of those intangibles cooks can tell as soon as the process of cookery begins. I kept thinking about that day at Don Alfonso. And I remembered Faith told me this was an important dish to learn. Now I was making it on my own. The only foil was the amount of steam and spiraling humidity in the galley, making every pore in my body open up, adding more heat to the already sweltering work space. A total contrast in ambience to the relaxing and jovial banter I could hear from the mid-deck above me, all of the guests under the canopy at the table sipping champagne in anticipation of the dining event. Within such close range, hearing it made me want to be there.

Soon after I sent the fish up, I was summoned to the table. I quickly changed my shirt for a dry one before heading up on deck. Gianni looked at me with a long face and an even longer pause. Then he broke into a huge grin and said, "This is better than how my *paesani* make it. And from an American!" The table erupted with frivolity no doubt fueled by multiple bottles of champagne. *Il Dottore* offered a rare superlative beyond one of his hand signals to communicate exceptional taste: "This is *mitico*"—mythical.

"Bravo!" Dennis added, while to the chorus of praise his wife pronounced it *"da morire"*—to die for.

Gianni also basked in his glory. Having brought a treasure from the sea to the applause of guests and owners, he tried to stretch his moment of triumph by hanging with the crew on the foredeck until *la Signora* not so subtly hinted with a twirl of her finger that the time was ripe for him to don his fins and return to the water. He finally caught on, gave a quick wave, and dove over the side of the boat into the water.

I felt bad for Gianni, but the scene stayed with me because it reminded me of the other side of *la Signora*. When she wanted something, she expected it to happen, and our job was to make it so. Period. Maybe that was a good thing also. The fact that she set her standards high and that she expected the rest of us to reach up to those standards did make a lot of us stretch higher.

But still, whenever there seemed a chance that the two of us might intersect, I consciously avoided her. If I had to go aft, I passed on the other side of the deck. For the most part, she didn't say much to me except to inquire about the menu. *"Cosa c'e di buono a mangiare?"*—What good things are there to eat? Although it was always phrased as an innocent question, something about her tone made me feel it was a cover for a statement that went something like: "It better be what I want, make me look good, and be delicious."

I found it easier for me to communicate with her through the food.

On the eighth of August, we were scheduled to arrive in Ponza, the largest of the Pontine Islands, northwest of Ischia. By now, I was addicted to our trusty mariner's pilot guide. Every island and every port had its own story of lost ships, daring rescues, and exiled monarchs. Ponza would not let me down.

The Romans, it seems, didn't just banish from the court those who found themselves in disfavor or had recently lost power. When necessary, they exported them to the Pontine Islands, whose most famous exiles were the brothers and sisters of the emperor Caligula. When Rome fell, pirates were said to take over the island and with the aid of assorted other sociopaths became its effective rulers for more than a thousand years.

As soon as we approached the island, I was surprised. It didn't look like the other islands we had visited, with chiseled mountains rising from rocky coastlines. Just the opposite, the rock formations were low and seemed to rise right out of the sea, as if the water table had once been lower and the island larger. The island, I would soon learn, is ringed with underwater rock formations. Apparently the others knew what I was just learning—that Ponza, and the other islands in the Pontine archipelago, are merely the highest points of a volcanic eruption that created a much larger landmass, most of it barely underwater and often visible to the naked eye.

Nigel and I stood by the starboard rail on approach, only to see *Serenity* skirt one of the volcanic daggers by what seemed like no more than inches. Neither of us said a word. As we pulled in closer, I saw young people riding inflatable skiffs dashing in and out of Ponza's coves to bask on the smooth rock formations and small white sand beaches. There was something about the island that radiated youth.

Later that morning, as Rick and I were cleaning up after breakfast, *la Signora* came into the pantry.

"Richard and Davide, tomorrow we are going to a small cove where there are some natural *fango*"—mud baths—"nearby. I am taking the ladies onshore for the day. We'd like to leave no later than eleven, so, Richard, we will need the *scafo*"—the launch—"in the water and loaded with everything we'll need. Davide, we'll take lunch with us, so if you can prepare a simple menu, that would be great. We will serve ourselves. The men can fend for themselves."

"No problem, *signora*," Rick quickly replied.

"*Hai capito, Davide?*" she said, snapping me to full concentration.

"*Sì, signora,* I'll take care of it."

The good thing about working for the superrich is that you get to see how they live. That's the bad part as well. Ponza's romantic coves and the inflatable skiffs I saw buzzing in and out of them made me envious. I wanted to be in one of those little boats myself, just once, with a girlfriend of my own, spending a sultry afternoon exploring the island's fascinating coastline—not assembling antipasti in a galley where the temperature easily topped a hundred degrees and was trapped nicely by *Serenity*'s steel hull.

I wasn't well equipped to handle a picnic, but once I put some thought into it, I realized a beach menu wasn't too difficult to compose: marinated chickpeas with arugula to be served with sliced prosciutto, the Tuscan bread salad *panzanella*, and grilled tuna *panini* inspired by *pan bagnat* from the French coast, replacing the canned tuna that is usually used with thin slices of grilled fillets. The ladies wouldn't be cooking anything onshore, just finishing. I figured that with the heat, and without proper refrigeration, I should create a menu made with as much from the pantry as possible since many of those ingredients are already shelf stable. At the same time, I wanted the food to be light, refreshing, and easy to assemble.

One of the challenges I faced was how to keep the salads over a period of time so that they could be dressed and not wilted at the desired time of service. The trick was in the packing, keeping the dressing at the bottom of the container and then layering the salad ingredients, each in order starting from the wettest such as tomatoes on the bottom to the driest such as any herbs or greens. This way, everything on top of the wet ingredients stayed "dry" until lunchtime.

We didn't have a cooler on board, so the bigger challenge was how to keep the food chilled, safe, and in good shape under the hot

August sun. It wasn't as if there were shops along a boardwalk like on the Jersey shore where I could get one. I told Rick I'd figure something out. But his look suggested that this was the least interesting thing he had heard all day. Then I scrambled and came up with a plan. Maybe at the fish shop in town I could get a couple of Styrofoam fish boxes and buy some ice. Once they were thoroughly washed, I could fill the boxes with a layer of ice, then sprinkle a thin layer of salt to solidify the ice to slow down the melting, place the food inside, add another layer of ice to cover, put the lid on, and wrap the boxes in aluminum foil and then garbage bags. If Rick placed them in the shade under some rocks nestled in cool, wet sand, they should be fine. One for food, the other for beverages.

"Don't forget your corkscrew," I needled a miserable-looking Rick as he started the launch's small putt-putt motor and got it ready to pull around to the boarding ladder. It was the first time we put the restored original wood dinghy in the water, a different vessel from the inflatable tender that we normally used.

"I'll be back soon," he said with a grimace. But I noticed he was all smiles when he piloted the boat to the other side of the yacht and offered a hand to each of the women as they boarded—all sporting large designer sunglasses and wide-brimmed sun hats.

It was a girl's day out. "*Adagio*," I heard *la Signora* say to Rick as they pulled away, using the classical music term for a movement that should be played slowly, no doubt a directive to dampen Rick's reputation for speed.

The next morning *il Dottore* invited me to join him onshore as he grabbed Alex's red leash and brought him with us. This was a first—*il Dottore* never spent any social time with me—and I liked the idea. Maybe the "crazy water" lunch with Gianni's grouper finally inspired him to take a deeper look into my world. Nigel and Scott were already in the cockpit polishing the brass when we went to board the tender. Nigel looked like he was off to a slow start that day. Ian told me in the galley they had snuck off in the tender late the night before, rowing it a good distance from *Serenity* before starting the engine and heading to a beachfront discotheque, Frontone, not far down the coast.

Il Dottore and I went into the small commercial port and walked along the stone quay. I was in my *Serenity* uniform while *il Dottore* was in his casual summer attire complete with designer Italian driving shoes. Alex walked ahead of us. At first, we didn't say much aside from small comments about the beauty of Ponza and the tranquillity of the morning. Then I told him I used my early-morning walks to unwind— that they were as much a part of my physical regimen as my sit-ups.

"I see," he said. "Very smart of you." And we ambled a bit farther down the quay. Then he popped a request that coiled me up again.

"Davide, do you think it's possible we could have some meat for dinner one of these nights?" At that moment, even Alex perked up and stared at both of us.

My first sinking thought was *la Signora*'s insistence about eating only fish and seafood. *Il Dottore,* during my interview, sat right next to her when she said that. He knew her rules. Unsure how I would clear this with *la Signora,* I coughed up, "I'll get some on board." At least this would buy me time until I figured out what to do.

Then the inevitable happened. Alex's leash tugged. He circled around one of the bollards next to a pile of fishnets, furrowed his brow, assumed a squatting position, and relieved himself. *Il Dottore* and I looked at each other. Since Alex wasn't mine, I just stood there, not feeling that it was my job to clean up after his dog. Plus, I was about to embark on procuring the day's food. *Il Dottore* had the "I don't take care of this type of thing" expression on his face. Alone, he no doubt would have just kept walking. Now there was a witness. We found ourselves at a crucial impasse. We looked at each other again, looked back at Alex, who didn't care one way or the other, shrugged our shoulders, and walked on. I now felt a little closer to *il Dottore* since I was privy to yet another of his quiet conspiracies. First the pasta fix, then the meat request, now this. I vowed to get him some meat.

After a few days at Ponza and another small island nearby, Palmarola, we weighed anchor for our next destination. I had never felt lower on departure. I loved Ponza. One can claim those little beaches nestled under the cliffs for a day. Even its name is cool.

But there was nothing wrong with Capri. Then again, I had to remind myself, I was seeing these islands, even during high season, from an offshore base. No crowds at sea. And early-morning forays onshore before the world took to the streets continually offered the chance to get a taste of a day in the life from the places we were in, and this was a great one.

I walked up a fairly steep and narrow road to the town of Capri, a route I remembered from a previous visit. The wildflowers in full bloom were as colorful as I remembered them. Along an old stone wall at the side of the road, a massive growth of purplish blue morning glories were basking in the sun. I was struck by the hand-painted ceramic tiles posted or inserted in the walls in front of the homes with the residents' names or house numbers adorned with caricatures of fish or sea creatures swimming around them. And the view of the sea, with *Serenity* at anchor below, gently bobbing in the shimmering water, was glorious.

A quick cappuccino in one of the *caffès* in the *piazzetta* at the town center was apropos before starting my quest. The key was being *in* the *caffè*, since at the bar a cappuccino would be a couple of bucks. Had I taken a seat outside, it could easily be ten or even twelve. It's one of those fairly consistent things throughout the land, but in highbrow places like Capri, especially in summer, prices were a little higher. Plus, a little harmless eavesdropping on the locals was a great pastime. Women spoke about social gatherings, men about soccer.

As had become the norm, I let the markets and shops drive my menu planning. I went to the *forno* to get in on the first bake, and asked if they could hold my purchase until I returned. This way there would be less bulk in transit through the very narrow and bustling pedestrian-only streets in town. Then I passed one of the *latterie,* and the feature for that day's lunch jumped out. The delivery must have been dropped off minutes before I arrived because what was in front of me was incredible. Three cheeses from the same vat of milk: *caciotta,* the first cheese pulled from the curds that are then formed in small wicker baskets, was still draining whey in the tub it was delivered in; jumbo egg-shaped balls of *fior di latte* mozzarella, made from those same curds and so fresh they were still tepid, were floating in a milky brine to season them; puffy snow-white ricotta—curds from the reboiled whey—in little plastic conical baskets had a little steam rising from their milk-fatty tops as the cheese settled into the molds. The only other way to get cheese fresher than this would be to have a cow on the boat! I took a kilo of each on sight alone. They'd be in perfect shape by the time they were served at lunch with thick slices of tomato, a healthy drizzle of extra virgin olive oil, and crystals of coarse sea salt. A slight departure from the ubiquitous *insalata caprese,* this version with a trio of fresh cheeses was true to form.

I *had* to take one of the little convertible taxis, unique to the island, back down the hill. These modified Fiats from the 1950s are to Capri what yellow cabs are to Manhattan. And the drivers were funny guys. The taxi I chose was bright blue, others were red, and I saw a couple that were pink and yellow. Most of them had a decoration attached to the front grille, like a bouquet of plastic flowers or some kind of stuffed animal.

But back on board, the long days and incessant heat were beginning to take their toll down below. Scott, our regulator of power distribution, refrained from turning on the air conditioner in the fo'c'sle. With the owners and guests on board and our constant nights at anchor, most of the available juice went to the aft areas of the boat. We had to be satisfied with the occasional slight breeze that came through our small portholes.

"Get used to it" was all he said in answer to our pleas for cool air.

It was also in Capri that *la Signora* first began to venture into the galley. She walked in one day with a bagful of hard-to-find *tartufi di mare*—sea truffles—small clams whose shells resemble truffles. Apparently, she hit the fish shop at just the right moment. "They don't show up every day and are gone quickly when they do come in," she explained to me, adding, "Delicacies like this are valued by those who have an eye for them.

"*Per favore,*" she asked me, "could we have them on the half shell, nice and cold, with a little lemon on the side? That can be our first course at lunch."

She was keen on having them, like the sea urchins, *crudo*—raw.

It wasn't long before *il Dottore* made his way to the galley to see his companion's catch.

"How did she ask you to prepare them?" he asked.

"Raw with just a little lemon," I replied, following directions.

"I want them steamed," he shot back.

I didn't know what to say or what to do.

"It's unhealthy how she wants them. Who knows what kind of water they were in," he said.

He excused himself and went up on deck. Moments later, *la Signora* called for me to come to the deck, and I found myself dead center in a debate over a sack of clams.

"Raw is the right way—it is summer—this is how you eat them," she lobbied.

"You don't know what the water is like," he answered.

"*Amore,* look at the blue—there is nothing wrong with this water."

"I just want you to be healthy. Steaming them will make sure you don't get sick."

"Do you think I would eat something to make me or any of my guests sick?"

"Why take the chance? What's wrong with steaming them?" *Il Dottore* looked to the guests, trying to sway support to his side. No one blinked an eye, fearing it might be taken as support one way or the other.

"*Scusi,* if I may," I said, realizing that an intervention was in order. "How about if I make them half one way and half the other?"

They both looked at me. It was quiet for a few seconds, and then they both said, "*Va bene.*"

A day later, news came down to me through Rick that I was about to have another chef in the kitchen. Rick, ever the crew conduit for owner gossip, reported that *la Signora* had announced to her guests that she would be preparing her signature dish, *spaghetti con astice—*spaghetti with lobster—the next afternoon.

Rick continued that the guests, led by Dennis of course, lustily clapped and cheered at this announcement.

La Signora came down to the galley the next day, her hair pulled back into a ponytail and tied with a scarf that gently fell over her chocolate brown one-piece bathing suit. A large white towel was wrapped around her middle. This was the first time we had ever been alone, for the rest of the crew somehow disappeared on deck.

She prodded and inspected the ingredients I had prepared in advance. She had requested lobsters with claws—*astice*—not the local spiny lobsters—*aragosta*—that didn't have claws. "More meat and more flavor," she told me. I was curious about this preference since *astice* are not indigenous to the Mediterranean. By the time she arrived in the galley, I had broken them down into pieces—claws, knuckles, the tails cut into three, and the bodies—according to her instructions. I also provided two kinds of oil, extra virgin and sunflower; a couple of onions; garlic cloves; fresh, ripe, peeled and halved San Marzano tomatoes; whole *peperoncini;* parsley; and of course spaghetti. She gave a quiet "*perfetto*" as she touched each ingredient.

To fill the silence, I stammered some unintelligible stream of nonsense about the day, realizing too late that my hard-earned knowledge of formal Italian had suddenly failed me. I looked up only to see Alex watching *la Signora* through the hatch above.

She dipped a finger into the oil and touched it to her tongue approving my choice. I helped her get the burners on the stove started and adjusted two flames, since the pan was large and the stove was small.

La Signora started to cook, placing a little of each oil in the pan while contemplating if she should add more of either. The onions and garlic went into the pan to heat with the oil, then simmered slowly to soften and release their aromatics. She slowly tossed them with a wooden spoon, giving this initial step a lot of concentration to seemingly find the place where a cook becomes focused on the pace of cookery. She added some of the drained tomato water to the oil to help braise and soften the onions. After tossing them around for a couple of minutes, she scraped out the pulp from each piece of onion and removed the remaining outer layers from the pan, voicing her theory that onions should not be visible in a dish since the solids are hard to digest. I had never seen anyone do this before. No wonder she cooked with low heat and asked me to cut them into large pieces.

Then she added the tomatoes and chiles to the pan. As the tomatoes heated up and the liquid around them came back to a simmer, she carefully crushed them to release more juice. At the same time, the tomato pulp began to blend with the oil in the pan. Then she added the lobster—claws, knuckles, and bodies first with any of the water that had fallen to the bottom of the bowl. After four or five minutes, while she tossed the pieces in the oil, she added the tails, all the time keeping the heat at an even simmer.

I had no idea if I should be making any conversation, and I certainly didn't want to correct any of her cooking, so I found it easier to just sit at the edge of the mess table bench and watch. In fact, she didn't need my help. She cooked with a confidence that impressed me, not only her handling of the ingredients but what her eyes and hands were telling her. But even better than how she cooked was the way she looked—calm, always in perfect posture, every movement and task methodical and precise. It was clear she'd done this before.

Finally the silence got to me, and out of left field I asked her a question: "Just curious, *signora*, how come there are no women in the crew?"

She chuckled and made a gesture toward the fo'c'sle. "With those conditions, do you think a woman could stand it? There'd be too many problems."

She checked for seasoning, added another chile, and pulled the pan from the stove when the lobster meat in the tails turned opaque. She kept the bodies in the sauce for a short while longer, gently crushing them with a wooden spoon to get as much flavor out of them as possible before discarding them. It was hot and humid in the galley, the air thick with the smell of cooked lobster and simmering tomato sauce. I noticed a light mist of perspiration had formed across the back of *la Signora*'s neck and shoulders.

"*Bene,*" she said, smiling at the results as if just completing a painting, "now I leave the rest to you.

"Just before it goes to the table, roughly chop the parsley and add on top of the pasta. And make sure you taste some of it," she said, indicating with a look that if I could improve it I should. I noticed she had left without a touch of sauce on her bright white towel. On the way through the pantry she asked Rick in perfect French to give the five-minute call to table so that everyone could be seated.

"It's incredible," he said when he came into the galley to inspect her culinary prowess. "She speaks better French than I do. Make sure you save a little for me, too, *d'accord?*"

I tasted the spaghetti with a morsel of lobster. Should I have been surprised? Like everything else about her, the dish was elegant. No one ingredient overpowered the others. Even the chile pepper, so easy to overdo, was strong enough to make the sauce hot but not spicy. The lobster was succulent and tender and had just enough briny sweetness to retain its noble status. Obeying my chef for the day, I roughly chopped the parsley and sprinkled it over the pasta to add a little herbal freshness that cut through the rich sauce. My only regret was that I couldn't add a note to the platter expressing my compliments.

The next morning we set sail, heading toward the southern side of the Sorrento Peninsula, our destination the Amalfi coast. Our first stop was to be the small harbor of Marina del Cantone. It was a leisurely three-hour ride that took us to what many believe is the most beautiful coastline in Italy. Before we got to the tip of the peninsula, Mount Vesuvius was in constant view in the hazy distance. I was grateful to be on deck the moment we passed the tip of the peninsula, for high up and long abandoned sat the Church of San Costanzo. I had visited it when I worked at Don Alfonso. Except for a single tree, it sat alone guarding the high point of the peak of the peninsula, remote and stark. I can only imagine what the eyes of this church had seen over the centuries, with its unobstructed view of the open sea. I remembered Alfonso telling me that along the winding road that leads up to that landmark grows peppery *rucola selvatica*—wild arugula. Out of respect to the foragers who brought it to market, *la rucola* is served on virtually every local menu.

When we arrived, a nice perk was in store for us. The owners invited the entire crew to celebrate *la Signora*'s birthday at the popular restaurant Lo Scoglio in Marina del Cantone, a quaint little seaside encampment huddled next to a line of waterside restaurants where we dined among locals and the well-heeled visitors that flock to the coast.

A table for fifteen waited for us on a shaded deck reaching out over the water's edge.

All of us in the crew sat to one end—perhaps a force of habit since we weren't directed that way—a group of seven men in *Serenity* uniforms, white short-sleeved button-down shirts with blue shorts and dock shoes. *Il Dottore* and his friends were in pastel shirts and khaki-type shorts, somewhat conspicuous in the fine leather loafers they wore without socks. The yachtie saying "You can always tell who is who on the boat . . . the one with the Swatch is the owner, and the one with the Rolex is the crew member" rang true since apart from his uniform, Kevin proudly wore the fancy new chronograph he picked up just before leaving France. The ladies came onshore with their de rigueur casual style—brilliant-colored sheer blouses over their bathing suits with sarongs or pullover short dresses, all sporting plenty of jewelry. It was amazing how they could carry on with all of the hand gestures that accompanies the Italian language and not be impeded by their large and ornate bracelets, watches, and necklaces.

La Signora ordered for everyone: *involtini di melanzane*—rolled eggplants filled with mozzarella; *antipasti di pesci*—various marinated fish and seafood; *frittelle di frutti di mare*—crisp shellfish beignets; vegetable dishes; pastas; whole roasted fish entrées; Neapolitan pastries like *baba au rhum* yeast cakes soaked in rum syrup and crispy ricotta-filled *sfogliatelle*.

We were all having fun until a dock attendant passed word that *Serenity* was dragging anchor and starting to drift. Kevin immediately excused himself to deal with the emergency. To those of us who knew him, the look on his face showed what he was really thinking: Patrick should have been the first to jump upon hearing any news about a boat emergency. But Patrick sat still, and off Kevin went while the rest of us finished lunch with ice-cold shots of homemade *limoncello*—a local cordial made with lemons macerated in grain alcohol and sugar.

The alcohol content must have been really high, for after a single glass my movements slowed.

A couple of hours later, we motored along the magnificent coast to Positano, arriving just before dusk. Patrick had slowed the boat down to a crawl as we approached the anchorage in perfectly still air. We were the only ones, about a hundred yards offshore, where we'd stay at night for the next short week. I had grown up with a vague idea about this fishing village turned upscale destination, having been told stories of wonderment from my parents. And from working at Don Alfonso, I knew this was where expensive boutique hotels and rental homes were embedded among the multigenerational neighborhoods of the locals. As sunset turned into evening, the colorful glazed majolica dome of the Church of Santa Maria Assunta just behind the center of the beach gave way to an expanse of small white lights adorning the buildings on the two hillsides that flanked us.

The next day I was getting ready for lunch service when Rick came down below, seemingly excited. "*La Signora* is in a very good mood and is holding court. The drinks are working extra fast today!" he shot out, preparing another round.

Amused, I asked, "What's going on up there?"

"They're doing what they always do—talk about all the people in the gossip magazines!" Then he flashed his mischievous grin. "But soon it will shift, and then it will be over."

"What will be over?" I wasn't sure what he meant.

"Yes, *finito*. There are two things I've noticed that tone her down," he said before sharing his theory. "If we're sailing hard, she doesn't ask for much and only looks at the water. And while out in the sun, after a second drink, she'll take a nap on deck for the rest of the day."

When *la Signora* and her guests took to seclusion, there wasn't much for him to do. Now I understood. Rick was after a little downtime.

He looked like a mad scientist as he began to assemble another tray of *caipirinhas,* a spirited Brazilian drink made with *cachaça*—a clear distillate made from sugarcane—shaken with slices of limes muddled with sugar and ice. Earlier in the season, *il Dottore* had instructed Rick how to mix this potent cocktail by making it a little strong, almost a double.

"Time to party!" he said as he left with a full tray of filled rocks glasses. "Then maybe I'll have the afternoon off!" I wondered if *la Signora* appreciated how often Rick became the instigator of a good time *for everyone.*

My only downtime—very early morning or late evening—bookended each day. A cappuccino among locals onshore in the morning and a whiskey after service on the foredeck at night. Alex, a smart pedigree hunting dog, also knew where to go for a late-night treat, for each night I put leftovers from the owners' meals in a dish for him. Why not? I'd look at him and remember an Italian proverb, *"Si lavorato come un cane"*—to work like a dog. I thought about this as I watched him lick his bowl clean and lie down near my feet. Alex lived like a king while I worked. Now deep into August I found myself working *più d'un cane*—harder than a dog. I am sure Alex somehow understood, as suggested by the tilt of his head, when I lamented about the heat and hours.

In a resort town where it seemed most folks dined in restaurants, called for room service, or were served on private terraces, procurement became its own problem, especially for fifteen. By now, I no longer cared about the inflated food prices and readily told Patrick I needed more money. But still, I had to find the food. There was no open-air market, so that was out. Eventually I realized I would have to make do with a cache of boutique shops for fruits and vegetables, a small *alimentario*—grocery shop for other things—and a fish shop near the beach that actually wasn't bad. The wife of the fishmonger was proud to have us as a customer, noting how beautiful the boat was and even asking about the cruise. I think she was taken by the romance of living on a boat—going somewhere, eating well, and coming back to the anchorage at night. And *Serenity* did look attractive from the shop's front door while at anchor just offshore.

Of course, she was also surprised that Italians who could afford such a large boat would have a foreign cook. But eventually we became friends, and on my last day in port she gave me a gift of homemade *limoncello*. It was another one of those very genuine Italian gestures.

I returned to the galley to find Scott peacefully reading at the mess table, sipping his comforting cup of steaming tea. The engine room door was wide open, and the heat just about knocked me down.

"This climate is brutal," I said, lifting my marketing bags onto the counter next to the stove. Scott didn't offer to help as I began to unpack.

"We're going to the Galli islands tomorrow," he finally said a half minute later, never looking up from his book.

"Where's that?" I asked.

"They're just down the coast," Scott answered. "We passed them the other day. Didn't you see them?"

I hadn't, probably because I was in the galley.

I sat down, relieved to have a momentary diversion from dealing with the stores, and looked at the book in Scott's hands. Homer's *Odyssey*.

A little heavy for a summer read, I thought to myself. Scott turned the book around to show me a passage.

"Here, mate, read about the Sirens. That's where we're going." He finished his tea in one enormous gulp and walked out, leaving the dirty cup on the mess table, and also the book, facedown, open to the page he was reading.

I pushed the cup away, slid into the mess bench, and started reading. A particular passage caught my eye, the section, I think, that Scott was referring to. It was the part where Circe, the sorceress, warns Odysseus about the Sirens at Galli:

> *But if you yourself should wish to listen to the Sirens, get your men to bind you hand and foot with ropes against the mast-step. In this way you may listen in rapture to the voices of the two Sirens. But should you begin to beg your comrades to unloose you, you must make sure that they bind you even more tightly.*

The next day I heard the guests *and the crew* splash in the cool, deep waters at the anchorage between the three small islands of Galli while I continued to slave away in the galley. It slowly drove me nuts. It may have been my imagination, but something about the place seemed to pull me. Maybe Homer was onto something.

Emerald Blues

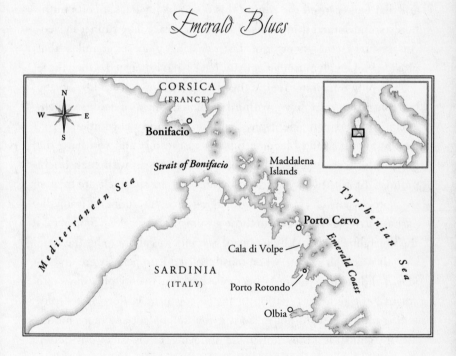

Sardinia and the Emerald Coast

*M*arathoners know the feeling. It's called "hitting the wall." It happens as mile twenty approaches, when all the training and grit that have carried the runner this far suddenly flags. Sports nutritionists understand it in terms of body chemistry. The runner's glycogen reserves, the storage of fast-releasing glucose granules that provide fuel for all muscular activity, have been exhausted. Once these go, the only remaining fuel is the slower-burning fatty acids. So the body begins to shut down, with exhaustion acting as a defense mechanism to avoid permanent physical damage. Add dehydration, overheating, nausea, and bleeding nipples to the mix and you have the makings of a miserable end to an event that began with such bright promise. At mile twenty-six, those witnessing the spectacle are treated to a procession of contorted, grimacing faces as runners, from the earliest-arriving champions to those gasping last stragglers, limp across the finish line in pain. Life on board *Serenity* was about to hit the wall.

It was high season, when most civilized Europeans were on holiday. I didn't think I would become sour, but twenty-plus days into August, the *ferie* was getting to me. I began to wallow in self-pity, telling myself I might not make it if the fatigue got any more numbing, my gimbal-less stove any more annoying, or my galley any hotter. I calculated that since the owners had moved on board, I was working about 112 hours of the 168 hours in each week. When not shopping, prepping, cooking, or cleaning up a galley hot enough to fry an egg on any flat surface, I was on deck, lending a hand to the crew, hoisting sails, coiling lines, or helping with maneuvers. That left me a grand total of fifty-six hours to myself, something like eight hours per twenty-four-hour cycle for all my own needs, of which sleep took six. Although I was getting sounder sleep, I wondered what had changed about my bunk. I recalled tossing and turning on it through many an interrupted night during my early months on board. Now I fell asleep within seconds of my head hitting the pillow. I guessed that if you work a man hard enough, a stone slab will feel like a king's feather bed.

We remained at anchor in front of Positano for a couple more nights before heading west to the island of Sardinia. After calculating it would take us thirty-five hours to cross the Tyrrhenian Sea, we planned to leave on Saturday evening, allowing for a dawn arrival on Monday. For the first time, we would be making a two-night passage with owners and guests on board.

Rick and I were excused from daytime watch duties so we could prepare and serve, should the owners need us. By early evening, the owners and their six guests had finished their meal and were lounging around the cockpit enjoying the ambient glow of looming dusk that covered the open sea as we headed toward the setting sun. From what Rick was able to understand, the talk was about taking it easy and the next night, repairing to bed early in order to awaken upon our arrival at one of the near-deserted white sand and clear water coves that can be found all along the Costa Smeralda—the Emerald Coast—the name given to Sardinia's exclusive northeastern coastline. As I washed the last pots and pans and tidied the galley, Rick joined me at the mess table to share the few end-of-day minutes that we had to ourselves.

We motor-sailed for this passage, meaning we used the engine with a few of the sails up to give us extra propulsion and, at the same time, lessen our fuel consumption. Once the boat was far enough offshore, the evening sea breezes gave some relief from the August heat. But it was not just the break of the heat that was so welcome. When under way, you feel as if you are cutting through the sea with the sharpest of knives, and I was savoring the smoothness of the ride as well.

The rest of the night and the whole of the next day we carried on with our duties to keep the boat in transit, the hum of the engines constant below deck. The owners and guests took on the slumbered look of a long voyage, didn't ask for much, read a lot, and I am sure got something from staring at nothing but water and the horizon on all sides for hours on end. It's amazing how seductive that view can be. A couple of times we watched dolphins swim with the boat and frolic in the bow wake. *La Signora's* only request for the meals was to keep things *molto semplice*—very simple—a directive I welcomed. And my friend Alex spent most of his time out of the sun in the chart house.

By eight or eight-thirty on the second night, a little chop was starting to build up, nothing big, just a slight change in the calm seas. Neither Rick nor I remarked on it, until our conversation was inter-rupted by the sound of footsteps—fast, assertive footsteps—coming down from the deck. Whoever it was, he was not coming down for a cup of coffee. It was Patrick who popped into the galley. "Suit up, guys. There's some bad weather coming our way."

Damn, I thought. There went those extra couple hours of sleep I desperately needed.

Normally a gale forecast would have kept us in port or required a move to a safe anchorage or protected marina that could handle a boat as large as *Serenity.* But by the time the squall hit us, we were on the open sea. With no place to hide, we would have to face the ele-ments. It was going to be one of the blowing forces of Mother Nature that the Mediterranean Sea is known for—a mistral from France, the *libeccio, ponente,* or *tramontana* from Italy, or the African *scirocco* that can bring with it the red sand of the Sahara desert—that would con-front us.

I had been on stormy seas before, and although gales are never pleasant, especially for those who get the least bit queasy under any circumstances, fear wasn't first on my mind. Work was. Everything in the galley had to be secured as quickly as possible. Then I had to go on deck to help the crew. Within minutes, I was pretty confident that nothing in the galley was capable of becoming a missile. Before climbing the ladder, I put on my foul-weather gear, which included a life vest and harnesses that could quickly be hooked to the boat in case we had to leave the cockpit and move about the deck. I took a minute to remind myself of the first law of working at sea in heavy conditions: One hand firmly on the boat, the other for the task.

Even before I reached the top step of the ladder I could feel that the wind had already kicked up and I could hear Patrick and Kevin yelling out their commands. On deck I understood why. You need to yell to be heard above the sound of the angry, building sea and increasing wind. When I got to the aft deck, I peered skyward, but the heavens and all the stars were gone, replaced by a huge black bowl that seemed to have been placed facedown over the boat and the sea around us. Patrick had the decklights turned on, but the circle of light they created around the boat emphasized the blackness that extended in every direction.

Every member of the crew was already on deck diligently tying down or stowing anything still loose, double-checking each other's efforts to be sure that nothing could come free at an inopportune time. Rick came to tell me that the owners, guests, and Alex were in the salon. He also told me that Patrick's plan was to hold on and keep going rather than run away from it. I was impressed. You don't rush to meet a gale unless you believe in not only your own seamanship but that of the crew. Still, I thought, it was going to be a long night.

A few minutes later, Patrick altered course and brought the boat into the wind. Kevin, Ian, Rick, and I went out to the foredeck, the most dangerous part of the boat in heavy conditions, to drop the headsails and tie them down while Nigel pulled the storm jib from below in the forepeak. We hanked the small sail on the forestay and raised it to help stabilize the boat. This early preparation was precautionary, so no one would have to go forward later with the heavier weather on us.

Kevin was wound up tight, yelling crisp commands. "We need to put a double reef in the mainsail! Ian, ease off the main halyard jigs! Scott, center the boom! Nigel, bring on the backstays hard! Rick and David, get on the halyards and ease down the sail. Everyone else flake it as it comes down, and then haul out the reefing lines and tie them off at their points—*quick*!" This would decrease the area of the sail to compensate for the stronger winds and also help stabilize the boat at the aft end. Then we dropped the foresail and furled it securely as fast as we could, sans our normal meticulous sail-folding procedure.

By midnight, the swirling wind had grown to a force that I guessed to be between thirty and forty knots, with irregular gusts even higher. The boat was jumping in the deepening chop. A fluke *libeccio*, I was told, had met up with northwesterly winds, and we were about to be caught in the maelstrom.

With each roll from side to side or pitching up-and-down movement of the boat, I could hear the pots, pans, kitchenwares, and the bottles, jars, and cans of the pantry ingredients banging against the walls of the cabinets and against each other. I decided to go down below again to check it out. Better to have them play bumper car with each other than for them to be flying around, I decided. Then I double-checked to see that all the portholes were tightly closed in the galley and fo'c'sle. Earlier, Rick had gone into the salon and cabins to do the same. At the same time, Scott was coming out of the engine room after battening down and stowing anything loose. With the engine running at high RPM, the noise was deafening.

Back on deck I could see wave crests breaking in every direction, filling the air with clusters of spraying seawater. As we were heading into the seas, those that came on deck slapped us from head to toe, drenching us. Sometimes, the slaps came so hard I wondered if with just a little carelessness on my part, one would finally knock me down and wash me out into the black sea. It was safest to stay aft since that was the only part of the boat rigged with lifelines. Which explained the second law of prudence in foul weather: Look out for your mates, so that when the gale was over, everyone could be accounted for. I could see that the others were always looking around, taking a mental count of everyone else on deck. Patrick also ordered us to be on the lookout for other boats that might present a risk of collision.

Occasionally, between slaps, the seas calmed themselves, a momentary break between wave sets. But I kept alert while waiting for the next assault, knowing that the Mediterranean can be a tricky sea. There was a sensation of being in a car driven along a deeply pitted road, not knowing when the car and its passengers would dunk into one really deep ditch from which we would never climb out again.

The boat may have been taking a beating, but Patrick's skill at the helm was gaining my respect. From crest to trough, the boat was pointed directly into and up over the next rising wave. He never seemed to lose control.

There are times, of course, when even the most competent captain cannot guarantee survival in a serious storm at sea. Sometimes the best chances of riding through heavy weather lie in keeping a boat like this "hove to," which would point us almost directly into the face of the wind. But that wasn't the end of our woes. We had to constantly make sure nothing broke in the rig or on deck. Once a boat starts to break up, things get even more challenging while the wind is howling.

Serenity's 150 tons seemed light in the violent weather, and I caught myself wondering if the vessel had been tested in storm conditions similar to these. I was constantly listening for the sounds I had been told come before a breakup. But I heard not a creak, shimmer, or whine. Her rigid submarine-standard construction was more than enough to ward off the pounding seas being thrown at her. After sixty years of handling the forces of Mother Nature, *Serenity* gave us a great sense of security.

During a lull, Rick and I went down below to the salon to see if the guests needed anything. There was no way that I would be asked to prepare meals or even snacks under these conditions, but Rick offered everyone bottled water. *Il Dottore* nodded in the direction of *la Signora,* who was sitting in the corner of the salon with Alex's head on her lap, uncharacteristically quiet and looking even more uncomfortable than the others, showing clear signs of *mal di mare*—seasickness.

"Richard," *il Dottore* said to Rick, "maybe we can make some tisane for the ladies?"

Scott was really good about keeping the batteries fully charged, so I decided we'd use the electric teapot rather than try to heat water on the stove. I placed it in the sink in the galley to deal with hotwater splashes following a violent pitch of the boat. We also used the crew's deep coffee mugs so that we could fill them halfway.

By now the conditions had picked up again, and even the simplest movement, such as walking from the mess table to the sink, took extraordinary effort. You attempt to use your thigh muscles to counteract the pitch and yaw of the boat and keep your body vertical. But after a period of time struggling to process the flood of ever-changing messages it is getting, your inner ear goes on strike. You are no longer able to signal whether you are straight upright or leaning one way or another, and so moving around becomes difficult. It was maddening for both Rick and me, especially since we were in the forward section of the boat, where it rolls the most. At one point, he sneered upward at the unseen guests. "Let's see if Dennis wants his American breakfast now."

Through the long night, the heavy weather would intermittently abate, then intensify, and we would be called up on deck again. I lost all sense of the clock. My only measure of time was that the boat was still afloat and we were all still alive. We had a berth reservation in Porto Cervo on the northwest tip of the Emerald Coast for arrival at some point later that day, but Patrick notified us that he planned to head considerably farther south to tuck ourselves into the lee of the island, south of the port of Olbia, to escape the continuing wrath of the wind.

A few hours later it worked. There was no single moment when we all knew we had passed out of the storm, but as the winds died down, we exchanged simple smiles that communicated more than hoops and hollers could ever have conveyed. By late morning, we were cruising up the coast of Sardinia headed for Porto Cervo. After the storm, the distant sea and the sky were a mirrored crystalline blue. The air had that hyper-clean, post-squall smell. The calm waters beneath us were truly emerald green, and the residual swell of the sea was easier to take than the night of bouncing and pounding.

After midday, we finally anchored a few miles below our destination, late but safe. The original plan, from what seemed like a lifetime ago, called for the owners and their guests to retire early, to get an early start on their first day in Sardinia in one of those secluded bays or inlets the coast is known for. Instead, they had not retired until close to dawn, when they, too, knew the danger was over. *Il Dottore* was the first to come up on deck. He wanted to see for himself what damage the boat had sustained and to make sure none of his crew had been injured. Everyone was tired, soaked, even bruised. But we all assured him we were okay. He suggested we take a rest as well.

We rinsed off some of the saltwater residue that had found its way into our crew quarters and tidied up the fallen clutter. Rick and I did an inventory of service ware to see what, if anything, had been broken. Nothing had been. The custom cutout shelves in the cabinets for holding the china vertical and glassware rigid proved their worthiness. Then everyone took a round of naps. *Il Dottore* made clear we were in no rush to get anywhere, that resting in the anchorage was fine with him.

Throughout the afternoon, the guests were awakening. As they arrived on deck, *la Signora* convinced them that the best remedy for the remnants of seasickness was toast with soft but not melted mozzarella and an anchovy fillet on top. No oil, no seasoning. Good thing

I had provisioned some of the iconic cheese before leaving the region of Campania. I made a platter, and all were satisfied.

In the early evening, we pulled up the hook and motored until the distinctive architecture of Porto Cervo came into sight. On what was once an uninhabited coastline, buildings and homes had been designed to blend with the natural landscape by virtue of shape, color, and materials used. The curved, organic forms of the roofs and walls blended modernism with a nod to Sardinia's dramatic coastal geography. From a distance, many of the structures were hard to see. The low rise and forms of the edifices followed the contours of the rocky terrain. In addition, clever landscaping matched the natural growth of island plants and brush. It is a fascinating sight, like nothing anywhere else. The view of the sea from these hillside residences, terraces, and private gardens must have been magnificent.

We entered the harbor under the guidance of the showy marina attendants in their overpowered inflatable skiffs that served as tugboats. The modern marina was ringed with restaurants and high-end designer boutiques. Everything was very clean and well maintained.

After the events of the past forty-eight hours I needed to take a quick walk onshore just to get off the boat. And it only took a few steps to experience what it felt like to have sea legs. It was kind of funny, walking on land with a slight, uncontrollable sway as if still in a rolling sea. Others onshore probably thought I was either drunk or a neophyte. Regardless, I knew this would be our final port of call with the owners on board, and I experienced a momentary lift.

Sardinia is Italy's second-largest island, a rugged mountainous land that lies about as close to North Africa as to the mother country only 112 miles away. Because of its colorful history, the island can be described as part Italian and part none of your business. Its motto could be "Don't bother us." So if the *sardi*—Sardinians—are a bit xenophobic, it's with good cause. The island has been held by just about every invading force in Mediterranean history. As the coast was vulnerable to numerous attacks, the mountainous interior hosted longer occupations.

First it was the Phoenicians who decided the island was a perfect base for western Mediterranean trading. The Carthaginians under Hannibal followed, giving way in a skirmish to the Romans, who in turn let the prior inhabitants move inland. After the Romans, the Vandals arrived, while the *sardi* staged a guerrilla war on the coastal occupiers until they grew weary, allowing the *sardi* to come back and reclaim their shoreline cities. But conquest didn't end, as Byzantines, Saracens, Spaniards, Genovese, and Pisans all had a hand in Sardinia's affairs, the latter two being called upon in an effort to keep the Moors out. The kingdom of Sardinia formed during the later occupations, and eventually, while under the rule of the house of Savoy, Sardinia was annexed to Piedmont. Finally, both regions joined what was to become a unified Italy in 1861. With such a pedigree, even though Sardinians speak Italian, they remain a distinct kind of Italian.

That is, until speculators and entrepreneurs armed with blueprints and cold cash did what the invading armies didn't do—develop a section of the island's northeastern coastline into an exclusive reserve for the very rich. A longtime yachtsman's secret, one of the last undiscovered stretches of land in the Mediterranean offered small coves and bays, white sandy beaches, and some of the clearest water in the sea. Development began in 1961, led by Aga Khan IV—a prominent Middle Eastern philanthropist whose hereditary post required him to engage in social and community leadership—and a consortium of high-profile Italian architects. With strict building codes and high costs of entry, the result was the Costa Smeralda—the Emerald Coast—an aesthetically and environmentally pleasing luxury oasis.

If I harbored any hope of even a brief Sardinian vacation, it was dashed by a visit the next morning from *la Signora,* clearly past her *mal de mare.* "Davide," she said, "we will be hosting a final end-of-*ferie* party at the end of the week." She told me there would be somewhere in the "*vicino*"—neighborhood—of sixty guests. I made it a point to hit the *supermercato* as soon as we got back to port that day. It was the only food near the harbor, and I had to make sure I could provision the event. If I couldn't find it all there, I'd have to figure something out fast.

But further bad news was awaiting me when I went up to the foredeck a short while later. Another boat was approaching us, a fairly large motor yacht.

"It's the kids," Rick said.

Sure enough, even from the distance, it looked like the yacht that was next to us in Monte Carlo.

"See that boat behind them," Rick said, pointing to what looked like a maxi-class sailboat in tow. "That's the kids' day sailer. What a toy."

The yacht was heading right for us. Rick then reported he had caught *la Signora*'s voice saying over the radio in the chart house, "*Vieni, vieni,*"—come, come—and I realized this was no random meeting but a prearranged rendezvous. I soon caught sight of the owners' children, and then it hit me.

La Signora was not going to welcome the children without serving them something. I went below, like a kid slumping way down in his seat to avoid being called on. *La Signora* followed me down to the galley. "There will be fourteen at the table, and I'd like to sit down in forty-five minutes."

When she saw the lack of joy on my face, she reminded me, "Davide, an emergency menu, *per favore*, like we discussed." She gave me approval to use pasta for the main course.

I had made plans to serve eight a lunch of shrimp and tomato salad with basil dressing, baked *ricciola*—an amberjack—with *peperonata*, and a parfait dessert of peaches and strawberries with whipped mascarpone. I wasn't going to throw away my earlier prep. This is where the great extenders—bread, pasta, and cookies—came in.

I began with assorted crostini—thinly sliced pieces of toasted bread served with a variety of toppings. For the first, I gently baked the amberjack, flaked it, carefully mixed it with some julienned pieces of green olive, lemon zest, lots of minced parsley, and light-style extra virgin olive oil. For number two, reworked canned chickpeas became a spread to be topped by the cooked shrimp, which I sliced in half lengthwise, thereby doubling the yield. I finished these with a drizzle of olive oil and a few turns of black pepper. I diced the tomatoes, added a little garlic and more seasonings, mixed in the basil dressing, and used that as the third topping.

For the second course, I chopped the *peperonata* and blended it with some marinara—another great extender—that I had made previously for the crew lunch. Some crushed chiles to make it *pepitoso,* the way they liked it, and *ecco!,* instant pasta sauce. *La Signora* preferred penne since it was easier to eat at a crowded table. I finished the dish by grating over the pasta Sardinian pecorino—a dry and pungent sheep's milk cheese that I had picked up earlier at the supermarket.

Once the guests began eating, I turned to dessert. My original idea of layering the fruits and mascarpone in individual glasses like a parfait had to be shelved. As if a lightbulb suddenly flashed in my mind, I recalled a syrup method I had seen the great chef Jacques Pépin make on television years ago. I grabbed some apricot preserves from the pantry and blended them with a nice splash of cognac, thinned the mixture to light-syrup consistency with a little tepid water, and strained out the pieces of fruit. I brushed *savoiardi*—ladyfinger cookies—in the syrup, the same way as when making tiramisu. The cookies were arranged on the platter as a base, topped by a layer of sliced peaches, then a layer of halved strawberries. I spooned the remaining syrup over the fruits and stirred freshly grated nutmeg into the cream that was to be served on the side. A slightly grandiose presentation on a platter offered a bit of that *abbondanza* thing *la Signora* liked at dining events. Kevin, curious as to how I was going to handle the last-minute crisis, watched from the mess table, offering a hand if needed, and was impressed with how I spun the menu. As he left the galley, knowing how much time and effort were put into a meal that went through a last-minute makeover, he offered a roundabout compliment: "Better you than me."

To be truthful, even though I might complain about not having been given sufficient warning, I knew I could handle this type of situation. It took just a little bit of flexibility and ingenuity to extend a meal. But the lack of an open-air market in our part of Sardinia gave me a little anxiety about dinner and the upcoming party. Long before Sardinia, I had worried about running out of ideas and how to keep the menus fresh and exciting. And I had conditioned the owners to assume that regardless of our location, I would surpass their expectations with freshly minted, authentic regional cuisine. Now I was in a quandary.

I tried to explain my problem to Patrick, but his answer was: "I'm sure you'll figure it out, you're the chef." Rick at least offered sympathy, but for once he, too, had no quick answer.

If I couldn't find decent fresh ingredients, what could I do? With nowhere else to turn, I decided it was time to go on a treasure hunt below—in the stores of the galley.

As a safety net, I routinely kept a large inventory of pantry ingredients on board, but prior to Sardinia the open-air markets and shops had been so rich with choices that I used pantry items only as add-ons. Now it was time to rifle through my stockpile, not just to augment my daily buy, but to create dishes anew. Before this European sojourn, it was easy to view a pantry as nothing more than a home for collected staples—a small bottle of some type of sauce or condiment here, used-once spices there—not a valuable cache of conserved foodstuffs. Now I would have to do what Italian cooks did in times of war and occupation—use what I had.

It's not as if I didn't have experience varying a single basic ingredient in my pantry to make a dish a little more special each time. And by using these ingredients in different proportions and combinations, I had almost endless variety. I had been doing just that in creating flavored mayonnaises as well as *la Signora*'s new favorite canapé with *spuma di tonno*—spreadable tuna mousse—adapted from a recipe given to me by the chef at Albergo del Sole, one of my *stages*. At first it stood alone very well with a drizzle of extra virgin olive oil and a few hot red pepper flakes, but while in Sardinia I shaved a little heady *bottarga di muggine*—cured and dried gray mullet roe—over the top. Thus, an ingredient of modest beginnings, fish roe, became a delicacy, and I was using a preserved foodstuff indigenous to an area. The same went for many of the crew pasta sauces, and items on the dessert menu such as *panna cotta*, the chocolate cake, and the *crema di mascarpone*. It had become time to turn some of my most everyday pantry items into true "hero" ingredients, which in turn lessened what I needed to find onshore.

On an evening when the owners were invited by one of the guests to a restaurant for dinner, the crew took their own well-deserved night on the town. I decided to join them.

We prowled the manicured streets of this jet-set community smitten by the very *per bene* women everywhere, before hopping into taxis to Sottovento, Sardinia's infamous nightclub. Rick in particular appeared energized, like a long-caged animal finally let loose back in the wild, darting off this way and that, not yet fully confident that he was really free. He said words I had not heard since Antibes: "Hot, hot, hot 'cause it makes you feel good, good, good!" Our old Rick had reappeared, and it elevated the mood of everyone in our group.

I was really relaxed and having a great time in the club, but my cash was evaporating quickly with drinks priced at thirty-five bucks each. I also wished I had better clothes to wear as everyone looked sharp in summer casual attire. Tanned women were in very short colorful dresses, men wore linen slacks and summer knit tops. I would have liked to stay longer, but the responsible side of me took over. I still had to shop for the big party, and I knew that when I woke up less crisp after a late night, my foreign-language skills slowed considerably and it was hard to put thoughts into words. I couldn't afford that, especially in August. So I made my regrets to everyone, including Rick, who was now anchored next to the bar buying rounds for every woman within hailing distance.

The next morning, while I prepared to make my way to the market, I realized Rick was still not up to start breakfast. I had never known him to oversleep. I went into the fo'c'sle.

"Rick," I said, shaking him. "What time did you get in?"

"Five-thirty," he said groggily, his cheeks blotched and puffy, looking like a prizefighter halfway through a tough bout.

"You need to get out there, the owners are almost up."

"I can't go out there," he murmured, burying his head under the pillow.

"Why not?" I became concerned.

Rick recounted his last moments at Sottovento, when the club owner presented him with the bill for the night. Rick was shocked by its size and informed him that he did not have anywhere near the four and a half million lira, about three thousand dollars, with him. He suggested since the money was on the boat, he would come back the next day to settle up. Clearly, the owner of the club had been down this road before, so along with the head bouncer he drove Rick back to *Serenity*. With no resources to pay the tab, Rick was forced to wake *il Dottore*, who came out of his cabin and paid the bill by check without many words. *La Signora* never stirred, which is why Rick still had a job today.

"*Il Dottore* immediately sent me to the quarters and dealt with the club owner himself," he told me.

"Then he's the only one who knows," I reminded him. "Let it go and get out there."

But Rick knew he had crossed a line and broken a code, humiliating himself in the process. He could not bear facing up to the damage he had done to his reputation with his boss. He kept repeating, "This is *so* not me."

With the humidity in the confined crew quarters, I could smell the alcohol emanating from his pores. I offered to help him up, just as he had stuck out his hand to me when we first met on deck four months back. "Come on, *mon pote,*" I said. He let me pull him up, but there wasn't much more I could do. As much as I wanted to stick around, talk him through the day, and let him know it would be okay, sixty people would soon be descending on *Serenity,* and I had to feed every hungry mouth among them or two of us would be in trouble with the owners.

Like a moth drawn to a flame, I also put myself in a spot that became my most embarrassing moment of the voyage. When the attractive cashier at the supermarket saw *Serenity*'s embroidered insignia on my uniform, she was jubilant because one of her favorite yachts was in the marina. When she asked if it was *my* yacht, I lied and said I was the son of the owner. She told me how lucky I was, to which I responded that every time I came to the boat, I was delegated to be the cook. As ridiculous as that line was, she bought it. She beamed with pride to be in the company of a member of the well-known family standing before her. I paid about eighteen hundred dollars in cash for two carts of groceries and hurried out.

I hadn't counted on how much of a favorite *Serenity* was to her. She came by on the morning of party day to see the boat. The owners were in the cockpit having breakfast, but in the confidence born of the belief that she was a friend of one of the family members, she called up to them and asked to speak to their son Davide. *La Signora* looked over the rail of the aft deck and must have asked her, "And this son of mine, Davide, what does he look like?" The girl must have described me to a tee, for *la Signora* came directly to the galley to inform me that there was a young lady on the quay asking to speak to her son. She was not amused. But when I went out to deal with my visitor, I had to pass the cockpit. *Il Dottore* looked up, smiled, and said in a low voice in front of his friends, "*Bravo, bravo.*"

Guitar players will sometimes reverse hands to reinforce how much they've improved their fretwork. Switch-hitting baseball players are so adept at home plate it looks reflexive. And with professional soccer players, it is very hard to tell which foot is stronger. This is what the end-of-season party did for me and the crew. The large dining events in Monte Carlo had left such an impression that I had thought long and hard about how to establish procurement, prep, and service as routine. Ian assumed the role of second waiter. Once the party began, Rick balanced his time between plating and pouring. Scott received and scraped plates through the crew passageway. Nigel took his station in the crew shower for rinse duty, and Kevin loitered by the galley to help in whatever way he could. Patrick donned his blue blazer and tried to appear comfortable making small talk with the Italian guests.

As I faced my ordeal, I remembered Patrick fully in control of the boat the night of the squall and how we all carried off any job he gave us without question or grumble. It became clear to me that we might not have survived that night had he shown any failure of resolve. Pulling off this dinner was not on the same scale of importance as getting us through gale forces, but that night had hammered home an important lesson of leadership. If the leader has no confidence in doing the job his way, why should those who have to carry out his instructions follow?

On this night I had to show my own resolve, and I went about my business with the words of one of my mentors in my mind: "Be a chef in the kitchen." The evening went smoothly. The menu, thankfully, was shorter than the first time, from the antipasti to the finish of petits fours purchased at a great *pasticceria* in town. And I was grateful *la Signora* sanctioned a meat course, giving me a free pass to take care of *il Dottore*'s request.

When everything had been done, with no calamities, I took my first break. I then realized there might be calls for the late-evening snack, so I put the water on to be ready for the *spaghettoni*. The chanting never came. I heard the next morning that the chef on the neighboring yacht had his turn in the barrel and had got beaten up pretty badly. Antipasti, pasta, *panini,* salads, more drinking until three or four in the morning.

As it became clear that the party had proved the ultimate bash for the owners, I took more than a little satisfaction in the way it had all come off. I had taken charge, made the galley my galley. There's an old saying that goes, "Responsibility without authority is hell on earth." Well, the responsibility had been all mine, and I wasn't bashful about taking the full authority I needed. The best part of the experience was that my fellow crew members, with whom I had a relationship of equals, had not resented my barking out orders. To the contrary, they remained eager throughout the long evening to communicate that they were ready for the next task.

A day later, Patrick lined the crew on the aft deck for the owners' end of August parting ceremony. I got to the line a little late and took a place in my usual penultimate position, feeling bad for being tardy because I knew it was noticed. The owners and guests shook the hand of each crew member with a firm grip and a pause until their eyes met, then made some statement of unabashed gratitude. Dennis obviously loved his American-style breakfasts so much he gushed, "Absolutely great—you worked so hard. Don't think it went unnoticed." He then stuck a tip in Rick's hand and mine, a nice gesture, but something we weren't supposed to accept. Rick shot a quick look in my direction that said, "He ran us through so many hoops, take it." We slipped the bills in our pockets, both knowing we would divvy the money up with the rest of the crew. *Il Dottore* continued on to me and said, *"Bravo, grande chef."* *La Signora* added her own *"Bravo, Davide. Everything was wonderful."* Flattering remarks like these were rare, but this time they felt particularly sincere and I basked in the praise.

The minute the owners disappeared into their waiting car service, beers cracked open, and we all migrated to the cockpit, forbidden territory in August. Everybody breathed sighs of relief.

The boat was "ours" again, and Patrick announced that we would sail to Corsica's coastal towns of Bonifacio and Calvi to clean the boat and enjoy a little needed rest and relaxation. As we toasted Sardinia and the Emerald Coast, the *passerelle* and lines came on board, and we motored toward the Strait of Bonifacio. Once under way, I retreated from my mates to sort things out in the galley and figure out what was next.

Eleven

The Last Regatta

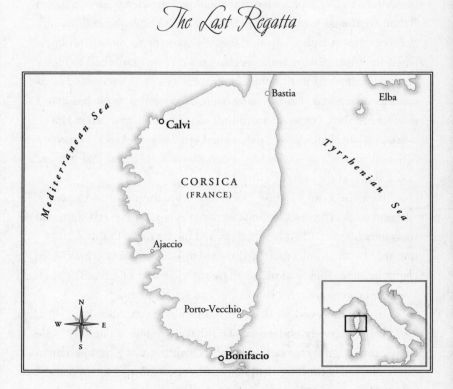

Corsica and the Côte d'Azur

*T*he ride from Sardinia to Corsica, sans owners, sans stress, on our way to a week of mostly rest and relaxation, took no more than a couple of hours. We could be considered *genti okay,* an Italian shorthand way to refer to those that visit after the high season. A silent respect extends from those who provide to those who know when to arrive, making for a pleasant stay. As we continued to motor toward Bonifacio, I was hoping the hospitalities shown us would be as good as advertised. I must have been daydreaming a bit because I didn't hear Rick come up to the aft deck behind me. "Hey, David, don't look out, look down," Rick called out as he flicked his cigarette ashes overboard, as if the sea around us was his personal ashtray. "Look down at the water."

How had I missed this? The waters were turquoise and aquamarine and so clear I could see rock formations of sand-colored stones on the sandy bottom. I had been fascinated by the rocks in this region— not only by their color but by their shape—and these were all worn round by time. Rick told me to enjoy the view and said that the shallow waters were great for snorkeling and scuba diving.

"But not so good for deep-keeled boats," he cautioned.

I could see what he meant. The shallow waters apparently made transit through the channels along the north coast of Sardinia treacherous and not a time for distraction. Every so often, I spotted these submarine islands of perfectly rounded rocks that seemed to have bubbled up from the sea's floor and somehow anchored themselves in place, there to seduce and destroy those who pass through these waters incautiously.

A short while after we passed the small, almost barren islands of the Maddalena archipelago, I began to see in the distance across the

Bonifacio Strait—known to be a treacherous wind funnel and seafaring challenge to cross because of the powerful mistral—vertical, sheet white cliffs rising majestically along the southern coastline of Corsica. Right in the middle of the palisades, I could see the outlines of what appeared to be a town that followed the crest and looked as if it had grown out of the stone below it. I was soon to find out that this was the *vieille ville*—the old town—of Bonifacio that rested above the hidden harbor area behind it.

For some reason, for all of history's conquerors, we remember learning early in life that Napoleon was born here and that the island is a part of France. But the locals—any local—on the island will proudly declare that they are Corsicans first and foremost. One look at the map tells you that most of its towns have Italian names or a close derivative, which is probably a result of the Genovese stronghold that reigned on the island. And Italians will remind you that the people are ethnically Italian, and some will even take the time to inform you that Napoleon's birth record spells his name Napoleone Buonaparte. What intrigued me from reading about the island was that in the eighteenth century, the Corsican patriot Pasquale Paoli tried to set up Corsica as one of Europe's earliest republics. In doing so, he adopted the profile of a Moor—*la testa di moro*—to be the image displayed on the island's black and white flag, a nod back to an earlier time of rule and a symbol for pride and separatism.

As we got closer, it became easier to make out where the cliffs flatten out and the buildings of the old town begin. Patrick, seeing me gaze in awe at this unique spectacle, completely different from anywhere we had been, came over and explained to me that every structure in the town is cut from the same white cliff rocks. The citadel at the top and the other freestanding watchtowers are said to be found all along the coast, outposts from another time that served to warn of possible enemy invasions. But the distant coastline was all a blur under the haze of the early September sun.

Bonifacio is situated at the southernmost tip of the island, and as we approached the shoreline, I could see more clearly the true dimension of that slice in the coastline. We were heading into what seemed like a sharp ravine that flanked a narrow waterway inland, called a *calanque* in French, in essence a fjord-like inlet. Nature and her handmaiden time had cut through the cliffs to create one of the most protected harbors on the planet.

Everyone kept up the merriment that started the moment of the owners' departure. I had never seen Kevin this relaxed or jovial. The serious, sober, diligent guy who set the standard for everyone else when it came to doing his fair share was now passing out beers and big pats on the back. "Job well done, here's to us," and we all saluted each other and took another swig. Slowly, the party drifted toward the foredeck. For a moment, *Serenity* was our boat and the Mediterranean our private sea.

Once we docked, reality set in as everyone scampered to take care of the chores that came with dockage. The boat's fuel and water tanks needed to be refilled. There was also plenty of scrubbing, touch-up painting, and varnishing that had to be done. Washing the hull got me out of the galley and finally back into the sun. It felt good even if the work was mindless because it was all that I wanted to do. My body after the August *ferie* felt like it had been hit by a truck. Down below, table and bed linens, towels, and uniforms all had to be sent out for cleaning. Rick was taking care of that. Later in the day, I went onshore to provision, first climbing the steep cobblestoned streets to get a look at the town itself. Knowing the crew had had its fill of fish and pasta, I bought racks of lamb and *contre-filet*—big, thick strip steaks.

Three days in Bonifacio to take care of business and load up on red meat and potatoes, and then we were off for Calvi, in the northern part of the island. Normally, the mistral comes down the very jagged western coast of Corsica, hitting parts of the shoreline head-on, which is why, after centuries, the coast is so rough. So most sailors choose instead to head north on the protected eastern coast. But with no sign of the fabled wind, we headed up the western coast, hoping for an event-free ride. We chose right.

The citadel that has protected Calvi for centuries during its fabled history is conspicuous after rounding the Punta della Revellata just west. Nothing fancy about it, the fort rests on the top of a hill at the end of a small peninsula, its high stone walls standing guard to one of the most beautiful land and seascapes I'd ever seen. The quaint town and small marina below are well protected in the shadow of the citadel, and a sweeping look across the bay reveals a long stretch of desolated beach. With the rolling hills and mountains behind, this expanse of terrain is very inviting.

After dinner our second night there, Nigel and I decided to head for one of the sailor bars in Calvi. Normally, Nigel is not the type of person to talk to strangers, even friendly ones. But when he heard a familiar accent at the next table—the unmistakable lilt of a fellow New Zealander—he brightened up. The man at the next table responded immediately with a friendly "hello." But then he introduced himself as Henri, saying it with a faux French accent. Registering our confusion, he explained that he was in the French Foreign Legion and was based in the citadel, the legion being the only tenants in the monument. No wonder it seemed off-limits when I went up to take a look. We asked him what his real name was, but he answered, "Henri," and we left it at that.

What had turned into a jovial evening of conversation was interrupted by the roar and gunning of a motorcycle engine somewhere extremely close to the bar. We and everyone else in the room looked toward the doorway to see what was making the racket. Over the threshold stood a bear of a man in a black leather rider's jacket, black jeans, and black boots, easing his shiny Harley-Davidson Sportster—engine still running with an occasional rev—into the bar and finally parking it in the space between the stools and the tables before shutting it down. A few women cheered the visitor on as he came in. It was, unquestionably, a grand entrance.

"That is Gaston. He likes to keep his new bike as near as possible," Henri explained, using a tone of respect. "He doesn't want it touched by anyone."

To me, our visitor looked more like an outlaw biker than a Gaston, but I said nothing. Henri then told us that Gaston was his superior officer.

I wondered for a minute if Nigel was thinking what I was thinking—what an act! The false French names, the macho image. But if Nigel was thinking that, his face didn't reveal it.

With his bike secure, Gaston sauntered right over to our table. He had a scar across his right cheek.

"Who are your friends?" he asked Henri, in a menacing tone consistent with the image he conveyed.

"Sailors on a yacht that called, mate," Henri replied. "Good guys on leave."

We introduced ourselves as David and Nigel, and Gaston, waving his finger at us and referring to me as Dave, leaned over and said, "One hard-and-fast rule of the island—Corsican women are off-limits to foreigners." Then he ordered us another beer.

While Henri and Nigel mused about New Zealand, all I could think about was why anyone would join the legion, adopt a new French name, and basically shed one's identity. Did these guys really think people didn't see through their bravado? Then I began to wonder if Gaston had joined by choice or had signed up to avoid some messy situation in the country of his birth. We landed on their good side, but at the same time I became a little uncomfortable. Maybe in the back of my mind, I wasn't thinking about the contrived élan of the legionnaires. Maybe seeing Gaston in his shielded but transparent posturing lit up a dark corner in my own psyche.

As the months of my sojourn turned into years, I had taken more and more satisfaction in the fact that I could pass as a native-born Italian. It was more than pride in learning to think and converse in another language, reflexively use its idioms, and speak with my hands. And it was more than conforming to the country's customs and traditions and wearing its clothes. I wanted to pass as authentic because I felt comfortable with the notion of *la bella figura*—the impression I made on others—the part of myself that wanted to be Italian.

Now I wondered, was I as transparent to others as Gaston was to me?

In one more day, *Serenity* would be sailing back to Antibes and then on to Saint-Tropez. Then the season would be over, the job done. And yet I wasn't thinking, as I would have in the past, "Okay, where do I want to go next?" What restaurant, what part of Italy, what type of work? And I knew why. For the first time during my years abroad I had a sense not only of time passing but also of time passing me by.

While we walked back to the boat, I firmed up a plan. Once we hit Antibes, I would find a moment to ask Michele what he thought about my approaching the owners with the idea of their backing me to open a restaurant or perhaps a food store in the States. I was more than a little anxious about what I might learn. Michele knew what the owners thought of me and would not hold back out of concern for how I would take it. I didn't know if I was ready to hear bad news. But I promised myself that I would make the inquiry.

We left Calvi toward evening, when the sun had a brilliant red-orange glow. "Red sky at night, sailor's delight," so the adage goes. Patrick passed his off-watch hours by trolling a long monofilament fishing line between the stern. He caught a good-sized tuna at three in the morning, and Ian quickly grabbed a bottle of gin to pour over the fish's gills—knocking it out instantly. I planned on having it broken down into fillets by daybreak.

During my watch, while manning a halyard jig, I was working out in my head how I would open the conversation with Michele when, absentmindedly, I took the last wrap of the line off the pin when a sail trim was called. The load on the rope made it ride fast and hard through my right hand, burning a deep and nasty red channel across my palm. It stung terribly, and the sea salt from the rope only added to the pain. Washing it was going to be excruciating. I was able to take the paid-out line and make it fast to the desired trim and immediately thought how sore my hand was going to be while at the stove. When I showed my wound to Patrick, he displayed no sympathy. "You'd better heal quickly because I need you on deck for the regatta. And don't mention it to Michele," he added, suggesting it would be a bad way to end a cruise.

Within days, everyone was so focused on getting ready for the race that I held off speaking to Michele. But when I decided to go ahead and ask him, he responded positively. "You should talk to *il Dottore* and *la Signora*. They were pleased with your work. They may well want to help you."

Then he gave me some heartfelt advice. Understand whom you are talking to, he warned gently but with a seriousness that caught my attention.

"In America, when you approach a businessman to bankroll you, he will expect you to show him a business plan and some financial projections. But it won't work that way with the owners. If they do it, they will do it as a gesture of honor, because you have earned their respect, but they will expect honor on your part in fulfilling your end of the bargain. It is not only business. It is personal. This is a big responsibility. Think about it. There will be more time to talk. I will be sailing on *Serenity* for the regatta."

But there was little time for talk. No one was doing or thinking of anything except preparing for the races. To make the boat as light as possible, Rick and I were assigned to unload anything that was not needed. After we removed everything that wasn't to be tied down, we loaded a new inventory of sails, which we all had to learn to handle. We practiced hoisting the gollywobbler, a huge sail that would encompass the entire area between the masts; using the genoa, a humongous light air jib; the fisherman, an almost trapezoid-shaped sail that was flown between the two topmasts to catch precious wind above; and finally a new addition to our heavy lifting, the main jackyard topsail, a larger topsail than the one we carried complete with two yards—heavy spruce pieces of timber that held the sail—adding another ton to our regimen when used and apparently could help provide another knot of speed. We'd need at least a dozen strong pairs of arms to hoist and trim this one. Patrick took his extra speed very seriously. Thankfully, he invited others to race with us—Peter, a captain and master in classic schooner sailing, some very capable maxi-boat sailors, a dedicated rigger, and our sailmaker. Also, *Serenity* had to be sparkling, not just race ready, for this was as much a social event as a sailing event. We washed and polished everything. Finally we were ready to leave for Saint-Tropez.

By the time we arrived, nearly all the motorboats had been cleared out of the harbor by the authorities, and hundreds of sailboats, of every size, age, and shape, took their place. We passed slender America's Cup race boats from past eras, fleets of yawls, ketches, and sloops. In the *belle classe* category a remarkable collection of schooners and cutters were assembled: *Camille* and *Juliette,* the huge yacht *Danzer, Maiden Sea, Pegasus, Aurora, Beguine,* restored large J-boat racing beauties from the 1930s, and of course, our nemesis, the gorgeous and perfectly maintained *Carina.* We backed in next to her. Grudgingly we all admitted that she looked divine.

That evening we checked out the bars and nightclubs. Usually the sailors hang out at one kind of place and the owners and their friends at another. But during regatta week, these barriers break down. One night, *la Signora* was seen working her way through the sailor-packed Hotel Sube bar, obviously curious as to the goings-on. One of my mates from another boat gave me an elbow and said, "Isn't that your boss over there?" A minute or so later, she was gone, her curiosity apparently satisfied.

In two days the races would begin. For all of us except Patrick, winning meant one thing—winning. But Patrick was looking for some degree of acceptance with a different crowd—professional racers. Being the skipper of the family's personal yacht meant something to him, but the regatta was his chance to prove he had what it took to do more—to be an elite yacht racer.

The chilly morning dawned bright on the harbor at Saint-Tropez, and by the time I climbed on deck, there were already helicopters flying above, spectator boats getting ready to leave, and chase boats outside filled with paparazzi snapping shots for the sailing and gossip magazines. On the quay there were hundreds of people, most of them with hopes of catching a glimpse of an international celebrity or boat. The temperature rose to a pleasant sixty degrees, and although I could feel a small bite of autumn, I didn't have an opportunity to get cold from the breeze. Too much work remained to be done. I still had to prepare lunch for twenty people prior to the start of the race, baskets of the ever-present yacht race lunch—sandwiches, cut fruits and cheeses, candy bars.

Within an hour the harbor emptied, and everyone was sailing in front of Saint-Tropez. We would race three times—today, tomorrow, and then, after a day's break, a third and final race. Patrick was tightly focused, and everyone else knew the drill and was alerted to what had to be done. He also gave *il Dottore* and *la Signora* new Windbreaker jackets like ours, but to honor them as owners, theirs were beige instead of navy blue. *Il Dottore* and Michele stood by the helm acting as navigators and tacticians. *La Signora* wore binoculars around her neck and was standing up, well positioned to observe everything. For someone who gets seasick, she seemed oblivious to anything but winning the race. Rick had gone aft to trim one of the jib sheets. This would also keep him close to the owners in case they needed something. Everyone else was positioned as assigned by Kevin. I was stationed at the foredeck. As amped up as we all were, we had no illusions. *Carina's* hull design made her a faster boat for this kind of race, and we needed more than a little help from the wind if we were to beat her.

Patrick set the radio to the race channel and turned the volume up so we could all hear what was happening. Excitement on deck built. The fleets of small boats would be first. The announcement was made: "This is the race committee. All six-meter boats will start in fifteen minutes."

In a predetermined sequence, flags rose and guns went off as the first boats were off. All morning long, class by class, the boats left, and the next classification got ready.

It was about an hour and a half before we received our call: "Ten minutes, *la belle classe.*"

Now it was our turn. Until then we had been trying to stay out of the way, cruising around the bay until we got close to the start, which was about a couple hundred yards from the breakwater. The fleet was assembling near the line, maneuvering around each other under full sail. It was amazing how much physical labor and seamanship it required to make these glorious and magnificent yachts appear graceful, slightly heeling to one side, as they cut through the water. And then the gun fired, our class's coded flag went up, and the voice on the radio hailed, "*belle classe,* this is your start!"

Just as in a foot race, there is a challenge in crossing the starting line of a sailing race. Getting out of the blocks at the first possible moment but not a split second earlier is paramount. The idea was to approach the starting line under perfect trim and at full boat speed when the final gun went off. If you cross the line before the official start, you will be penalized and have to go around and start again. And if you are not yet at the line when the race starts, you will be playing catch-up, trying to make up lost time against those correctly under way. We all knew that if *Carina* took a significant lead on us at the start, we would not be able to make up the loss.

We had a strong wind that morning, which was good for us but also made for a very physical day. All of the sail changes, the lack of electric winches for most of the sails, and the need for six or seven of us to trim the topsails entailed a lot of active work. Kevin, I could see, had a competitive edge and was comfortable driving his troops. During the race, we'd heave the lines and growl together while Kevin, excited and fired up, shouted, "C'mon guys, HAUL IT, DAMN IT! PULL! PULL! Keep going! PULL THAT BASTARD!"

For the first few hours, things looked good, with *Serenity* holding her own and staying within close range of *Carina*. We all watched her every move. I was told by one of the maxi sailors to keep an eye on *Carina*'s crew. The activity on deck would let us know if a tack or sail change was coming up. This way we could respond as quickly as possible.

Aurora was being expertly handled not far behind us. But slowly, *Carina* began to take off. At that moment, we knew it was over. We crossed the finish line a few hours later, a far second.

In the second race, the course was slightly altered. This was to our advantage because there would be more off-wind opportunities, and that's where we excelled. *Serenity*'s long keel was suited for those situations where the wind blew across her beam or from all points behind. She was probably designed to satisfy the yachtsman's motto "Gentlemen sail off the wind." With the winds that we'd been having, the extra weapon in our sail wardrobe, the fisherman, would be a powerful tool and no doubt add boat speed. Also, long off-wind legs of the racecourse were great opportunities for me to do prep work, since the boat in these conditions was leveled off and the ride much smoother than anything upwind.

Serenity must have been a happy boat that day as she powered through the course because we could hear the hum along her hull. We were pretty happy ourselves. With the help of the extra crew, every maneuver, sail change, and trim went off without a hitch. Not one mistake occurred, nothing broke, and none of the other yachts caught us. Victory was ours.

When we crossed the finish line, the first gun sharply declaring us the winner, a cheer went up throughout the deck. There was a lot of excitement from the cockpit, and *la Signora* looked the proudest I had ever seen her. But we all knew that if we were going to win the third race, we would have to stay close to *Carina* right from the start or she would leave us in her wake.

As pumped up as I was about the race itself, I wasn't excused from my day job. I was still the cook on board, and the owners were still expecting a first-class dinner. Given that we were in France, I decided to create a sequence of dishes inspired by coastal French cookery. I bought some salt cod and made savory profiteroles using the recipe for *brandade de morue* that Madame Quillier, from the shop in Antibes, had given me at the beginning of the summer, when I bought my kitchenwares from her. Then I made a fish soup served with the traditional accompaniments: croutons, rouille—a spicy type of mayonnaise—and grated Gruyère cheese on the side. Rick served the soup from a porcelain tureen. For the entrée, a beautiful *saint-pierre*—John Dory—caught that morning just outside the bay that was baked, as per the fisherman's advice, with locally foraged chanterelle mushrooms and served with roasted new potatoes scented with garlic and thyme. On the way back from the famous open-air market in the Place des Lices, I picked up a classic local dessert, *tarte tropézienne,* and I made a berry coulis to serve with it. It was the owners' kids who came into the galley later to deliver the compliments.

The off day gave the crew a chance to relax and take care of personal business. Patrick spent time at the race committee office checking our ratings and standings. The rest of the crew did what had to be done on deck, and then ran off with friends from other boats. But Rick and I had scheduled time to speak with the owners—Rick with *il Dottore* and me with *la Signora*. Rick told me about his meeting after I had mine.

The morning after he woke *il Dottore* in the middle of the night to pay his bar tab in Sardinia, Rick made a pledge to himself. He was not going to ease the pain of his family situation with drink anymore. And he was going to repay the money *il Dottore* had laid out for him.

Alone with *il Dottore,* he unfolded a wad of colorful French currency, explaining that he would repay the rest of the money shortly. But *il Dottore* looked at the money and placed it back in his hand. "Richard," he said, "I don't need your money. You know I don't need your money. This is not about money. This is about you. If this is how you wish to continue in life, then you may not get much further than this boat. I want to believe that there is better for you."

Sitting in the same cockpit seat as I had during my interview, I spoke to *la Signora* about the marvelous experience I had been having on *Serenity.* She let me speak without interruption. Finally I got the courage up to ask her if she would be interested in helping me financially with a restaurant project.

She thought for a moment, and then said, "Davide, I have another idea. I would like to propose this offer: we would like you to be our 'special events' chef. In addition to summers here on *Serenity,* we have much entertaining to do for business, social, and family events at many of our homes. We can find a place of your choosing for you to live and schedule your responsibilities for the various occasions. You have done a wonderful job this season and have pleased us greatly. I know you like being in Italy. I think you should consider this, not opening a restaurant somewhere back in America with all the work that entails."

It was not the answer I wanted, but in a way I was relieved. I had not forgotten what Michele said about the personal obligations I would incur if the owners bankrolled me.

"This is a great offer, and I thank you for it," I answered her. Then I opened up to her more than I ever had before.

"I, too, have been thinking seriously about staying and settling down somewhere in Italy. Also, I have flattered myself into believing that if I stay long enough, I'll no longer be a foreigner and become an Italian. But maybe not. I don't know."

"Davide, you have been looking for something of great value, but you have been looking in the wrong direction. Out instead of in. Let me tell you something you must never forget. To be an Italian is to be yourself."

I sat stunned. "Think about my offer," she said, and then excused herself to go down below.

The next morning was the rubber match. The crowds were even bigger, this being the last race of the week and the most important.

The start was brilliant. Patrick must have waited for this opportunity his entire sailing career. We were a little over a boat length ahead of *Carina* to her right side on port tack as we approached the line. Patrick told Rick to spread the word for everyone to stay calm and not move too much on deck. With thirty seconds to go we were in perfect trim and boat speed to make the start. Seconds later Patrick yelled, "TACKING!" while he started to turn the boat through the wind, changing which side the wind would come across our deck. This maneuver caught everyone on *Carina* by surprise. He slam-dunked 'em! They couldn't turn off the wind to avoid or pass us astern because *Beguine* was close behind and she started to tack as well. *Carina* was forced to immediately tack, and because of their position near the start, they had to duck under the far buoy of the line, denying them any chance to exercise their right-of-way. By missing the start, they had to come back around again behind the other yachts passing en route for their start. This gave us a comfortable lead from the outset. The view from the press helicopters hovering above must have been spectacular. Patrick's strategy was sure to be a topic in the bars that night.

And then it happened. Out of nowhere, on the second upwind leg, *Carina* came alongside us, and then pulled ahead, the distance between us increasing with every passing minute. We watched her transom in shock as it got smaller and smaller. At the speed she was going, even with corrected time and our handicap, there was no way we could beat her. Ironically, it was Patrick who pulled us out of our daze. "Great job, everyone; really great." In that moment, the Riviera yachting season came to an end.

After the awards ceremony the next day, we gathered on the aft deck for our final parting-line ceremony. Patrick directed me to take the last position—the honor position. *Il Dottore* passed through first and gave me a firm handshake with a powerful "*Bravo*." "We'll see you soon," he said. I wondered if he knew something I didn't.

Then *la Signora* came to me. She put her hand out, and I shook it.

"I hope everything was to your liking," I said.

The handshake stopped. Her eyes bored into mine.

"You hope?" She paused for a moment with a growing fire in her eyes. "You are kidding, aren't you?" This was all said in Italian. Loud, clear, assertive Italian. Only *il Dottore* and I knew what she was saying. I could see the crew out of the corner of my eye. They couldn't understand what she was getting excited about, but they knew it wasn't just a pleasant "thanks for everything" conversation. They began to fidget, feeling badly for me. I could feel their angst.

"HOW CAN YOU HOPE EVERYTHING WAS TO MY LIKING?" she flashed. "Look at where you are! Look at where you work! Look at what you've done!"

At that point *il Dottore* cut in to say, "Let's go, *amore*," to which she snapped back, "No, dear, this is important."

She continued, "You need to be proud of what you have done. We've been your biggest fans. Hope has nothing to do with it. You have worked hard all summer and earned our respect. Your food is always a pleasure to eat, you wear the cuisine better than most Italians, and your crew members feel lucky to have you on board. That's not the result of hope. Make me feel your confidence. It's deserved. You've already proved what you can do."

She stuck out her hand again and repeated what *il Dottore* had said in a much more relaxed tone, "We'll see you soon."

The owners left and I just stood still, looking past my crew members, across the rail, past the other yachts across the harbor, and into the cyan Riviera sky. The guys asked me what happened, was I okay? I turned and said to Rick, *"Tutto bene"*—All is well.

Twelve

~

Ciao, Italia

~ ~ ~ ~

Like taking down ornaments from a Christmas tree, preparing *Serenity* for the off-season gave everyone a feeling that the holidays were over. The interior furnishings, drapes, slipcovers, service ware, and kitchenwares were removed and put into storage. On deck, all of the sails and most of the rig would be dismantled and stored in a rented shipping container. Day by day, the yacht was getting barer and barer to the point of being stark and lifeless, unlike her magnificent presence while cruising on the Mediterranean. *Il Dottore* and *la Signora* would probably never see her in this state. The crew would be reduced to two, Patrick and Scott, with ongoing upgrades and mechanical maintenance keeping them busy through the winter. Ian was hired to cross the Atlantic for the winter in the Caribbean, Nigel was heading to Greece, Kevin landed a job on a new yacht that was getting finished in Viareggio, and Rick had his life onshore in Antibes.

I was going to miss these guys. Professional sailors are an interesting group, and I wished I had spent more time on deck learning about their world. We may not have been destined to be lifelong best friends, but we quickly adapted to coexist in small quarters, tried to accept each other's ways, and, as a result, possibly discovered new thresholds within ourselves. At the same time, the waste-not, want-not lifestyle on board enabled us to get by with less. And in respect to the elements, we were efficient with our limited resources and didn't leave a trail behind us. Even though it had its challenges, it was a fascinating way to see beautiful places. But most important, through it all, there was no shortage of laughs.

Michele arranged a final dinner for us at a small restaurant in town, the Safranier, one of our favorite hangouts. With his office staff, we honored *Serenity*'s strong showing in the races and celebrated the end of the season with friends from other boats.

But as the evening wore on, Rick, ever sensitive to my moods, could tell my attention was elsewhere. He asked me to go with him to the bar area and tried to engage me in another of those "what next?" sessions we had been having. I surprised him when I said I would not be returning to Italy to look for any new jobs. After five years living abroad, I would be returning to the States.

"When did you finally decide this?" he asked me, rather taken aback.

"Tonight," I answered, "while we were talking about the summer. Even though there is still plenty I'd like to do, I've accomplished a lot. I want to leave Europe on a high note."

"But will *la Signora* let you go?" he said in an instant. "The superrich are different. They can be very proprietary toward the help, especially the ones they like."

"I'm already steeling myself for that," I said, knowing that I had to call and let her know my decision.

Once convinced I would be leaving Europe, Rick invited me to spend the last two weeks before my flight to New York at his family's house in the Pauillac wine region of Bordeaux. I quickly accepted. My first stop on the Continent had been in the south of France, and a last couple of weeks near where it all started seemed an appropriate close of the loop before heading home.

At dinner one night, Rick's mother raised her glass and called for a toast.

"To David." She paused, then added, "And to going home. Compliments. In France we say, '*Les voyages forment la jeunesse.*' Traveling matures youth."

Now, sitting at Rick's parents' table, he and I were spinning out war stories from our season at sea—the nonstop entertaining in

Monte Carlo during the Grand Prix, the relentless heat below deck in August, and the night of the big storm en route to Sardinia—when the telephone rang. Rick's mother excused herself to answer it in the kitchen. Within moments, she returned to say the call was for me. I was puzzled. Who knew I was there? I went into the kitchen to take the call.

"*Ciao, Davide!*" It was *la Signora,* her voice, as always, rich with exuberance. I wondered how she knew where to reach me.

"*Buona sera, signora,*" I answered, trying to perk up my voice and sound more sober than I was.

"How wonderful that you and Rick are spending some time together before you depart. *Che bella,*" she said in her sharp and crystal-clear Italian. "Is this a good time to talk? There is something I would like to speak to you about. We have a project for you."

I hesitated before responding. Just a week before I had told her of my decision to return home. Now I wondered if her project was a way to keep me in Europe so that I'd be available the next spring for another season on the yacht.

She didn't wait for my answer. "Davide, listen carefully. This is business. It is for our annual New Year's pheasant shoot at our house in England. I am putting together *la mia ottima squadra di servizio*"—my ultimate service team—"and we would like you to cook for the occasion. Can we discuss menus?"

There was a moment during which neither of us said anything. Finally, I said something like, "I am leaving for New York soon from Paris. Why don't you tell me what you have in mind, and I can fax you some ideas."

"I don't have time for faxes!" I could almost see her hand flying through the air dismissively. "Too much back-and-forth. We can meet before you leave and go over the entire menu program in one meeting. Two hours and it's done."

"But I'm leaving the country this Saturday."

"Here is my schedule. I am in Padua through Wednesday, Modena on Thursday, and Como on Friday. Call me tomorrow and tell me which city you are going to meet me in."

Sheepishly I said, "Como might be the easiest."

"Perfect. Then it is settled. Friday morning, ten-thirty, at our apartment in Como. *Grazie, Davide.*"

The call had taken no more than a few minutes, but it was long enough to put me in disarray.

"What does *la Signora* want?" Rick asked when I was back at the table.

"She wants me to cater for them and their friends in England over the holidays. She also wants to meet with me this week to go over the menus. How am I going to manage that?"

"You call Michele first thing tomorrow and have him book a flight for you from Paris to Como. She wants to speak with you in person. She doesn't care what it costs."

"She has probably already called him," I said as I reached for my wineglass.

"Are you pissed that she called you or that you agreed to meet her?" Rick asked.

"I don't know," I answered honestly.

As soon as the commuter flight to Como took off, I started to question my decision to agree to this trip. In my last face-to-face conversation with *la Signora*, her way of presenting my role as the family's "special events" chef was characteristic of her savvy and made the offer hard to refuse. "You love Italy," she said. "Why don't you stay here? We very much like your work. We can set you up anywhere you want in Italy. Think about it carefully."

It wasn't bad what she had proposed. The idea was tempting and would satisfy most of my concerns about staying in Europe. I'd find an apartment, most likely in Florence, and be able to enjoy many of the pleasures of an Italian lifestyle. But I kept reminding myself I didn't spend the past five years angling for a personal chef job. Of course, she had too much pride to bring up the offer once I had turned it down, but she had to expect I would see the two offers as part of one campaign.

"*How nice that you* have arrived early," *la Signora* said as she approached me while I waited in front of her apartment near the lake in Como, in one of the fashionable neighborhoods in this silk and textile capital of Italy. I had only known her around the boat, so I had never seen her in business attire. She was certainly very well put together in a red Chanel dress. I took the few shopping bags she carried and followed her up a short flight of steps.

She walked me through a large apartment sparsely decorated with furnishings that whispered, not shouted, extreme wealth. As we got to the dining area, she directed me to a seat near the end of a polished walnut dining table that was an antique of regal proportions. Two pads and two pens had already been laid out. She went into the kitchen to greet the housekeeper and request a beverage service.

"It's nice to see you again," she said as she sat across from me, then pulled a few folders from her briefcase. Always cordial, she was not one to extend opening pleasantries. I could see she was ready to get down to business.

"Every year we do a traditional New Year's pheasant shoot at our farmhouse in Oxfordshire with our friends," she started. "But this year we want it to be more than special. I want to plan the menus for each day."

She laid out the marching orders, including details of the house, the schedule, the rest of the staff, and travel arrangements. Each dinner would have a theme. As the food changed, so too would the wines, the flowers, the table linens, service wares, even the uniforms of the service staff. Now I understood her impatience to have the menus settled. All the other decisions hung on the food.

"I would like every dish to blend in with the idea of Italians being in England during the winter for this special occasion. You can make Italian dishes some nights and classic English on others. But for sure, on New Year's Eve, we are going to have a very traditional Milanese menu. I will bring some of the food for it." She mentioned *cotechino*—a type of sausage served over lentils. The lentils symbolize coins in Italian folklore, so the more lentils you eat, the better your chances for financial success in the New Year. And *tortellini in brodo*—a classic winter dish from northern Italy.

She had clearly thought it all through. "One night we would like to have roast beef with Yorkshire pudding. The house manager has a great recipe." I took "roast beef" to mean prime rib. "On another night, let's do rack of lamb. They have delicious lamb in England," she made a point of telling me. There would be a large ham to bake already ordered from the local butcher, Scottish salmon, and Dover sole. Once again she wanted the meals to convey a sense of place.

There were many other details she mentioned—from local sourcing to the layout of the kitchen, including a coal-burning Aga stove and cold rooms in lieu of refrigerators. I listened intently, sometimes taking notes, most of the time just trying to get a feel for what she wanted, never once interrupting her. At one point she paused and leaned back in her chair, signaling that she was ready for any questions or comments I might have.

I had none for the moment, and she went on. "Lunch will be served every day out in the field. We will mark predetermined places in the forest where the stewards can meet us for service. You'll need to have this ready in time for them to pack and get set up."

I had to think about England in winter—it was going to be pretty cold. All summer on the Mediterranean, I had cooked coastal Italian dishes for them, a very different cuisine. She was clear and specific about the English food she wanted included, so while she spoke, I started to scratch out on my clean white pad menu ideas that made sense.

By now *la Signora* was waiting for my reaction. I was certain she had finished with her dictates.

Before I spoke, I tested in my head what I might say. Then I jumped in, never more confident of my cooking instincts.

"I assume there will be cocktails and canapés as we did before dinner last summer," I said, "so I will locate some foie gras in London on the way up to the house. That, as you know, makes for a great start. Warm Stilton cheese on crostini would be another. I think a winter vegetable minestrone might be a nice *primo,* and this is certainly the season for risotto. I can even make gnocchi with brown butter and sage if you'd like, and better yet, I will make them with squash as they do in Friuli. It would be perfect before the ham. If I can find guinea fowl, they would be great braised with apples and served with polenta. With the bounty of the shoot, I wonder if we should think about roasting pheasants one night. And many of the meats you mentioned can also be carved for warm *panini* at lunch. Even consommé with porcini mushrooms will work well in the field. For desserts, I'd like to bake pears in sweetened red wine, make *panna cotta* with that wonderful clotted cream from Devon, and definitely the chocolate *torta caprese* that you like."

"Maybe twice," *la Signora* threw in. I had to suppress a smile. Rick had always commented on the impact of my *torta* on her usually minuscule appetite for sweets.

Instead, I said, "I am curious about breakfast. What are your thoughts?"

"We leave by seven in the morning, so maybe an American-style breakfast buffet would be the most practical. At that hour, it's nice to have choices."

"How about a changing egg preparation each day?" I asked to offer variety and keep her from asking for too much. As a restaurant cook, I was used to hitting the sack late and sleeping till well past breakfast. Breakfast had always been my least favorite meal to prepare.

"It sounds like you are on the right track, so let's go ahead and assign the dishes to menus and the days they will be served."

When we were finished, she smiled and closed the business discussion by saying, "Now, isn't this better than faxing back and forth? Two hours and we have it all done."

"You're right," I answered.

There was a silence that she broke. "And how long has it been since you've been home?"

"About five years," I answered.

"This must be exciting for you, going home after all this time. Are you nervous? Are you going back to California or New York? And what are you going to do when you get there?"

I smiled. "I don't even know yet. I need to think about that for a little while."

"But are you certain of your decision?" she asked, as if trying to discern if there was any wiggle room in my earlier decision to turn down her offer.

"I may not be certain about where I am going to live, but I do know that I found what I was looking for in Italy."

"*Bene,*" she said, smiling. "I hope we had a small part in this."

"More than a small part."

"After January, are we ever going to see you again?"

"Of course," I answered without a minute's pause. But it pleased me she had asked the question.

She smiled, and I smiled back. "That's wonderful news," she said. "See you on the twenty-seventh of December, and have a great holiday. And remember to have some fun in New York."

We shook hands. Italians will invariably greet or part from friends with a perfunctory kiss on each cheek. But as closely as we had worked all summer, a kiss on *la Signora*'s cheek would have been entirely inappropriate.

I walked down the steps. Outside, it was Europe in autumn, a beautiful season. The air outside felt fresh and tangy. A driver stepped out of a dark green Alfa Romeo sedan parked in front of the building, came around, and held the door open for me.

"*La Signora* arranged transit for you."

"Malpensa Airport, *per favore*," I said to the driver as I climbed in.

"I know," he responded with a smile.

On my way back to the airport my thoughts were on getting started with this as soon as I got home, because I needed to contact her people in England and start sourcing the ingredients I would need.

As the plane lifted off the runway, I looked out the window and half muttered, "*Ciao, Italia.*" The man next to me heard me and smiled. He was an American, and we began to talk.

Avanti

~ ~ ~ ~

Like the conclusion of any milestone in one's life, the season on *Serenity* ended with good intentions and the promise to keep in touch. I knew that in the small world of the yachting community, as long as I checked in periodically, I would hear about everyone else's whereabouts.

Il Dottore and *la Signora*'s annual New Year's pheasant hunt was quite a production, hosted on a farming estate used only for the occasion. It was cold, but the staff and I were warmed up by the arrival of Rick, who was called to be part of *la Signora*'s international team. For the owners and four other couples, we were a service staff of eight. Everything had gone as planned, even though the days were longer than those in August. I had wonderful winter-season ingredients to cook and a well-equipped kitchen to work in. The cold rooms for food storage performed phenomenally well, maybe even better than refrigerators, but the coal-powered stove took some getting used to. And by the end of the week, it was no surprise *la Signora* proved to be the most successful hunter of the group.

Michele built his yacht management business and moved to a very upscale office in Cannes, France. He continues to manage

Serenity and remains my point person for tracking the other members of the crew.

Patrick eventually moved on to become the skipper of another classic schooner, *Bellatrix,* managed a refit, spent a couple years on board, and then relocated to Chiavari in Liguria, where he became the restoration director for an Italian yacht-building company.

Kevin went back to Viareggio to begin his tenure aboard *Tirion,* a new state-of-the-art sailing yacht. He quickly proved his worth and was promoted to the job he was really after—fully licensed captain. When the yacht was sold to a European statesman, Kevin stayed on while keeping homes in both the United Kingdom and the south of France.

Scott proved tougher to track down, but I heard he spent the next couple of years working on yachts both in the Mediterranean and in the Caribbean. He became, so I was told by Michele, a master at marine engineering and moved on to motor yachts.

Ian completed his home-training course to become an accredited sailing yacht captain. After a few stints as skipper on smaller private yachts, he took the necessary tests and put in the required hours to extend his license to larger craft. He married a stewardess he had met on one of the boats, and they make the Côte d'Azur home.

Nigel returned to New Zealand and opened a marine repair facility—with the sole purpose of allowing him to pursue his main passion, diving. No one had heard from him since.

Rick also found himself becoming the skipper of motor and sailing yachts. But more important, he finally gained custody of his son, got remarried, and had another child. I heard there was talk about him taking his wife and kids on an around-the-world voyage on a good-sized sailboat he was going to build.

For me, another journey was just beginning. I thought I could pick up where I left off, but it would not prove to be that easy. A lot of time had passed. You don't notice how fast things change in America until you're out of it for a while.

I started on the line in a couple of high-end restaurants, first in New York, then in California, to work my way back into the business. I quickly became a sous-chef and then *chef de cuisine,* always fortifying the menus with what I had learned abroad. A decade later, I successfully fused my restaurant background with my college degree in set and lighting design into the specialized position of culinary producer for food television. A great assignment came my way when I was hired to work with one of the masters of the medium, Chef Jacques Pépin, and the television series to his companion cookbook, *Fast Food My Way.*

For each show, Jacques and I would do a final walk-through before the recipes to be taped. These occasions brought every element together for the first time—ingredients, steps in the cooking, movement around the set, the arrangement of kitchenwares, when to swap for a "twin" of what was being made to save production time, the finish plates, and table settings. He looked through his recipe while I worked from blocking sheets, choreographed blueprints of the segment. Occasionally there would be a few last-minute changes.

At the same time, the director followed Jacques and gave guidance to the cameramen for angles and shots. The producer watched for content and presentation while stage managers, prop stylists, and assistants stood by for any last-minute needs. Off the set, video, sound, and lighting engineers watched from the control room while the back-kitchen staff viewed and listened from a monitor.

One morning camera three was in need of a little tuning, and we were on hold for a short while. I looked around the beautifully decorated set, everything bright, clean, and perfectly lit under the studio lights—created for comfort with some elements from Jacques's home. On one of the walls hung a model of a classic yacht.

"Nice boat," I said to Jacques.

"You like boats?" he asked.

"I worked on one like that when I lived in Europe."

"Did you cook on board?"

"For Italians," I replied.

"That's a good job. It's a wonderful cuisine," he said, admiringly.

"It was a lot of work, but I learned a lot."

"I am sure you played hard, too," he said with a smile.

I found out later that Jacques had spent some time early in his career cooking for officers in the French navy, moved up the chain of command, and became the personal chef to the president of France.

A couple weeks later, Jacques and I were going through our pre-taping steps. We were about to shoot the last of twenty-six shows. Just before the walk-through, while we were standing at the stove waiting for the others to assemble, he pointed to the boat.

"When the show is over," he said to me, "that's yours."

I wasn't sure what to say.

Jacques answered my question for me. "Memories."

Recipes

SAUCES AND CONDIMENTS
Sughi e Condimenti

Fresh Tomato Sauce
Serenity Marinara
Dijon Mustard Vinaigrette
Porcini Mayonnaise
Madame Quillier's Rouille

APPETIZERS, SALADS, SANDWICHES
Antipasti, Insalate, Panini

The *Original* Spreadable Tuna Mousse
Marinated Chickpea and Arugula Salad
Shrimp, Summer Vegetable, and Rice Salad
Panzanella
Romano's Warm Shrimp and White Beans
Grilled Tuna *Panini*
Mozzarella in a Carriage, sort of

PASTAS
Primi

Baked Crêpes with the Don's Filling
Shrimp and Garden Vegetable Cannelloni
Linguine with Clams and Zucchini
Spaghettini with San Marzano Red Clam Sauce
Dried Pasta with Tuna Sauce

ENTRÉES
Secondi

Baked Snapper with Tomatoes and Olives

Halibut in Crazy Water

Grilled Swordfish with Naked Caponata

Leghorn-Style Fish Stew

DESSERTS
Dolci

Fresh Fruit *Macedonia* with Mock Limoncello Syrup

Baked Stone Fruit with Sweetened Ricotta and Crushed Amaretti Cookies

Chocolate Capri Cake

Whipped Mascarpone Cream

Very Rich Cooked Cream

Fresh Tomato Sauce

~

Sugo di Pomodoro

MAKES ABOUT 3 CUPS

Ripe and dense plum tomatoes—pomodori maturi in Italian—are crucial for making this very simple sauce. This base can be used wherever tomato sauce is called for and will marry beautifully with other flavors added to it, whether herbs, olives, diced prosciutto or salami, seafood, mushrooms, or cheese. Multiply the recipe to have it on hand. A good trick after peeling the tomatoes is to squeeze the skins a handful at a time to release the precious pulp and tomato water and add it to the puree.

2 1/2 pounds ripe roma tomatoes, peeled
1/2 cup finely chopped yellow onion
2 tablespoons pure olive oil
1 1/2 teaspoons fine sea salt
1 teaspoon sugar

Puree the tomatoes in a food processor or pass through a food mill. Heat the onion and olive oil together in a nonreactive saucepan large enough to hold the tomato puree over medium-low heat. A pot lined with stainless steel works best because it will not affect the flavor of the sauce. Cook, stirring from time to time, until the onion is very soft, translucent, but not caramelized, 5 to 8 minutes from when the onion starts to sizzle.

Add the tomato puree, salt, and sugar. Stir to combine with the onion and oil. Adjust the heat so that the sauce boils slowly and evenly, stirring from time to time from the bottom so the tomato solids do not cluster and burn. Boil until most of the water has been cooked out and the sauce starts to thicken, 35 to 40 minutes. The bubbles in the sauce will appear to be resting in the top surface of the sauce. Check the seasoning and add salt or sugar to taste if needed. The sauce can be refrigerated for up to a week or frozen for up to 3 months.

Serenity Marinara

~

La Nostra Marinara

MAKES ABOUT 4 CUPS

Make this on terra firma. It's a good one. The root of the word marinara *commonly used for tomato sauce is* marinaio—*sailor*—*so it made sense to have a version for* Serenity. *The hot pepper adds a nice element of heat that isn't overpowering, but you can always add more. The subtle layer of seasoning added by the anchovy marries beautifully with fish and seafood, but since there is so little in the recipe, the sauce works with everything. A bonus to having this recipe in your repertoire is that all the ingredients come from the pantry. Perfect for emergencies and remote locations.*

1/4 cup pure olive oil
1 medium yellow onion, peeled, cut into 6 wedges, and the
  layers separated
3 large garlic cloves, peeled and lightly crushed
1 tablespoon roughly chopped anchovy fillet
2 tablespoons finely chopped Italian parsley
Two 28-ounce cans whole peeled tomatoes, pureed with their
  liquid

- 1/2 teaspoon dried oregano
- 1/2 teaspoon hot red pepper flakes
- 1 1/2 teaspoons fine sea salt
- 1 teaspoon sugar

Heat the olive oil, onion, and garlic together in a nonreactive saucepan large enough to hold the tomato puree over medium-low heat. A pot lined with stainless steel works best because it will not affect the flavor of the sauce. Cook, stirring from time to time, until the onion and garlic are soft but not browned, 8 to 10 minutes from when the onion starts to sizzle. Remove the onion and add the anchovy. Using a wooden spoon, mash the anchovy with the garlic so that they combine into a paste. Add the parsley, stir, and continue to cook for 30 seconds, then add the tomato puree, oregano, hot pepper, salt, and sugar. Adjust the heat to keep the sauce at a low, steady boil and cook, stirring from time to time to keep the sauce from burning on the bottom, until the sauce starts to thicken, 30 to 40 minutes. The sauce will have lightened in color, and the bubbles will pop on the surface rather than coming from within. Check the seasoning and add oregano, hot pepper, or salt to taste if needed.

Dijon Mustard Vinaigrette

~

Vinaigrette di Senape

MAKES ABOUT 1/2 CUP

This is French dressing, and it goes with just about any salad or vegetable and even grilled meats. Whisking the oil into the vinegar and mustard will suspend it in the liquid, creating an emulsion that will hold for only an hour or so. This means the vinaigrette has to be made for each use—a bonus, because it will always be fresh. To vary the basic dressing, add crumbled blue cheese, chopped fresh herbs, crushed green peppercorns, honey, or minced black truffle after the last step.

1 tablespoon minced shallot or red onion
1 tablespoon red wine vinegar
1/4 teaspoon fine sea salt
1/8 teaspoon freshly ground black pepper
1 tablespoon plus 1 teaspoon Dijon mustard
1/3 cup plus 1 tablespoon pure olive oil

Blend the shallot, vinegar, salt, pepper, and mustard in a 1- to 2-quart mixing bowl. Let rest for 5 or 10 minutes to soften the shallots. While whisking, add the olive oil in a slow, steady stream to start and keep the emulsion. Then add 1 teaspoon lukewarm water in the same manner to thin the consistency. Set aside for up to an hour so the flavors open up and evolve—or, as chefs like to say, "bloom."

Porcini Mayonnaise

~

Maionese di Porcini

MAKES ABOUT 2 CUPS

At Gastronomia Peck in Milan, one of the greatest food stores on the planet, a signature pairing on their beautiful cold platters is spiny lobster or scampi with porcini mushrooms. This recipe takes from that elegant combination, making a perfect accompaniment for baked, grilled, or poached fish like salmon, sea bass, and halibut. Try it instead of plain mayonnaise in shrimp or lobster salad or as a great alternative to Louis dressing with cocktail shrimp and crab. And for land-based occasions, have it in sandwiches with cold roasted meats or chicken salad.

3/4 cup pure olive oil

3/4 cup canola oil

1/2 ounce dried porcini mushrooms

1 large egg (see Note)

1 large egg yolk

1 tablespoon Dijon mustard

1 tablespoon fresh lemon juice

3/4 teaspoon fine sea salt

1/4 teaspoon freshly ground black pepper

Blend the oils and set aside. Bring 1/2 cup water to a boil in a small saucepan and add the mushrooms. Remove from the heat and set aside to steep for 10 minutes to reconstitute. Place the egg, yolk, mustard, lemon juice, salt, and pepper in a food processor. Lift the mushrooms out of the water and gently squeeze out as much water as possible over the sink. Set aside the mushroom water left in the pan. Roughly chop the mushrooms and add to the food processor. Puree the mixture and, with the machine running, slowly add the blended oils in a thin, steady stream to make an emulsion. Spoon 2 table-spoons of the lukewarm mushroom water off the top and add in a steady stream while the machine is running. The mayonnaise can be used immediately or covered with plastic wrap and refrigerated for up to a week.

Note: This recipe contains raw eggs. People with health prob-lems, the elderly, or those who are pregnant should avoid consuming foods with uncooked eggs, which, in rare cases, carry the potential for Salmonella infections.

Madame Quillier's Rouille

~

Rouille

MAKES ABOUT 1 CUP

How often does one get a handwritten recipe as a bonus when making a purchase at a restaurant supply store? It was quite a gesture when the Madame insisted on giving me her recipe for rouille—"rust"—when I bought, among many things, a mortar and pestle in her shop. This not-so-shy emulsified concoction is to Provençal cookery what tartar sauce is to the world of continental condiments. Traditionally served with fish soup, it is wonderful with fish, shellfish, or things from the grill like chicken and leg of lamb. I made my first few batches in the mortar, but don't worry—a food processor works just fine.

> 1/2 cup (about 5) roughly chopped canned Spanish piquillo
>   peppers
> 1/2 teaspoon minced garlic
> 1/8 teaspoon hot red pepper flakes
> 3/4 cup fresh bread crumbs
> 1/4 cup plus 2 tablespoons pure olive oil
> 1/4 teaspoon fine sea salt

Place the peppers, garlic, and hot pepper flakes in a food processor. Pulse to combine and break down the peppers. You may need to stop the machine to scrape the peppers from the side of the bowl so everything gets pureed evenly. Blend the bread crumbs with 1 tablespoon lukewarm water to combine and form into a thick and pasty mass. Break it up and add to the mixture in the food processor. Puree to a smooth consistency. With the motor running, add the olive oil in a thin, steady stream to combine and create an emulsion. Season with salt.

Chef's Tip: Since raw garlic is being used, cut the garlic clove in half lengthwise before mincing. If there is a green germ inside, pull it out with the tip of a paring knife and discard. Removing it will make the raw garlic flavor less pungent.

The Original Spreadable Tuna Mousse

~

Spuma di Tonno

MAKES ABOUT 1 1/2 CUPS

If I could bring anything to the world of gastronomy, this would be my first entry. The best testimonial was from la Signora. After her first taste it was one of the items she asked for on more than a few occasions. I learned to make it at Albergo del Sole in Maleo, Italy. The chef, Franco, made his with poached John Dory, and he suggested trying it with tuna in olive oil. Serve it as an hors d'oeuvre, snack, or first course. It is especially important to use good-quality tuna. A number are available from Europe: A's Do Mar, Flott, Callipo, and Ortiz. Since there doesn't seem to be a standard for retail tuna packing, I have specified the amount of drained tuna to use.

Serve the mousse with bread sticks, small toasts, croutons, crackers, or in celery stalks. It can be topped with a drizzle of extra virgin olive oil, thinly sliced radish, a few turns of coarsely ground black pepper, a pinch of toasted and ground fennel seeds or Basque espelette chili powder. For a first course, spread a liberal amount on a crouton and serve alongside a nice cluster of green beans in a vinaigrette. It also makes a great tuna sandwich.

1 tablespoon soy sauce

1 tablespoon balsamic vinegar

1 tablespoon fresh lemon juice

10 ounces (about 2 cups) drained Italian, Spanish,
    or Portuguese tuna packed in oil

5 tablespoons unsalted butter, cut into small pieces

2 tablespoons heavy cream

Combine the soy sauce, vinegar, and lemon juice. Break down the tuna in a food processor by pulsing first, then running, until it is evenly chopped but not pureed. Add the liquid seasonings and process until the mixture is smooth. After a few seconds, stop the machine and scrape down the sides of the bowl to incorporate the tuna that didn't get into the puree. With the machine running, add the butter, piece by piece, adding the next only after each is incorporated. Do not overmix. The butter needs to be blended with the tuna but not whipped to the point that it will melt because of the heat generated in the bowl. Add the cream while pulsing the machine, and as soon as it appears incorporated, *basta*—that's it. This will take only a few seconds.

Transfer the mousse to a bowl or storage container and keep refrigerated. The mousse can be made up to 3 days before serving. Take it out of the refrigerator 45 minutes before serving to let it soften.

Wine Recommendation: From Lombardy, a sparkling Franciacorta from Castellino or Bellavista

Marinated Chickpea and Arugula Salad

~

Insalata di Ceci e Ruchetta

MAKES 6 TO 8 FIRST-COURSE OR LUNCH SERVINGS

Except for the arugula, this is right out of the pantry. This classic southern Italian antipasto is a great accompaniment to tuna grilled or packed in oil; seafood; grilled leg of lamb, whether whole, cut into steaks, or as brochettes; or sliced prosciutto.

2 tablespoons minced red onion

1/4 teaspoon minced garlic

2 tablespoons red wine vinegar

1/4 teaspoon fine sea salt

1/4 teaspoon hot red pepper flakes

1/4 cup plus 2 tablespoons extra virgin olive oil

Two 15-ounce cans chickpeas, drained and rinsed

1 medium carrot, grated

1 tablespoon chopped Italian parsley

2 cups loosely packed arugula

In a small bowl, blend the onion, garlic, vinegar, salt, and hot pepper. Let rest for 10 minutes to allow the flavors to open up and evolve—or bloom. While whisking, add the olive oil in a steady stream. In another bowl, combine the chickpeas, carrot, and parsley. Add the dressing and mix gently so the chickpeas are well coated. Cover and refrigerate for 2 to 3 hours, tossing from time to time.

Remove from the refrigerator 30 minutes before serving. Toss the ingredients and adjust the seasoning. Just before serving, add the arugula and blend until the leaves are lightly coated. Serve *subito* (immediately)!

Entertaining Note: If taking this to a picnic or a dinner party, place the marinated chickpeas in the bottom of a container that is more deep than wide. Add a layer of olive oil–packed tuna, cooked shrimp, or steamed and shelled mussels, and then the arugula. Keep chilled. Just before serving, toss from the bottom.

Wine Recommendation: A southern white Fiano di Avellino from Mastroberardino or Feudi di San Gregorio

Shrimp, Summer Vegetable, and Rice Salad

~

Insalata di Riso con Gamberetti e Verdure

MAKES 8 TO 10 FIRST-COURSE OR LUNCH SERVINGS

In summer, rice salads are a great alternative to hot bowls of risotto, and there is certainly no shortage of ingredients that can go into them. Here the high ratio of vegetables and shrimp to the rice makes this a meal in itself, but it is also a great antipasto. Try other vegetables, as long as you have about 7 cups cooked. This recipe is perfect for entertaining since it can be made in advance.

1 cup (7 ounces) Arborio rice

1/2 cup plus 1 tablespoon extra virgin olive oil

1 pound thick or jumbo asparagus

2 to 3 medium (about 1 pound) leeks

1 pound fresh peas in pods or 1 cup frozen

3 medium (about 1 pound) zucchini

2 to 3 medium (about 1/2 pound) carrots, peeled and halved
   lengthwise

1 pound small (31–35 per pound) shrimp, peeled and
   deveined

1 1/2 teaspoons grated lemon zest

1/2 cup roughly chopped Italian parsley

1/2 cup lightly packed torn fresh basil leaves

3 tablespoons fresh lemon juice

1 1/2 teaspoons fine sea salt

1/2 teaspoon freshly cracked black pepper

Put the rice into a quart of boiling water and cook until tender but still slightly firm, 15 to 18 minutes. Drain and then toss with 1 tablespoon of the olive oil. Set aside. While the rice is cooking, prepare the vegetables, keeping each separate. Break the tough bottoms from the asparagus and then peel the fibrous outer green layer from the bottom 2 inches of each stalk. Trim the roots from the bottom of the leeks, then remove the tough outer leaves. Cut each crosswise into 1/4-inch rounds. Rinse under cold water in a strainer to remove all of the sand. Shuck the peas if you're using fresh ones.

Boil the zucchini in boiling salted water in a sauté pan large enough to hold them in a single layer until tender, 10 to 12 minutes. Transfer to a baking sheet to cool, keeping the water boiling. Cook the other vegetables in the same water, cooking each just until tender: the asparagus for 2 to 3 minutes, the leeks for 2 to 3 minutes, the peas for 1 to 2 minutes, the carrots for 6 to 8 minutes. Transfer each to the baking sheet to cool after cooking. There should be enough water left in the pot to cook the shrimp. Adjust the heat to produce a slow boil and simmer the shrimp for 2 to 3 minutes, or until opaque and slightly firm.

When the vegetables have cooled, cut the zucchini and carrots into 3/8-inch pieces and the asparagus into 1/2-inch slices. Place the rice, vegetables, lemon zest, parsley, and basil in a large mixing bowl. Slice the shrimp in half lengthwise and add to the bowl. Keep refrigerated. The salad can be made up to 6 hours before serving.

Take the salad out of the refrigerator 30 minutes before serving and make the dressing. Place the lemon juice, salt, and pepper in a small bowl. Whisk in the remaining olive oil. Add and toss with the salad just before serving. Adjust the seasoning, transfer to a platter, and serve.

Wine Recommendation: A unique Ligurian white Pigato from Bruno or Lupi

Panzanella

~

Panzanella

MAKES 6 FIRST-COURSE OR LUNCH SERVINGS

This Tuscan classic is great as a first course by itself or as a side dish with roasted or grilled meats and fowl. It will become a regular in your stable of go-to recipes, especially in summer, with aromatic sun-ripened tomatoes. Use day-old good-quality bread so it's easier to work with and doesn't get too spongy when tossed in the vinaigrette. Great for picnics too.

1/4 cup plus 2 tablespoons extra virgin olive oil, plus more for
    drizzling
2 tablespoons grated Parmigiano-Reggiano or Grana Padano
    cheese, plus a little more for garnish if desired
6 cups day-old Italian bread, crusts removed, cut into 3/4-inch
    cubes

1 1/2 tablespoons red wine vinegar

1/4 teaspoon fine sea salt

1/8 teaspoon freshly ground black pepper

1 teaspoon anchovy paste (mashed from about 1 anchovy fillet)

1/2 teaspoon dried oregano

2 pounds ripe but not soft tomatoes, cut into 1/2-inch cubes (about 4 cups)

2 cups arugula or chopped dandelion greens

1/2 cup thinly sliced celery heart

1/3 cup very thinly sliced red onion

1/2 cup torn fresh basil leaves

Preheat the oven to 350°F.

Blend 2 tablespoons of the olive oil with the cheese in a large mixing bowl. Coat the bread in this mixture, then spread it out in a single layer on a baking sheet. Keep the bowl for making the dressing in the next step. Bake the croutons until lightly golden, 10 to 12 minutes, tossing from time to time to cook all sides. The bread should be lightly crispy on the outside but still soft on the inside. Set aside to cool.

Make the dressing. Combine the vinegar, salt, pepper, anchovy paste, and oregano. Whisk in the remaining olive oil in a steady stream.

Toss the tomatoes and croutons in the dressing so that the bread absorbs the residual tomato juice and the dressing. Add the arugula, celery, onion, and basil. Toss gently to coat these ingredients, but don't let them get too wilted. Season to taste with salt, pepper, and an extra splash of vinegar if necessary.

Transfer to a serving platter or individual plates. Finish with a drizzle of extra virgin olive oil. A little extra grated cheese isn't a bad thing either. Serve *subito* (immediately)!

Entertaining Note: This salad can be made up to 3 hours before serving. Layer but do not mix the tomatoes, then the bread, arugula, celery, onion, and basil. Cover with plastic wrap and keep refrigerated. Take out 30 minutes before serving and then toss with the dressing. Adjust the seasoning as necessary.

Wine Recommendation: A coastal Tuscan white from the Bolgheri region, Grattamacco Bianco, or Tenuta Belvedere

Romano's Warm Shrimp and White Beans

~

Gamberi e Fagioli con Pomodori e Basilico

MAKES 8 FIRST-COURSE OR LUNCH SERVINGS

This coastal Tuscan antipasto makes a regular appearance during the parade of antipasti at Ristorante Romano in Viareggio. The beans are warm and creamy. The shrimp are cooked in broth just before serving. Sun-ripened tomatoes are perfumed with fresh basil and a great olive oil. When the layers of this dish all come together, this is optimal summer fare and perfect for entertaining once the base components are prepared. Cannellini beans are the most traditional, but other varieties like White Runner or Great Northern will do just fine. Cooking times, as with all beans, will vary, and this will also be a result of their freshness, but plan on up to 3 hours. The rest of the prep work can be done while they are cooking. Or the beans can be cooked a day ahead and will actually benefit from sitting overnight in their flavorful broth.

2¹/4 cups (about 1 pound) dried white cannellini beans
1 medium yellow onion, roots trimmed but bottom still
      attached so the layers stay together, halved lengthwise
4 garlic cloves

2 Turkish bay leaves

4¹/₂ teaspoons fine sea salt

2 large strips lemon zest

¹/₄ teaspoon hot red pepper flakes

1¹/₂ pounds large (16–20 per pound) shrimp, peeled and
    deveined but shells reserved

2 large (about 1¹/₄ pounds) tomatoes, ripe but not too soft,
    seeded and cut into ³/₈-inch dice

¹/₄ cup plus 2 tablespoons extra virgin olive oil

¹/₂ cup lightly packed torn fresh basil leaves

¹/₂ teaspoon freshly ground black pepper

3 or 4 scallions

To cook the beans, cover with cold water by 2 to 3 inches in a
medium saucepan. Bring the water to a boil, then remove the pan
from the heat, cover the pot, and let rest for 1 hour. Strain and rinse
the beans, place back in the pot, then add enough cold water to cover
by 2 to 3 inches, half the onion, 3 of the garlic cloves, and 1 bay leaf.
Bring the water to a very slow boil—a little more than a simmer—and
cook for 1¹/₂ to 2 hours, adding 2 teaspoons of salt after 1 hour. (If
added too soon, the salt will toughen the beans.) Cook until the beans
are tender—soft and creamy but not falling apart—if you're going to
serve the dish right away, in which case keep the beans warm over
very low heat. If you're making the beans a day ahead, cook them until tender but not soft, since they will continue to cook while they
cool and also when reheated later, and then cool them in the water.
Do not strain or remove them from the liquid while hot or their outer
skin will peel. Also, the cooking liquid has a lot of flavor that will only
make them better the longer they are in it. When cool, cover and refrigerate.

While the beans are cooking, prepare the shrimp broth. Boil 6
cups of water with the remaining onion, garlic clove, and bay leaf, the

lemon zest, hot pepper, and 2 teaspoons of salt for a few minutes. Add the shrimp shells and boil slowly for 10 minutes. Pour the broth through a strainer into a bowl and then pour the broth back into the original pot.

If necessary, add a little more water to the beans so they are completely immersed in liquid. Gently stir from time to time and season with salt if necessary. Keep the liquid from boiling so as not to break or overcook the beans. At this point they should have a creamy texture. Bring the shrimp broth to a steady boil.

Blend the tomatoes with the olive oil, basil, and pepper. Set aside. Thinly slice the scallions, including a few inches of the greens.

Working with half the shrimp at a time, simmer them in the broth until opaque and slightly firm, 2 to 3 minutes. Transfer to a baking sheet.

With a slotted spoon, place the beans on a warm serving platter or individual plates. It's fine if some of the flavorful liquid comes with them as you remove from the pot. Place the shrimp on the beans, arranging in a single layer of 3 or 4 per serving. Add the remaining 1/2 teaspoon salt to the tomatoes, then spoon them with the residual oil over the shrimp. Sprinkle the top with the scallions. Serve immediately.

Wine Recommendation: A Tuscan white Vermentino from Cima or a Montecarlo Bianco by Fattoria del Buonamico

Grilled Tuna Panini

~

Panini di Tonno alla Griglia

MAKES 8 SANDWICHES

This is a version of a common sandwich found in cafés and snack bars all along the French coast called pan bagnat, *typically made with canned tuna. Using a grilled piece of tuna takes it to another level. Have your fishmonger cut thin slices from a piece of center-cut loin. Instead of a gas or charcoal grill, you can also make this by using a grill pan on a stove. Either way, make a couple extra; they may leave you wanting more!*

$1/2$ cup black olive paste (tapenade)

2 tablespoons fresh lemon juice

$1/4$ cup extra virgin olive oil

Eight 4-ounce slices fresh tuna

Fine sea salt

Freshly ground black pepper

8 rolls large enough to hold the slices of tuna or 16 thick
     slices country bread like Italian or a French *bâtard*

8 leaves Bibb lettuce

1 large red bell pepper, thinly sliced crosswise

1 green bell pepper, thinly sliced crosswise

1 large tomato, cut into 8 thin slices

4 hard-cooked eggs, sliced

Preheat a grill or a grill pan over medium-high heat. Blend the olive paste with the lemon juice and 2 tablespoons of the olive oil. Set aside.

Season the tuna on both sides with salt and pepper and coat with the remaining olive oil. Grill for 3 to 4 minutes, turning once halfway through the cooking. Transfer to a baking sheet.

Cut the rolls or divide the bread to make sandwiches. Spread the inside surface of each piece with the olive paste. On the bottom slice of bread or roll, place a piece of tuna and add a lettuce leaf, a few slices of red and green bell pepper, and a slice of tomato. Season with salt and pepper. Add a few slices of egg to each sandwich. Cover with the top of the roll and gently press on the sandwich with just enough pressure to blend the ingredients and let any residual liquid get absorbed by the bread.

Chef's Tip: You can also use good-quality tuna in olive oil right out of the can or jar. It's fine and actually true to the original.

Wine Recommendation: A white from Piedmont, Roero Arneis from Bruno Giacosa, or a red Dolcetto d'Alba from Aldo Conterno

Mozzarella in a Carriage, sort of

~

Mozzarella in Carrozza

MAKES 8 SANDWICHES

Attenzione! *These are very addictive. Grilled cheese meets French toast in this hot, savory sandwich perfect for lunch, as an appetizer, or cut into small pieces for a snack. With this version of the Neapolitan classic, you build the sandwich on the griddle. This seems odd at first, but what you end up with is a lighter version of the original—and cleaner hands. The melted cheese and a little adornment of tomato, basil, or other savories inside will be enveloped in a "carriage" of the griddled and baked bread that is coated in a Parmesan-laden egg crust.*

6 large eggs

1/4 cup plus 2 tablespoons finely grated Parmigiano-Reggiano cheese

1 teaspoon fine sea salt

1/2 teaspoon freshly ground black pepper

16 slices white bread, crusts removed

3 tablespoons unsalted butter

8 ounces whole-milk mozzarella, cut into 16 thin slices

1 large tomato, cut into 8 thin slices

16 fresh basil leaves

Preheat the oven to 275°F. Preheat a griddle or cast-iron pan over medium-low heat.

Whisk the eggs with 1/4 cup plus 2 tablespoons lukewarm water. Add the Parmesan, salt, and pepper. Transfer to a baking dish large enough to hold 4 pieces of bread. Only one side of the bread will be coated. Working with 4 slices of bread at a time, place them in the egg mixture. Let rest for 10 seconds or so.

Wipe some butter on the griddle, then place the bread on it egg side down. Put 2 pieces of mozzarella on each slice of bread and season with a pinch of salt. Add a slice of tomato to each and season with some salt. Place 2 basil leaves on each. Coat 4 more pieces of bread with the egg wash on one side then place one on each sandwich egg side up. Cook until golden brown on the underside, about 5 minutes. Place a small pat of butter on the top of each sandwich, gently pressing it into the bread. Carefully turn the sandwiches with a spatula. As they start to cook on the other side, gently press down on each to help bind everything together. Cook until the second side is golden brown, an additional 3 to 5 minutes. Transfer to a baking sheet. Repeat the procedure to make 8 sandwiches.

Bake until the cheese is completely melted and the egg absorbed by the bread is cooked throughout, 12 to 15 minutes. Hold for a couple of minutes or so before slicing, then serve immediately.

Entertaining Note: The sandwiches can be made up to 1 hour in advance. Just hold off on putting them in the oven until at least 15 minutes before serving. They may need a few more minutes of baking time since the sandwiches will have cooled.

Chef's Note: Pair the mozzarella with other fillings—sliced ham, prosciutto or salami, chopped olives, anchovies, hot red pepper flakes, oregano, cooked and chopped spinach, truffles, or try different cheeses like Fontina, Taleggio, or a young Montasio.

Wine Recommendation: A sparkling white from Sicily, Murgo brut NV or a sparkling red from Lombardy, Sangue di Giuda by Bruno Verde

Baked Crêpes with the Don's Filling

~

Crespelle al Forno, Ripiena di Don Alfonso

MAKES 8 FIRST-COURSE OR LUNCH SERVINGS (16 CRÊPES)

This sublime recipe is inspired by the signature ravioli made at Ristorante Don Alfonso near the Amalfi Coast. It is also a version of a Neapolitan dish called crespelle ripiene, simply put, stuffed crêpes. When baked, the filling ingredients

blossom to a light and cheesy flavor highlighted with ham and basil. When paired with a pungent tomato sauce that cuts through the cheese, the result is a flavor experience the Italians like to call ottimo (optimum)!

For the Crêpes:

> 2 cups all-purpose flour
> 6 large eggs
> 2¼ cups whole milk
> 2 tablespoons grated Parmigiano-Reggiano or
>> Grana Padano cheese
> 2 teaspoons fine sea salt
> 2 tablespoons unsalted butter

For the Ripiena (Filling):

> Two 15-ounce containers whole-milk ricotta
> 2 large egg yolks
> 8 ounces fresh mozzarella, grated
> 2 ounces baked ham (from a deli slice ⅛ inch thick),
>> cut into small dice
> ⅓ cup roughly chopped fresh basil, plus 8 sprigs for garnish
> 2 tablespoons grated Parmigiano-Reggiano or Grana Padano
>> cheese
> 1½ teaspoons fine sea salt
> ½ teaspoon freshly ground black pepper

> 3 cups Fresh Tomato Sauce (page 280)
> 2 tablespoons grated Parmigiano-Reggiano or Grana Padano
>> cheese
> 2 tablespoons extra virgin olive oil

To make the crêpe batter, sift the flour into a mixing bowl. In another bowl, beat the eggs, then mix to incorporate the milk. Slowly pour the egg mixture into the flour while whisking to create a smooth batter. Pour through a strainer. Add the cheese and the salt. Reserve at room temperature covered with plastic for 1 hour if making crêpes the same day or refrigerate the batter for up to 1 day ahead. Take the batter out of the refrigerator 1 hour before cooking.

To make the filling, stir the ricotta with the egg yolks in a mixing bowl to make them smooth. Mix in the remaining filling ingredients, adding more salt and pepper if needed. The flavor should be a touch salty as for pasta fillings. It can also be made a day in advance and in fact will be even better after the flavors develop overnight.

To make the crêpes, heat a 10-inch nonstick skillet over medium-low heat. Use a paper towel to coat the bottom surface of the pan with 1/2 teaspoon of the butter. It should lightly sizzle for optimal heat. Stir the crêpe batter, then add 1/4 cup to the pan. Keeping the pan near the heat, tilt in each direction so the batter coats the entire bottom surface in an even circle. If it is too thick and doesn't move easily, add a little milk to the rest of the batter to thin the consistency a touch. Cook the crêpe until dry on the top surface, about 3 minutes. With a rubber spatula, lift the crêpe and turn it over to cook on the other side, 10 to 15 seconds.

Transfer to a baking sheet, then repeat with the rest of the batter, buttering the pan in between crêpes. Space the crêpes on the baking sheet so as each one cools, the next one does not cover it, then make layers. To make the crêpes in advance, stack the cooled crêpes on a plate, cover with plastic wrap, and refrigerate for up to a day. Bring the crêpes to room temperature before separating and filling; otherwise they will tear.

To bake the crêpes, preheat the oven to 350°F. Butter a baking sheet. Spread a shy 1/3 cup of the filling evenly over the textured side of each crêpe to about 1/2 inch from the edge all around (the smooth surface is the side that was cooked first). Fold the crêpes in half, then with the back edge of your hand or index finger gently make an indentation in the crêpe and filling to form a crease perpendicular to the center of the fold. Fold the crêpes in half again to make a quarter of a circle. Transfer to the baking sheet, leaving some space between crêpes.

Bake until the crêpes start to brown and puff, 15 to 20 minutes. Meanwhile, warm the sauce. The consistency should be thin and smooth, so add a little water, a couple tablespoons at a time, if necessary. Arrange the crêpes on a serving platter or on individual plates and offer the sauce on the side or top each with some sauce, about 2 tablespoons per crêpe. Add some grated cheese and a drizzle of the olive oil, then garnish with the basil sprigs. Serve *subito* (immediately)!

Wine Recommendation: From Campania, a white Pallagrello Bianco from Terre del Principe or a red Aglianico from De Conciliis

Shrimp and Garden Vegetable Cannelloni

~

Cannelloni con Ripiena di Gamberi e Verdure

MAKES 6 FIRST-COURSE OR LUNCH SERVINGS

This wonderful filling made with shrimp, a few vegetables, and just a little heat from hot red pepper flakes is used to stuff tiny calamari—calamaretti—at Ristorante Romano in Viareggio. For flavor and economy, I've added fresh bread crumbs to the original recipe, making it delicious as a pasta filling. It is also great as a stuffing for vegetables like zucchini and tomatoes. Or make little patties, coat in dried bread crumbs, and cook as if making crab cakes. Best if the filling is made a day in advance to give the ingredients a chance to marry and develop better flavor.

1/4 cup plus 1 tablespoon pure olive oil
1 tablespoon sliced garlic

1/4 teaspoon hot red pepper flakes

1/2 pound green zucchini, grated (about 1 1/2 cups)

1/2 pound yellow zucchini, grated (about 1 1/2 cups)

1 medium carrot, grated

Fine sea salt

2 to 3 large garlic cloves, peeled and lightly crushed

1 pound large (16–20 per pound) shrimp, peeled, deveined, and cut into 1/2-inch pieces

2 tablespoons dry white wine

1 large egg yolk

2 cups fresh bread crumbs

2 tablespoons chopped fresh basil

12 cannelloni shells

3 cups Fresh Tomato Sauce (page 280)

Extra virgin olive oil for drizzling

2 tablespoons roughly chopped Italian parsley

Heat 2 tablespoons of the pure olive oil with the sliced garlic in a large sauté pan over medium heat until it starts to brown, about 3 minutes. Add the hot pepper flakes, swirl in the oil, and immediately add the zucchini and carrot. Stir from time to time until the vegetables are soft and begin to break apart, about 20 minutes. The mixture should be fairly dry at this point. Season with salt. Spread the mixture on a baking sheet to cool.

In the same pan, heat another 2 tablespoons of the oil with the crushed garlic cloves over medium heat. Gently shake and tilt the pan so the cloves are immersed and sizzling at one side of the pan in a pool of the oil. As the garlic starts to turn golden, lay the pan flat on the burner, then add the shrimp. Sauté until opaque but still tender, about 2 minutes. Season with salt. Deglaze the pan by adding the wine and scraping any bits from the bottom of the pan. Transfer the shrimp to the baking sheet with the vegetables to cool. Scrape any residual oil and cooking liquid with a rubber spatula out of the pan and onto the shrimp and vegetables.

When the mixture has cooled, working in 2 batches, pulse in a food processor to break down the shrimp into small pieces without pureeing. You can also do this by hand with a chef's knife. Make sure the mixture is combined evenly. Transfer to a bowl. Adjust the seasoning. Mix in the egg yolk, bread crumbs, and basil. The mixture should be fairly dry and should hold together. Make the mixture up to a day in advance and refrigerate to give the flavors a chance to develop.

Cook the cannelloni shells in salted boiling water until pliable but not too soft since they will cook again when filled. Have a tray ready to cool the pasta instead of running it under cold water. Carefully remove the pieces of pasta with a slotted spoon or skimmer so as not to break them. When the pasta is cool enough to be handled, carefully cut each along the length to open it into a flat piece.

Preheat the oven to 350°F.

Oil a baking dish large enough to hold all of the cannelloni when rolled. Form a log using slightly more than 1/4 cup of the filling that is the same length as an opened cannelloni shell. Place it along one edge of the pasta and roll it gently in the pasta, keeping the roll snug. There should be a slight overlap when you finish the roll. Place seam side down in the baking dish. Repeat with the remaining filling and cannelloni. Add 1/2 cup water to the pan, cover with aluminum foil, and bake for 25 to 30 minutes.

Warm the sauce in a nonreactive saucepan (stainless steel is best). Use a thin spatula to transfer 2 cannelloni per serving to warmed plates or put all of them on a serving platter. Spoon the sauce on top. Finish with a drizzle of extra virgin olive oil and the parsley. Serve *subito* (immediately)!

Wine Recommendation: From coastal Tuscany, a white Argentato Bianco from Le Pupille or a red Le Difese from Tenuta San Guido

Linguine with Clams and Zucchini

~

Linguine con Vongole e Zucchini

MAKES 4 FIRST-COURSE OR LUNCH SERVINGS

A popular and classic primo of the Amalfi Coast, this dish can be found on menus throughout the region in countless different versions. This recipe is an adaptation from Ristorante Lo Scoglio in Marina del Cantone. One of the waiters gave me the method after our epic lunch for la Signora's birthday. Small world. I knew him from when I worked at Don Alfonso. He grew up with Alfonso. This camaraderie led to the secret in the recipe to be revealed—the seemingly overcooked zucchini in the method is interesting and makes for very flavorful oil in which to cook the clams.

4 large garlic cloves, peeled

$1/4$ cup extra virgin olive oil

$1/4$ cup pure olive oil

4 medium (about $11/2$ pounds) zucchini, sliced into
$1/8$-inch-thick rounds

$1/2$ teaspoon fine sea salt

32 littleneck clams (about $31/2$ pounds), washed

$1/4$ teaspoon hot red pepper flakes, plus extra for serving

2 tablespoons chopped Italian parsley

12 ounces linguine

1 tablespoon unsalted butter

Lightly crush the garlic cloves and heat with both oils in a large nonreactive sauté pan over medium heat until they start to sizzle. Adjust the heat so the garlic continues to cook evenly in the oil, releasing its own essential oils and softens, but does not brown, about 2 minutes. Add the zucchini and carefully blend with the oil. Season with salt. Continue to cook slowly, stirring from time to time, until the squash is completely softened and starts to break apart but does not brown, about 20 minutes. Remove from the heat and let rest in the oil for 2 hours. Pour into a fine-mesh strainer, reserving the zucchini and oil separately. Keep the same pan, without cleaning, for cooking the clams.

Heat the zucchini oil in the pan over medium heat until it starts to sizzle. Add the clams, cover the pan, and turn the heat to medium-high. Cook the clams, gently shaking the pan from time to time, until they start to open, 5 to 6 minutes. Cooking time will vary, depending on the size of the clams and the thickness of the shells. Add the reserved zucchini, hot pepper flakes, and parsley. Gently stir with the clams. Set aside.

Boil the linguine in an abundant amount of salted water until done to taste. Reserve 1/2 cup of the pasta water before draining the linguine. Heat the clams and zucchini with the butter. Toss with the linguine, adding a little of the pasta water so that the zucchini and pan liquid coat the pasta like a sauce.

Transfer to a warm serving platter or individual pasta bowls. Start with the pasta, then top with the clams and zucchini. Serve *subito*—immediately—with extra hot pepper flakes on the side.

Wine Recommendation: Whites from Campania, a Falanghina from Castello Ducale or Lacrima Christi from Villa Carafa

Spaghettini with San Marzano Red Clam Sauce

~

Spaghettini con Vongole in Sugo Rosso

MAKES 4 FIRST-COURSE OR LUNCH SERVINGS

Everyone should have a red clam sauce in his or her repertoire. This one is particularly good for smaller clams like littlenecks or clams sold as vongole. *If you make this a couple hours ahead of serving, the sauce will take on a nice hint of clam flavor with the other aromatics. Except for the clams and the basil, all of the other ingredients come out of the pantry, making this an excellent recipe for getting on the express line at the store. With a few other things to round out the meal, you'll still be buying fewer than ten items!*

1 large garlic clove, peeled

2 tablespoons pure olive oil

4 pounds littleneck clams

2 tablespoons extra virgin olive oil, plus more for finishing

2 tablespoons minced onion

1 tablespoon sliced garlic

2 tablespoons chopped Italian parsley

1/4 teaspoon hot red pepper flakes

One 28-ounce can San Marzano tomatoes with their juice,
       pureed (2 cups)

1/2 teaspoon sugar

Fine sea salt

12 ounces spaghettini

1/4 cup torn fresh basil leaves

Lightly crush the garlic clove and heat with the pure olive oil in a large nonreactive sauté pan with a lid over medium heat. When the garlic starts to sizzle, gently shake and tilt the pan so the clove is immersed and sizzling at one side of the pan in a pool of the oil. As the clove starts to turn golden, lay the pan flat on the burner so the oil covers the entire surface. It is important the clams be dry so they don't flare up because of any water on them when added to the hot oil. Add the clams and immediately cover the pan. Gently shake the pan from time to time with the cover on and cook until the clams start to open, 5 to 6 minutes. Cooking time will vary, depending on the size of the clams and the thickness of the shells. As they start to open, remove them with a slotted spoon and transfer to a baking sheet to cool. Strain the remaining liquid in the pan through a fine-mesh strainer and set aside. You should have about 1/2 cup.

Wipe out the pan and return to the stove over medium-low heat. Add the extra virgin olive oil, onion, and sliced garlic. Cook, stirring from time to time, until the onion is softened and the garlic is just beginning to caramelize, about 4 minutes. Add half the parsley, the hot pepper flakes, the reserved clam juice, tomato puree, and sugar. Stir to produce an even consistency. If necessary, season with salt (this will depend on how salty the clam juice is). Adjust the heat to maintain a slow, even boil. Cook until the sauce begins to thicken and lightens in color, about 10 minutes. Stir from time to time, scraping the bottom with a wooden spoon or paddle.

While the sauce is cooking remove the clams from the shells. When the sauce is ready, turn off the heat and add the clams with any residual liquid to the pan.

Cook the spaghettini in a liberal amount of salted water to al dente. While the pasta is cooking, bring the sauce to a gentle simmer. Reserve 1/2 cup of the pasta water before draining the spaghettini.

A little at a time, add the pasta water to the sauce until it is a touch looser than seems correct. The pasta will absorb the sauce when it is added. Add the basil, then the spaghettini, and gently toss over the heat for a minute or so. If the pasta absorbs too much sauce and the pan looks dry, add a touch of pasta water as you work.

Transfer to a warm serving platter or individual pasta bowls. Finish with a drizzle of extra virgin olive oil and the remaining chopped parsley. Serve *subito* (immediately) because *la pasta fredda non' e buona!* Cold pasta is not good!

Entertaining Note: The sauce can be made up to 2 hours before serving, when the clams are added back in.

Wine Recommendation: From Campania, a white Greco di Tufo from Feudi di San Gregorio or a red Aglianico Murellaia from De Lucia

Dried Pasta with Tuna Sauce

~

Pasta Asciutta con Sugo di Tonno

MAKES 6 FIRST-COURSE OR LUNCH SERVINGS,

OR 4 MAIN-COURSE SERVINGS

Just a few ingredients from the pantry and you have a great lunch or dinner main course. The method works for other seafood like shrimp and mussels.

1 1/2 cups *Serenity* Marinara (page 281)

Fine sea salt

3 1/2 cups (12 ounces) dried short tube pasta like rigatoni, ziti, or penne rigate

One 6- to 8-ounce can or jar Italian, Spanish, or Portuguese tuna packed in oil, drained

2 tablespoons extra virgin olive oil
1 tablespoon freshly chopped Italian parsley

Bring the sauce to a simmer in a pan large enough for both the sauce and the cooked pasta. Bring an abundant amount of salted water to a boil. Cook the pasta in the boiling water according to the package instructions. Drain, keeping a little of the pasta water. Add the tuna to the sauce, but do not overmix as it will break down when the pasta is added. Thin the sauce if necessary with a little of the reserved pasta water and adjust the salt to taste. Gently toss the pasta with the sauce and cook for a minute or so in the sauce. If the pan gets too dry and there is no residual sauce in the bottom, add a little more of the reserved pasta water so that there is an even coating of sauce around the pasta and a little in the bottom of the pan. Transfer to a serving platter or individual pasta bowls. Drizzle the top with a little extra virgin olive oil and finish with the parsley. Serve *subito* (immediately)!

Wine Recommendation: A Sardinian Vermentino from Argiolas or Contini

Baked Snapper with Tomatoes and Olives

~

Pesce al Forno con Pomodori e Olive Neri

MAKES 8 MAIN-COURSE SERVINGS

This versatile recipe for baking fish calls for snapper, but you can use any other tender, flaky fish like bass, sole, or bream. Once you get comfortable with the baking method, try using different herbs, olives, and spices like ground coriander or

even a touch of cumin. Pitted Niçoise olives are available at specialty food stores
and are worth the hunt. Unpitted will work as well—just remember to tell your
guests! Serve with roasted summer squash.

1/4 cup plus 2 tablespoons extra virgin olive oil, plus a little oil
    for drizzling
Eight 6-ounce pieces snapper fillet
Fine sea salt
Freshly ground black pepper
1 teaspoon lightly toasted and ground fennel seeds
1 cup Niçoise olives, pitted
1/4 cup dry white wine
13/4 pounds ripe but firm tomatoes, seeded and cut into
    3/8-inch dice
1/2 cup lightly packed torn fresh basil leaves

Preheat the oven to 400°F.

Put 3 tablespoons of the olive oil in each of 2 baking dishes,
each large enough to hold 4 pieces of fish with space in between. Put
the dishes in the oven to heat the oil but don't let it get to the smoking point.

With a sharp utility or boning knife, make a few shallow slices
through the skin of each snapper fillet to keep them from curling in
the hot oil. Season each piece on both sides with salt, pepper, and fennel. Place the fish in the hot oil, skin side down, to coat with the oil,
then immediately turn with a fish spatula so that the skin side is up.
The oil is the correct temperature if you hear a light sizzle when the
fish is added. Divide the olives between the dishes, scattering them
around the fish, then splash equal amounts of wine into each dish.

Bake for 6 to 8 minutes, until the fish is slightly firm and starts
to flake when the tip of a knife is inserted into the flesh. The cooking
time will vary depending on the thickness of the fillets. Season the

tomatoes with salt and pepper, then divide them between the baking dishes, making sure they fall between the pieces of fish and into the hot pan juices. The tomatoes just need to get slightly wilted in the hot pans.

With a fish spatula, transfer the fish to warmed plates or a serving platter. Toss the basil in the olives and tomatoes, and when the leaves are coated with the pan juices, spoon the mixture over the fish. I always like to add a drizzle of extra virgin olive oil to finish for tradition's sake. Serve immediately.

Equipment Note: I don't recommend using aluminum baking pans since the wine and tomatoes will react unfavorably and become bitter. Glazed ceramic, stainless steel, enameled cast iron, and Spanish *cazuelas* offer the best heat. Ovenproof glass will work too.

Entertaining Note: You can bake the fish till about three-quarters done and hold it for up to an hour before serving. Drape plastic wrap over the fish to keep it moist. To serve, remove the plastic, spoon some of the pan juices over the fish, then finish in the oven. By the time you start to hear the ingredients in the baking dish sizzle, the fish will be ready. Continue as directed. To hold the tomatoes, coat them with a little olive oil and do not season until ready to add to the fish. Adding salt too soon will pull water from the tomatoes and make the finished dish too watery.

Wine Recommendation: A Ligurian white Vermentino from Lupi or Tenuta Giuncheo

Halibut in Crazy Water

~

Pesce in Acqua Pazza

MAKES 6 MAIN-COURSE SERVINGS

From the region of Campania and a classic of Neapolitan cooking, this recipe is all about a great piece of fish cooked in a wonderfully simple way. Since the list is short, using great ingredients is paramount. At the beginning of the cooking, everything in the pan is fairly dry, but by the time the fish is cooked, there will be a simmering bath of acqua pazza—*crazy water. This is a perfect way to cook halibut and other flaky fish like snapper, grouper, or bass. Use vine-ripened tomatoes that are not too soft. And by rinsing off the capers, you will get seasoning from the capers, not the flavor of the brine. Serve with roasted or steamed potatoes.*

Six 6-ounce pieces skinless halibut fillet

Fine sea salt

Freshly cracked black pepper

2 large garlic cloves, peeled

2 tablespoons extra virgin olive oil, plus a little oil for drizzling

About 1³/4 pounds ripe, firm tomatoes, seeded and cut into
      ³/8-inch dice (3 cups)

2 tablespoons finely chopped Italian parsley

1¹/2 tablespoons drained capers, rinsed and finely minced

Season the fish on both sides with salt and pepper. Lightly crush the garlic cloves and put in a sauté pan with a lid that is large enough to hold all the fish and some of the tomatoes in between in a single layer. Add the olive oil and heat over medium heat. When the garlic starts to sizzle, gently shake and tilt the pan so the cloves are immersed and sizzling at one side of the pan in a pool of the oil. As the cloves start to turn golden, lay the pan flat on the burner so the oil covers the entire surface. Place the fish in the pan, skin side down. Tilt the pan so you can spoon some of the garlic oil over the exposed side of the fish. Season the tomatoes with salt and pepper. Add the tomatoes and parsley, evenly distributing them over the entire surface of the fish and in between the fillets. Cover and lower the heat so the pan juices come to a slow, even boil. Add the capers 2 to 3 minutes later so their flavor will not overpower the rest of the dish. Continue to simmer until the fish is opaque and slightly firm, 3 to 4 minutes.

Transfer the fish with a thin spatula to warm plates or a serving platter. Using a slotted spoon, place the tomatoes over the fish, then with a regular spoon, place some of the residual "crazy water" in the pan over the fish and enough on the dish or platter to serve it in a shallow pool. Finish with a drizzle of olive oil. Serve *subito* (immediately)!

Entertaining Note: You can make this dish an hour ahead of serving; just don't cook the fish all the way. The best way to do this is to stop when the top of the fish is still raw. Keep the lid off until it cools so the condensation that would occur does not make the pan sauce too watery. Reheat, covered, over medium-low heat.

Wine Recommendation: From Campania, a white Pallagrello Bianco from Vestini Campagnano or a red Neranico Irpinia Rosso from Salvatore Molettieri

Grilled Swordfish with Naked Caponata

~

Pesce Spada alla Griglia con Caponata Nuda

MAKES 4 MAIN-COURSE SERVINGS

Caponata is typically an eggplant dish, but in this stripped-down variation, everything is included except the eggplant. And instead of using a tomato-based sauce, pomodorini—small tomatoes—are roasted before being combined with the rest of the ingredients, making for a lighter and very colorful blending of flavors and textures. It is perfect on swordfish but works just as well with other firm-fleshed fish, chicken, and lamb. Of course, you can add grilled, roasted, or fried eggplant to the mixture to make a great antipasto or side dish.

$1/4$ cup plus 1 tablespoon extra virgin olive oil

2 large garlic cloves, peeled and lightly crushed

2 cups (about 12 ounces) Sweet 100 cherry tomatoes

$3/4$ cup pitted and halved green olives

$1/3$ cup blanched almonds, toasted

$1/3$ cup golden raisins

$1/3$ cup thinly sliced celery heart

2 teaspoons minced drained capers

$1/4$ teaspoon hot red pepper flakes

$1/2$ teaspoon dried oregano

Four 8-ounce pieces 1-inch-thick center-cut swordfish

Fine sea salt

Freshly ground black pepper

$1^1/2$ teaspoons red wine vinegar

1 tablespoon chopped Italian parsley

Preheat the oven to 400°F. Preheat a grill or grill pan to medium-high heat.

Put 2 tablespoons of the olive oil and the garlic cloves in an ovenproof dish that will hold the tomatoes in a single layer, then place in the oven to heat the oil and lightly brown the garlic, about 8 minutes. Carefully add the tomatoes to the baking dish, toss gently to coat with the hot oil, then continue to bake until the skins crack but the tomatoes do not burst, about 5 minutes. Gently toss them from time to time. Add the olives, almonds, raisins, celery, capers, hot pepper, and oregano. Carefully mix the ingredients and continue to bake for another minute or two to warm everything together. Remove from the oven and set aside.

Season the fish on both sides with salt and pepper, then coat with 2 tablespoons of the remaining oil. Grill the fish until the steaks are opaque and slightly firm, 6 to 8 minutes, turning once halfway through the cooking. Transfer to warmed plates or a serving platter.

Add the remaining 1 tablespoon of oil, the vinegar, and parsley to the reserved topping and toss gently to combine. Season with salt and pepper to taste. Spoon over the fish. Serve immediately.

Entertaining Note: The topping can be made a couple of hours ahead. When the tomatoes are done, remove from the oven, let the pan cool for 10 or 15 minutes, then add the other ingredients. Reheat before serving, adding the vinegar and salt as directed. The recipe can be doubled for larger groups; just make sure the baking dish is larger or use two.

Wine Recommendation: Sicilian reds, Don Pietro Rosso from Principi di Spadafora or Rosso del Soprano from Palari

Leghorn-Style Fish Stew

~

Cacciucco Livornese

MAKES 8 MAIN-COURSE SERVINGS

From the Tuscan commercial port city of Leghorn (Livorno), this is one of Italy's best-known coastal fish stews. The four-seasons method lets the variety of market availability direct which fish to use. Typically, a combination of five different fish, shellfish, or seafood should be chosen, one for each c in the word cacciucco. *What's important is to cook them beginning with the firmest and finishing with the flakiest so as to not overcook. A great dish for entertaining, it should be served with thick slices of grilled bread, soft polenta, or steamed potatoes.*

8 garlic cloves, peeled

3 tablespoons pure olive oil

2 1/2 pounds littleneck clams, washed and shells dried

1/2 cup dry white wine

1 1/2 pounds mussels, washed, beards removed, and shells
    dried

4 cups *Serenity* Marinara (page 281)

1/4 teaspoon hot red pepper flakes

1 pound tuna or swordfish fillet, cut into 1 1/2-inch pieces

Fine sea salt

Freshly ground black pepper

1 pound sea bass or mahimahi, cut into 1 1/2-inch pieces

1 pound halibut or flounder, cut into 1 1/2-inch pieces

1 1/2 tablespoons chopped fresh oregano

Extra virgin olive oil for drizzling

2 tablespoons roughly chopped Italian parsley

Lightly crush the garlic cloves, then heat them with the pure olive oil in a large sauté pan with a lid over medium heat. When the garlic starts to sizzle, gently shake and tilt the pan so the cloves are immersed and sizzling at one side of the pan in a pool of the oil. As the cloves start to turn golden, lay the pan flat on the burner so the oil covers the entire surface. It is important the clams be dry so they don't flare up because of any water on them when added to the hot oil. Add the clams and immediately cover the pan. Gently shake the pan to roll the clams in the hot oil, then, with the cover slightly ajar, add the wine and immediately cover again. Continue to cook, gently shaking the pan from time to time, until the clams start to open, 5 to 6 minutes. Cooking time will vary, depending on the size of the clams and the thickness of the shells. Transfer them with a slotted spoon to a baking sheet to cool. Add the mussels to the pan and cook in the same manner. Their cooking time will be much shorter than for the clams.

Add the marinara sauce and hot pepper flakes to the pan and blend with the residual liquid from the shellfish. Adjust the heat to produce a steady simmer. When the clams and mussels are cool enough to handle, remove the top shells, being careful to reserve any residual liquid, and add it to the sauce. The clams and mussels will be added later in their half shells.

Season the tuna on all sides, then add the sauce, keeping enough space between pieces so that the next fish can be placed in between. Adjust the heat so that the sauce remains at a simmer. Cook for about 3 minutes, then season and add the sea bass. Repeat the cooking, then do the same for the halibut.

Add the oregano to the pan, then place the clams and mussels in the sauce and between the pieces of fish. Do this gently so as not to break the pieces of fish, and gently shake the pan to coat the shellfish with the sauce and create an even layer of seafood in the pan.

Using a large kitchen or serving spoon, divide the fish and shellfish with some of the sauce among warmed pasta bowls or arrange on a serving platter. Drizzle with the extra virgin olive oil, then finish with the parsley. Serve *subito* (immediately)!

Equipment Note: A 12-inch sauté pan or casserole is best, and remember that a stainless or enameled interior will keep the wine and tomato sauce from creating any off flavor or bitterness.

Entertaining Note: The stew can be made up to an hour before serving. To reheat, bring back to serving temperature over low heat, covered, so that the fish does not overcook or fall apart.

Wine Recommendation: A deep Tuscan white from the Chianti region, Querciabella Batar, or a coastal red from the Bolgheri region, Le Macchiole Rosso

Fresh Fruit Macedonia with Mock Limoncello Syrup

~

Macedonia di Frutte Fresche con Sciroppo di Limoncello

MAKES 8 DESSERT SERVINGS

By consensus, Italy's best-known fruit salad is named after the country of Macedonia, the first province of the Roman Empire, as a dedication to the many different people who have inhabited its territory throughout history. The mixture of fruits given here is a suggestion for choosing the best the season has to offer. Limoncello, the ubiquitous southern Italian digestivo made by infusing a clear liquor, sugar, and lemon peel, is the inspiration for this very refreshing syrup.

For the Syrup:

>¹/₄ cup water
>
>¹/₄ cup plus 1 tablespoon grappa
>
>¹/₂ cup sugar
>
>Strips of peel from ¹/₂ lemon

For the Fruit Salad:

>2 large (about 1¹/₄ pounds) white peaches
>
>2 large (about 1 pound) nectarines
>
>3 large (about 1 pound) plums
>
>4 to 6 (about ³/₄ pound) apricots
>
>1 pint strawberries, washed, stemmed, and cored
>
>¹/₂ pint blueberries

To make the syrup, heat the water and grappa in a small non-reactive saucepan over medium heat. Add the sugar. Stir to dissolve. Add the lemon peel. When the liquid comes to a boil, lower the heat to produce a slow, even boil and cook for a few minutes. Cool. Cover and keep refrigerated. The syrup can be held for up to a week.

To make the fruit salad, minimal handling of each fruit is important so as not to bruise since they will be mixed together when the syrup is added and will make for a better presentation. Cut the peaches and nectarines to remove the pits, then cut into ³/₄-inch pieces. Cut the plums and apricots to remove the pits, then cut into thin wedges. Halve or quarter the strawberries, depending on their size. Place the blueberries on top. Cover and keep refrigerated up to 3 hours before serving.

For serving, take the fruit out of the refrigerator an hour before serving. Just before serving, remove the lemon peel from the syrup and pour over the fruit. Toss gently to coat the fruit with syrup. Serve cold.

Baked Stone Fruit with Sweetened Ricotta and Crushed Amaretti Cookies

~

Frutte al Forno con Ricotta Dolce e Biscotti Rotti

MAKES 8 DESSERT SERVINGS

Except for the fruit, all of the ingredients can be in the pantry, leaving the trip to the market for finding what's best in summer. The fruit looks beautiful when baked, and if you're using oven-to-table baking dishes, this is a nice addition to a dessert buffet. This method is great in winter with baking pears like Bosc. Instead of the amaretti cookies, a little freshly grated nutmeg is a pleasant alternative.

1/2 cup golden raisins

1/2 cup heavy cream

2 tablespoons honey

2 tablespoons dark rum

One 15-ounce container ricotta cheese

8 (about 31/2 pounds) nectarines or peaches, slightly
    underripe

8 tablespoons (1 stick) unsalted butter, very soft but
    not melted

1/3 cup sugar

8 to 10 amaretti cookies

To prepare the ricotta, pour a cup of boiling water over the raisins in a small bowl. Set aside. When cool, drain the raisins. Whip the cream with the honey and the rum until it starts to thicken. Fold the ricotta into the cream, then continue to whisk until soft peaks form. Stir in the raisins. Keep refrigerated until serving time. The ricotta mixture can be made up to a day in advance.

To bake the fruit, place an oven rack on the lowest level and preheat the broiler. Cut the nectarines in half, remove the pit, then cut into quarters. Lightly butter 1 or 2 baking dishes large enough to hold the fruit in a single layer cut side up. Brush a little butter over the cut surface and pit cavity of each piece of fruit. Sprinkle the sugar in an even layer over the same surface. The butter will help keep the sugar on the fruit. Bake under the broiler until the butter and sugar caramelize and the fruit starts to become tender, about 12 minutes. Set aside.

To serve, place 4 pieces of fruit in a dessert or shallow bowl. Spoon a dollop of the ricotta over the fruit. Add crushed pieces of the cookies over the ricotta.

Chef's Tip: For a nice addition, reduce a cup of inexpensive balsamic vinegar by half in a small nonreactive saucepan. Set aside to cool. Drizzle on or around the fruit just before serving.

Wine Recommendation: A unique Tuscan sweet white wine from Montalcino, Moscadello di Montalcino from Col d'Orcia or Capanna

Chocolate Capri Cake

~

Torta di Cioccolato Caprese

MAKES 10 DESSERT SERVINGS

On the island of Capri, I saw in the pastry shops a cake called torta caprese—*a chocolate and almond cake that looked flourless—but finding a recipe proved*

difficult. I adapted the chocolate torta recipe from Albergo del Sole and created a new one by incorporating homemade almond flour. This nice addition to the repertoire is easy to make and is a great go-to recipe. Because the technique is very much like making a soufflé, it has a light, airy, and moist texture that is not shy in flavor. With the espresso crema, the flavor pairing is ottimo (optimal)!

12 tablespoons (1 1/2 sticks) unsalted butter, plus a little more
    for the cake pan
8 ounces unsweetened chocolate
1/2 cup (3 ounces) whole almonds, toasted
2 tablespoons all-purpose flour
6 large eggs, separated, at room temperature
1 cup granulated sugar
1 tablespoon confectioners' sugar for dusting
Whipped Mascarpone Cream (page 324), made with
    2 tablespoons strong brewed espresso in place of rum

Place a rack in the middle of the oven and preheat to 300°F. Butter a 9-inch cake pan and line the base with a circle of parchment paper. Butter the paper.

Place the butter and the chocolate in the top of a double boiler or in the microwave and melt, stirring to combine. Cool and set aside. Grind the almonds with the flour to a flourlike consistency in a food processor. Set aside. Beat the egg yolks with the granulated sugar on high speed until light yellow and fluffy, 3 to 4 minutes. Fold in the chocolate mixture. Fold in the almond flour until just incorporated. Beat the egg whites to soft peaks in a separate bowl, then carefully fold them into the batter. Pour the batter into the prepared pan and spread in an even layer.

Bake for 35 to 40 minutes, or until a skewer inserted into the center of the cake comes out dry. Cool completely on a wire rack. Invert the cake from the pan to a plate, carefully remove the parchment circle, then invert back onto a serving plate. Dust the top with confectioners' sugar.

To cut the torta, run a long, thin knife under hot water. Shake off the excess water, keeping the blade clean for each slice. Serve with a dollop of the espresso *crema* on the side.

Entertaining Note: The *torta* can be made up to a day in advance. Keep it in the pan and cover with plastic wrap. Store at room temperature. Add the confectioners' sugar just before serving.

Wine Recommendation: Small-production dessert wines from the island of Lipari, such as Malvasia delle Lipari from Hauner, or from the island of Elba, a sweet red Aleatico dell'Elba from Acquabuona

Whipped Mascarpone Cream

~

Crema di Mascarpone

MAKES ABOUT 3 CUPS

This luscious and elegant blend of sweetened mascarpone cheese with whipped egg whites was served with the torta sabbiosa—*sand cake—at Albergo del Sole near Milan. It's great with baked, poached, or fresh seasonal fruit, berries, and tarts. Instead of the rum, try it with other liquors like cognac or grappa. Or replace the liquor with 2 tablespoons of strong espresso. A little nutmeg or orange zest grated into it is divine too.*

3 large egg yolks (see Note)

1/4 cup sugar

One 250-gram container (about 9 ounces) Italian mascarpone
1 tablespoon dark rum
2 large egg whites at room temperature
$^1/_8$ teaspoon cream of tartar
$^1/_8$ teaspoon fine sea salt

Beat the yolks and sugar with an electric mixer on medium speed until the mixture is light yellow and ribbons fall from the beaters when they are lifted up. Add the mascarpone and rum. Mix at low speed and blend until smooth, then at high speed until soft peaks form.

Using clean, dry beaters, beat the egg whites in another bowl on low speed until foamy. Add the cream of tartar and salt, then continue to beat, increasing the speed in increments, until stiff peaks form. Fold the whites into the mascarpone mixture. Keep refrigerated.

The *crema* can be made 3 to 4 hours before serving. If it separates a little bit by becoming thin on the bottom and still fluffy on the top, give it a gentle stir to make it smooth throughout before serving.

Note: This recipe contains raw eggs. People with health problems, the elderly, or those who are pregnant should avoid consuming foods with uncooked eggs, which, in rare cases, carry the potential for Salmonella infections.

Very Rich Cooked Cream

~

Panna Cotta

MAKES 8 DESSERT SERVINGS

There's custard, flan, pudding, and then there's panna cotta, one of the mainstays of the Italian dessert repertoire. Even though the direct translation is "cooked cream," it is heated only enough for the flavors to marry and for the gelatin to melt into the base. With mascarpone it becomes sublime. If you have gelatin sheets, replace the powdered gelatin in this recipe with 2 sheets. Make sure you soften them in tepid water before adding to the cream. For forming, use the classic baba molds, available at better kitchenwares stores and online. Choose the 5-ounce size and look for those with a nonstick coating since they will not react and discolor the cream.

2 cups heavy cream

1/2 cup sugar

1/4 teaspoon fine sea salt

1 teaspoon pure vanilla extract

2 1/8 teaspoons granulated gelatin

1/2 cup whole milk

One 250-gram container (about 9 ounces) Italian mascarpone

Heat the cream with the sugar, salt, and vanilla in a nonreactive pot over medium heat (stainless steel is best). Stir to melt the sugar and salt. Meanwhile, dissolve the gelatin in the milk. When the cream starts to steam, add the milk mixture. Remove from the heat and cool to lukewarm. If the cream is too hot, it will melt the mascarpone, causing it to release some of its fat, which will rise to the top. Stir from time to time to make sure the gelatin is dissolved and not forming any clumps in the cream.

Place the mascarpone in a bowl large enough to hold all the liquid. Add 1 cup of the cream mixture and stir until smooth. Add the remaining cream, stir to combine, and strain with a fine-mesh sieve into another bowl.

Ladle 1/2 cup of the cream into each mold, then evenly divide any that remains among all of them. Place the molds on a small tray, cover with plastic wrap, and refrigerate for at least 12 hours. These can be made up to 2 days in advance.

To remove the *panna cotta* from the molds, run the blade of a small, thin knife under hot water, then insert into the mold between the edge and the cream. Follow the circumference to free it from the mold on the sides. Invert the mold in your hands and gently shake it to feel it release, then unmold on dessert plates.

Serve with fresh, baked, or poached seasonal fruit, purees, syrups, caramel, or slightly warmed chocolate sauce and ground toasted nuts.

Wine Recommendation: Tuscan Vin Santo from Fattoria di Felsina or La Sala

Bibliography

Artusi, Pellegrino. *L'arte di mangiar bene.* 111th ed. Florence: Giunti Marzocco, 1991.

Davidson, Alan. *Mediterranean Seafood.* Baton Rouge: Louisiana State University Press, 1981.

Gosetti della Salda, Anna. *Le ricette regionali Italiane.* 12th ed. Milan: Casa Editrice Solares, 1995.

Heikell, Rod. *Italian Waters Pilot.* 5th ed. St. Ives, UK: Imray, 1998.

———. *Mediterranean France and Corsica Pilot.* 3rd ed. St. Ives, UK: Imray, 2002.

Reboul, J.-B. *La cuisinière provençale.* 25th ed. Marseille: Tacussel, 1997.

Acknowledgments

David

Whole or in part, this book is the result of an extraordinary collaboration by several very talented people. It would not have occurred without the wisdom and support of photographer and bon vivant Steven Rothfeld. Our spirited editor Charlie Conrad saw promise from the beginning and was steadfast with his valuable mantra "show, don't tell" throughout the writing. My great friend and college roommate Erol Munuz was the perfect person to help me fulfill this effort, balancing voice with clever objectivity in the storytelling. Our agent Susan Rabiner expertly coached us in the essence of memoir writing, and Al Fortunato's literary talent helped us capture the impact and message of those stories.

Jenna Thompson and everyone at Broadway Books define efficiency, are wonderful to work with, and exude the values of caring and listening. The photographers Paul Moore and Nigel Pert have keen eyes behind their cameras. Ben Pease, our cartographer, has created spectacular maps. Many thanks to Margot Hirsch for letting me develop and test entertaining-size recipes in her kitchen, and Amy Vogler for guiding me in their writing. Kudos to Sergio Esposito of Italian Wine Merchants, whose passion and palate helped pair delicious wines with the recipes that together stimulate a sense of place through taste.

Faith Heller Willinger, a *bravissima* food and wine writer, took me under her wing and offered a chance to discover what was to become an enormous inspiration. Annie Benard, an enthusiastic yacht charter agent, untied my lines and introduced me to living at sea. Captain Peter Wood, with immense knowledge of the world offshore, helped to keep the maritime writing in the book on course.

My parents reared their sons with a no-limits attitude toward life, while my brother Adam advocated a "don't stop" position when I was abroad. The results have brought forth a new literary tradition in the family. To my extended family, Julie and Gary Wagner, thank you for urging me to write *this* story.

Erol

First and foremost, heartfelt thanks go to my dear friend David Shalleck for allowing me to vicariously tag along on his great adventure. It has been quite a journey.

Charlie Conrad, our editor at Broadway Books, consistently offered a steady hand and precise direction, always with sharp insight and good humor. Jenna Thompson provided terrific perspective and ensured the project (and its authors) stayed on track. Many thanks to the entire Broadway team who helped guide us to the finish.

Additionally, I would like to acknowledge John Butman, whose friendship and experience let me know what to expect next; Frank Sommerfield for his kind efforts; my friends at The Boston Consulting Group for their unwavering encouragement; Jimmy Gilroy, Rosalie Joseph, and Alan Duncan Ross for their much appreciated support.

Al Fortunato played an instrumental role influencing the tone of this book and his sense of styling and taste always inspires me. Finally, Susan Rabiner, my agent, who has stood by me for close to a decade dispensing priceless wisdom, along with healthy doses of tough love. Finally, I offer a special note of gratitude to my mother; my wife, Janet; and my children, Anna and Evan, for their limitless support, patience, and smiles.

About the Authors

© NIGEL PERT

David Shalleck has worked for over two decades in the food business as a chef and television culinary producer alongside some of America's most celebrated chefs. He has cooked in noted restaurants and for special events in New York, San Francisco, the Napa Valley, London, Provence, and throughout many of Italy's famous regions. Recent television credits include the PBS series *Chef's Story at the French Culinary Institute, Joanne Weir's Cooking Class, Fast Food My Way* with Jacques Pépin, and with Cat Cora on the Food Network's *Iron Chef America*. His recipe, menu, food styling, and food product development clients include respected cookbook authors, restaurant operators, and many national brands. He is the founder of VOLOCHEF™ Culinary Solutions, offering specialized services to the food service and media industries. A graduate of Syracuse University in set and lighting design, he currently lives in San Francisco.

© JANET RAPAPORT

Erol Munuz is an executive-level adviser and communications strategist who has worked across both public and private sectors. He is a graduate of Syracuse University and Harvard's Kennedy School of Government. Currently, he lives in Sudbury, Massachusetts, with his wife and two children.